STUDENT STUDY GUIDE

Prepared by

Steven A. Schneider
Pima Community College

to accompany

PSYCHOLOGY
AN INTRODUCTION

Fifth Edition

BENJAMIN B. LAHEY
University of Chicago

WCB Brown & Benchmark
PUBLISHERS
Madison, Wisconsin • Dubuque, Iowa

Cover design by Laura Von Thun

Cover image Detail:
© MIRIAM SCHAPIRO, 1988
Conservatory (Portrait of Frida Kahlo), 1988
Acrylic/collage on canvas, triptych
72" x 152"
Collection: Miami University Art Museum Purchase
through the Helen Kingseed Art Acquisition Fund and
the commemorative Acquisition Fund (Anonymous)
Courtesy Steinbaum Krauss Gallery, NYC

Copyright © 1983, 1986, 1989, 1992, 1995 by Wm. C. Brown Communications,
Inc. All rights reserved

A Times Mirror Company

ISBN 0-697-14521-2

Printed in the United States of America by Wm. C. Brown Communications, Inc.,
2460 Kerper Boulevard, Dubuque, Iowa, 52001

10 9 8 7 6 5 4 3 2 1

Contents

Tips for Successful Studying

Some students take an introductory psychology course because they are considering psychology as a major; others take it because it is a required course for another major; still others take psychology out of a general interest and curiosity about their fellow human beings. Whatever the reason, whatever your major, you are certain to find some topics in this course to be most interesting. Biology/pre-med students will find the chapters dealing with biological psychology and sensation and perception to be particularly interesting. Education majors, parents, and future parents will find the developmental psychology chapter applicable and interesting. Are your interested in health, diet, and exercise? If so, you will find the health psychology chapter to be intriguing. You don't have to be a social scientist to wonder whether intelligence tests are valid, how the human memory system works, what causes mental disorders, or what attracts people to each other. These issues and many others will be explored in your introductory psychology course.

I have taught thousands of introductory psychology students over the past 20 years, and I would like to share some observations about students who succeed in the course and those who fail to live up to their (and my) expectations in the course.

1. Successful students are well organized. Some of my most successful students have been some of my busiest students—those with parttime or fulltime jobs, parents with many familial obligations, and students carrying an incredible course load. Their ability to organize their lives and manage their time, however, allowed them to accomplish their tasks efficiently and effectively. To be well organized, you should use a semester calendar that clearly indicates deadlines for papers, exam dates, and other important dates. Keep your course outlines in a safe place so that you can refer to them during the semester. Be certain that you know the office hours and office phone numbers of your instructors. Make and adhere to a weekly schedule for yourself that builds in all the important activities, including class time, work time, study time, *and* relaxation time.

2. Successful students come to class. As you begin college, one difference you may note from your previous educational experiences is that your instructor may not take attendance. That doesn't signify a lack of concern on the part of your instructor—after all, it's *your* tuition and textbook money. What it does mean is that you are responsible for the decision to come to class or not. Both casual observation and the results of research studies show that students who attend class do better than those who don't attend.

3. Read the material before going to class. My most successful students over the years generally read the text before coming to class. They had a pretty good idea what the lecture was going to be about. This also helped them organize their notetaking while in class.

4. Take good notes and review them. In your efforts to be a good learner, it is usually a mistake to try to take down everything that is said in class. Instead, try to outline the lecture, using Roman numerals and letters for the major and minor points. This technique can be particularly effective if the instructor lectures from an outline. Review your notes as soon after class as possible. It is somewhat dismaying while studying for an exam to see notes in your handwriting that you don't even remember writing.

5. Focus on key terms and concepts. A large and important part of most introductory courses consists of learning the language of the field you are studying. This is necessary in order to communicate with and to think like the professionals in the field. The implication is that, when you study, you need to learn the language of psychology. You are likely to be tested on the terminology and, even if you are not tested directly on the terms, you will almost certainly be expected to know and understand them.

6. Consider using the SQ3R method for studying. The SQ3R method of studying is a tried and tested technique. Research conducted with students who use this technique indicates significantly greater comprehension of text material. This is how it works:

Survey: Although the temptation when you begin studying is to open the text and begin reading, this technique suggests that you should first get an overview of the material. Read the chapter outline (found in the text) and the chapter overview (found in this study guide). Skim through the text, noting the major headings as well as the charts and pictures. This activity will allow you to get a feel for the chapter, as well as to see how the chapter is organized.

Question: As you survey the chapter, begin noting questions about the material. You may use the Learning Objectives section in this study guide to help you formulate questions about the text. The questions that you formulate will help you pick out the most important parts of the text as you read.

Read: When you have formulated questions, reading the text now becomes purposeful; that is, you are reading in order to answer the questions. As you find the material that answers your questions, consider highlighting it or marking an *X* in the margin. Consider taking notes of the major points as you read the text.

Recite: After you have finished a section of the text, stop and state the answers to the questions in your own words (not the author's). This will help give you practice pronouncing some difficult terminology and will test whether the material you have just learned makes sense to you. Recitation is also a very efficient system; material that has been recited is remembered much longer than material not recited. Recitation is particularly effective when studying for essay exams, since it may stimulate the questions you will receive on the exam.

Review: Virtually everybody who sees a movie for the second time comments that the experience was much different from the first viewing. People often say they "got something completely different" from seeing the movie a second time. A similar situation exists when reading a chapter of your text. Review the material soon after reading it. You may test yourself by working through the guided review for each chapter that is included in this study guide. Try to answer the multiple-choice questions in the study guide. These are keyed to the learning objectives found at the beginning of each study guide chapter.*

7. Prepare for exams. The most widespread method used by instructors to asses what you have learned is to give you an exam. Whereas some students welcome the challenge, for many it provides an exercise in terror. Test anxiety is widely recognized to be a major problem for many students. Some hints for preparing for and taking exams can help. Find out as much as you can about the exam beforehand (remaining, of course, within the bounds of conventional morality and the law!). What material will be covered? Will it be multiple-choice, essay, fill-in, or matching? How much time will be allotted? How much weight will be given to various topics? The answers to these questions should help guide your preparation for the exam. Try to study always in the same place and on a regular basis. It should be a quiet, well-lit area and should contain minimal distractions. Use your study area only for studying. Generally speaking, you study most efficiently when you study alone. Take breaks when you study. Studying is a fatiguing activity, and most students can benefit from a short break every 20 minutes or so. It is certainly time to take a break when you reach the end of a page and then realize you haven't retained a word on the page. Take a break instead of fighting it. The type of test for which you are preparing should dictate how you prepare—for example, study for an essay exam by asking yourself essay questions and writing out good answers. Prepare for a multiple-choice exam by answering multiple-choice questions (be sure to review those in the study guide). Solid preparation, a good night's sleep the night before an exam, and relaxing instead of cramming just prior to the exam should help minimize test anxiety. If your anxiety is severe, seek the advice of a counselor. Many colleges now offer courses designed to help deal with test anxiety.

I hope you enjoy and benefit from your psychology course. I also hope that you find this *Student Study Guide* to be a helpful resource. I welcome your comments, opinions, and suggestions for improvements. My address is Steve Schneider, c/o Psychology Department, Pima Community College, 2202 W. Anklam Rd., Tucson AZ 85709.

---

*The SQ3R method is discussed in more detail in the "Application" section of Chapter 1 in the text.

To the Student: Before You Begin

This *Student Study Guide* has been written to assist you as you read the fifth edition of *Psychology: An Introduction* by Benjamin B. Lahey. This guide will help you to learn the essential concepts, facts, and theories that are covered in the text; please remember, however, that it is not intended to be used as a substitute for the textbook. This study guide should be used to help you identify essential information, to help you review, to indicate the gaps in your learning, to stimulate your thinking about the ideas in the text, and to test what you have learned. Each chapter of the *Student Study Guide* is divided into the following sections:

Learning Objectives

You can use the learning objectives in two different ways. First, examine the objectives *before* you read the chapter to get an overview of the major topics that will be covered in the text. Pay attention to the terms, concepts, and names mentioned in the objectives. Second, after you have completed reading the chapter, return to the objectives; you should now be able to perform the activities listed in the objectives. If you find an objective that seems unclear to you, return to the text and reread that section. The page numbers following each objective refer to the location of the material in the text.

Chapter Overview

The chapter overview is a relatively brief survey of the material in the chapter. It should be read before and after you read the text. The first reading will help to prepare (and intrigue) you for the topics covered in the textbook. The second reading will help you to see how the information you have just read in the chapter fits together.

Key Terms Exercise and Who Am I?

The key terms exercise is intended to test your understanding of the key terms that are listed at the beginning of each chapter in the textbook. These matching exercises are grouped according to topic; therefore, some exercises contain only a few terms while others contain more. For your convenience, the key terms are page-referenced to the textbook, and the correct answers immediately follow each exercise. To get the maximum benefit from this activity, keep the answers covered until you have completed all the answers.

Some chapters contain the names of a large number of psychologists. The "Who Am I?" exercise will test your ability to match the names of the psychologists with their contributions to the field. As with the key terms exercise, page references to the text follow the names of the psychologists, and the correct answers immediately follow each exercise (remember to keep the answers covered while you do the exercise).

Guided Review

The guided review is deigned to be a challenging and comprehensive fill-in-the-blanks exercise. Again, as you go through the exercise, try to resist the temptation to peek at the answers in the right margin until you have provided an answer. The page numbers following the answers refer to pages in the textbook. This exercise will help point out the terms or sections of the text you need to review. When all of the blanks have been correctly filled in, you will have a thorough summary of the chapter for future reference and review.

Concept Checks

These fill-in exercises are designed to allow you to check your understanding of several important concepts from each chapter.

Multiple-Choice Questions

These sample multiple-choice questions are similar to the type you might be asked to respond to on an exam. One important note: The multiple-choice questions correspond to the learning objectives found at the beginning of every Study Guide chapter. If you miss a multiple-choice question, you might want to review the corresponding learning objective. Page references to the text are given after the multiple-choice questions so that you may refer to the text for any items you answer incorrectly or do not understand completely. Also included is an expanded answer section for the multiple-choice questions. In addition to the correct answers, I have provided explanations for the answers. I hope you will find this to be a useful study tool.

Chapter 1 What Is Psychology?

Learning Objectives

1. Define psychology and describe the three key elements of the definition.
2. List and provide examples of the four goals of psychology.
3. Compare and contrast the concepts of theory, hypothesis, and law.
4. Compare the early schools of structuralism and functionalism and describe the contributions of Wilhelm Wundt, Edward Titchener, and William James.
5. Describe the school of thought called behaviorism and discuss the influence of Ivan Pavlov and John B. Watson.
6. Describe Hermann Ebbinghaus's research on human memory.
7. Explain the basic ideas involved in Gestalt psychology.
8. Discuss Binet's work in the area of measuring intelligence and Freud's work in developing psychoanalysis.
9. Describe the contributions of early female and minority psychologists.
10. Compare contemporary perspectives in psychology with earlier schools of thought and list and describe the six current perspectives.
11. Describe the differences between basic and applied areas of psychology; list and describe examples of both areas.
12. Distinguish between psychologists and psychiatrists.
13. Explain the key features of the scientific method.
14. Describe the following three descriptive methods: surveys, naturalistic observation, and the clinical method.
15. Discuss the correlational method; explain the statement "Correlation doesn't prove cause and effect."
16. Discuss the use of formal experiments.
17. Distinguish between a dependent and an independent variable; distinguish between a control group and an experimental group.
18. Explain the five major ethical principles of research using human beings.
19. Explain why psychologists use animals in research and describe the ethical principles associated with animal studies.
20. Summarize the beliefs commonly shared by psychologists about human nature and behavior.
21. (From the "Application" section) List and explain the elements of the SQ3R study method and describe other strategies designed to improve study skills.

Chapter Overview

Psychology is defined as the science of behavior and mental processes. Psychology is considered to be a science because psychologists acquire knowledge through systematic observation. The four main goals of psychology are to describe, predict, understand, and influence behavior and mental processes.

The influential early psychologists and their areas of interest include Wilhelm Wundt and Edward Titchener (structuralism), William James (functionalism), Ivan Pavlov and John B. Watson (behaviorism), Hermann Ebbinghaus (human memory), Max Wertheimer (Gestalt psychology), Alfred Binet (psychological measurement), and Sigmund Freud (psychoanalysis). The field of psychology has greatly increased the participation of females and ethnic minorities.

Although some contemporary behaviorists continue to rule out the study of mental processes, other behaviorists, like Bandura, stress the importance of cognition. Contemporary psychoanalysts continue to emphasize unconscious conflicts, but suggest that motives other than sex and aggression are important. A contemporary perspective that emphasizes culture, gender and ethnic factors is the sociocultural perspective.

Cognitive psychologists are interested in the intellectual processes of cognition, such as perceiving, believing, thinking, and remembering.

Another contemporary approach, the biological perspective, studies the relationship between the nervous system, heredity, hormones, and behavior. Humanistic psychologists believe that humans determine their own fates through the decisions they make.

Modern psychologists work in experimental or applied fields. Experimental psychologists conduct basic research, whereas applied psychologists put psychological knowledge to work helping people in a variety of settings.

The scientific method involves using careful observation, forming hypotheses, and testing these hypotheses. Psychologists use three major scientific methods: (1) descriptive methods, which help to describe behavior and which include the use of surveys, naturalistic observation, and clinical methods; (2) correlational methods, which help to predict behavior by studying the relationship between variables; and (3) formal experiments, which study the cause-and-effect relationships between variables and help psychologists to understand and influence behavior.

Formal experiments usually involve an experimental group, which receives the independent variable, and a control group. Differences in the dependent variable between the groups are believed to be caused by the independent variable.

Psychologists are interested in conducting ethical research, which protects the rights of human subjects by avoiding coercion, uninformed participation, and unnecessary deception, and by offering subjects the results of the studies in which they participate. In conducting research with animals, psychologists are guided by the principles of necessity, health, and humane treatment.

Most psychologists would agree with the following statements:

1. Human beings are biological creatures whose structure and physiology influence and limit behavior.
2. Each person is unique, yet enough similarities exist between individuals to allow a science of behavior.
3. People can be understood only by taking into account their culture, ethnic identity, and gender identity.
4. Human lives are in a continual process of change, evolving from birth to death.
5. Behavior is motivated, not random or aimless.
6. Humans are social animals working together in groups.
7. People play an active part in choosing their experiences and constructing perceptions.
8. Behavior has multiple causes.
9. Behavior can be either adaptive or maladaptive.

Key Terms Exercise

For each of the following exercises, match the key terms on the left with the correct definitions on the right. Page references to the text follow the terms so that you may refer to the text for any items you answer incorrectly or do not understand completely. You may check your responses immediately by referring to the answers that follow each exercise.

Psyche and Science-Psychology

_____ 1. psychology (p. 6)
_____ 2. behavior (p. 6)
_____ 3. mental processes (p. 6)
_____ 4. theory (p. 7)
_____ 5. hypothesis (p. 7)
_____ 6. law (p. 8)
_____ 7. introspection (p. 10)

a. psychological activities, including thinking, perceiving, and feeling
b. a proposed explanation for a phenomenon that can be tested
c. observable and measurable human action
d. a tentative explanation of facts and relationships in science
e. a strongly supported and widely accepted theory
f. the science of behavior and mental processes
g. looking inward at one's own consciousness

ANSWERS
1. f   5. b
2. c   6. e
3. a   7. g
4. d

The Many Faces of Psychology and Their Origins

_____ 1. structuralism (p. 11)
_____ 2. functionalism (p. 11)
_____ 3. behaviorism (p. 12)
_____ 4. Gestalt psychology (p. 13)
_____ 5. psychoanalysis (p. 14)

a. the approach that believes that people control their own fates
b. the school of psychology that emphasized the functions of consciousness
c. an approach that emphasizes learning and the measurement of behavior
d. an approach that studies the mind in terms of large, meaningful units
e. techniques based on Sigmund Freud's theory of the unconscious
f. the school of psychology that used introspection to determine the structure of the mind

ANSWERS
1. f   4. d
2. b   5. e
3. c

Contemporary Perspectives

_____ 1. sociocultural perspective (p. 19)
_____ 2. cognition (p. 21)
_____ 3. humanistic psychology (p. 22)
_____ 4. applied psychologist (p. 24)

a. mental processes of perceiving, believing, thinking, and so forth
b. an approach that emphasizes one's culture, ethnic identity, and gender identity
c. a psychologist who uses psychological knowledge to solve human problems
d. the approach that believes that people control their own fates

ANSWERS
1. b
2. a
3. d
4. c

Specialty Fields and Scientific Methods

_____ 1. scientific methods (p. 28)
_____ 2. survey method (p. 29)
_____ 3. naturalistic observation (p. 30)
_____ 4. clinical method (p. 30)

a. the method of observing people while they receive psychological help
b. a research method using interviews and questionnaires
c. a research method that records behavior in natural life settings
d. methods of gathering information based on systematic observation

ANSWERS
1. d
2. b
3. c
4. a

More Scientific Methods

_____ 1. correlational method (p. 31)
_____ 2. variable (p. 31)
_____ 3. formal experiment (p. 32)
_____ 4. dependent variable (p. 33)
_____ 5. independent variable (p. 33)
_____ 6. control group (p. 33)
_____ 7. experimental group (p. 33)

a. the group that receives none of the independent variable
b. a method that measures the strength of the relationship between two variables
c. the variable whose value can be controlled by the researcher
d. the group that receives the independent variable
e. the variable whose value depends on the independent variable
f. a factor whose numerical value can change
g. a method allowing the researcher to manipulate the independent variable to study the effect on the dependent variable

ANSWERS
1. b   5. c
2. f   6. a
3. g   7. d
4. e

Who Am I?

Match the psychologists on the left with their contributions to the field of psychology on the right. Page references to the text follow the names of the psychologists so that you may refer to the text for further review of these psychologists and their contributions. You may check your responses immediately by referring to the answers that follow each exercise.

Part I

_____ 1. Aristotle (p. 6)
_____ 2. William James (p. 11)
_____ 3. John B. Watson (p. 12)
_____ 4. Alfred Binet (p. 14)
_____ 5. Gilbert Jones (p. 16)
_____ 6. Albert Bandura (p. 19)
_____ 7. Carl Rogers (p. 16)

a. I taught the first course on psychology and founded the functionalist approach to psychology.
b. I was a philosopher who believed in the importance of observation.
c. As a humanistic psychologist, I believe that people determine their behavior by their own free will.
d. I am a cognitive behaviorist who believes mental processes can't be ignored.
e. I was the first African-American psychology professor in the United States.
f. At the request of the Paris Ministry of Education, I developed the first tests to measure intelligence.
g. I believed that only outward behavior can be studied, and I founded the behaviorist approach to psychology.

ANSWERS
1. b   5. e
2. a   6. d
3. g   7. c
4. f

Part II

_____ 1. Wilhelm Wundt (p. 10)
_____ 2. Ivan Pavlov (p. 11)
_____ 3. Hermann Ebbinghaus (p. 12)
_____ 4. Max Wertheimer (p. 13)
_____ 5. Sigmund Freud (p. 14)
_____ 6. Margaret Floy Washburn (p. 15)
_____ 7. B. F. Skinner (p. 19)

a. I studied perception and helped found the Gestalt approach to psychology.
b. As a behaviorist, I believed that learning shapes our behavior.
c. I opened the Laboratory for Psychology in Leipzig, Germany, in 1879 and used a technique called introspection.
d. I was the first woman to receive a Ph.D. in psychology and I taught at Vassar College.
e. My techniques of psychoanalysis helped patients to explore their unconscious minds.
f. My work with salivating dogs led to the discovery of classical conditioning.
g. I did a series of important experiments on human memory.

ANSWERS

1. c	5. e
2. f	6. d
3. g	7. b
4. a	

Guided Review

Psyche and Science-Psychology: Definition of Psychology

The ancient Greek philosopher Aristotle used the term _____ to   psyche (p. 6)

refer to the essence of life. Aristotle believed that psyche escaped as a

person took his last dying _____ .   breath (p. 6)

Psychology is defined as the science of _____ and   behavior (p. 6)

_____ processes. Modern psychology uses careful, controlled   mental (p. 6)

observation and therefore is considered to be a _____ .   science (p. 6)

Psychologists study the overt actions of people that can be directly

observed; these actions are referred to as _____ . Psychologists   behavior (p. 6)

also study thoughts, feelings, and motives that cannot be directly observed,

they make inferences about these mental _____ .   processes (p. 6)

Goals of Psychology

The goals of psychology are to _____, _____, _____, and _____ behavior and mental processes. Although psychology is a science, current explanations are always subject to revision. These tentative explanations of facts and relationships are known as _____. Theories allow scientists to make predictions or hypotheses that can be tested in _____. When a theory is consistently supported, it may be considered a _____.

describe (p. 7)/predict (p. 7)
understand (p. 7)/influence (p. 8)

theories (p. 7)

experiments (p. 7)
law (p. 8)

The Many Faces of Psychology and Their Origins

Psychology, like other sciences, emerged from the general field of _____. In 1879, Wilhelm _____ founded a psychological laboratory in Leipzig, Germany, Wundt and his student, Edward _____ studied consciousness using a method of looking inward at one's own experiences; this technique is called _____. Wundt and his followers were interested in the elements and structures of the mind; they were thus called _____.

philosophy (p. 10)/Wundt (p. 10)

Titchener (p. 10)

introspection (p. 10)

structuralists (p. 11)

The first course on psychology was taught in 1875 by William _____. He believed that the process of consciousness helps the human species to _____. His approach, which emphasized the purposes or functions of consciousness, is called _____.

James (p. 11)

survive (p. 11)

functionalism (p. 11)

In the 1890s, Russian physiologist Ivan Pavlov identified a simple form of learning called _____. Today this form of learning is called Pavlovian or _____ conditioning. Pavlov's ideas were popularized in the U.S. by John B. Watson, who believed that only outward behavior could be scientifically understood. The school of psychology based on the ideas of Pavlov and Watson is called _____.

conditioning (p. 12)

classical (p. 12)

behaviorism (p. 12)

In Germany, Hermann Ebbinghaus applied the experimental method to the study of human _____. Max Wertheimer and his associates studied _____. They believed that the mind could not be broken down into raw elements because "the

memory (p. 12)

perception (p. 13)

_____ is different than the sum of its parts." This approach is called _____ psychology.

whole (p. 13)

Gestalt (p. 13)

In the 1890s, in France, Alfred Binet and others sought to measure the mind's _____ capacities.

intellectual (p. 14)

Sigmund Freud was an influential founder of psychology who believed that conscious experiences were not as important as the _____ mind. He believed the roots of psychological problems involved _____ and _____ motives. The process Freud formulated to help people with psychological problems is called _____.

unconscious (p. 14)

sexual (p. 14)/aggressive (p. 14)

psychoanalysis (p. 14)

The majority of new doctorates in psychology today are earned by _____, and the number of minority psychologists has greatly increased in the past 20 years. The early history of psychology includes sexual discrimination in the treatment of women and prejudicial roadblocks against _____.

females (p. 15)

ethnic minorities (p. 16)

Contemporary Perspectives

Although no one approach has emerged as the correct approach to psychology, two early approaches that still exist in contemporary psychology are _____ and psychoanalysis. Another contemporary perspective that can be traced to the founders of psychology is the _____ perspective. Many contemporary behaviorists believe that mental processes such as _____ can be studied scientifically. This approach is referred to as _____ _____ theory. A contemporary perspective that emphasizes cultural, gender, and ethnic factors is called the _____ perspective. A group of people who descended from a common group of ancestors is called an _____ group. A person's sense of belonging to a particular ethnic group is referred to as ethnic _____. A person's view of himself or herself as male or female is called _____ _____. The sociocultural perspective encourages the view of other cultures as being different rather than inferior; this view is called cultural _____. The sociocultural perspective also emphasizes _____

behaviorism (p. 12)

cognitive (p. 21)

cognition (p. 21)

social learning (p. 19)

sociocultural (p. 19)

ethnic (p. 19)

identity (p. 19)

gender identity (p. 20)

relativity (p. 20)

individual (p. 19)

differences among members of different ethnic groups, cultures, and genders. Modern psychoanalysts still believe that conflicts regarding unconscious _____ and _____ motives are   sexual (p. 14)/aggressive (p. 14)
the chief source of psychological problems. Today, however, many psychoanalysts also stress the importance of other motives as well as cognitive processes of the _____ mind.   conscious (p. 14)

Recently, there has been increasing interest among psychologists in the intellectual processes of cognition, including _____, believing, and _____.   perceiving (p. 21)/thinking (p. 21)

Abraham Maslow, Carl Rogers, and Viktor Frankl have popularized the _____ approach, which holds that   humanistic (p. 22)
humans determine their own fates through the decisions they make.

Enormous progress has been made in unraveling the functions of the nervous system, heredity, and the hormonal systems; these psychologists approach the field from a _____   biological (p. 22)
perspective.

Specialty Areas of Modern Psychology

Psychologists who work in _____ areas conduct   basic (p. 24)
research. Psychologists who use basic knowledge to solve and prevent human problems are called _____ psychologists.   applied (p. 24)

The largest specialties within experimental psychology are
(1) _____ psychology, which studies the nervous system   biological (p. 24)
and its relationship to behavior; (2) _____ ____   sensation and
_____ which studies how the sense organs operate and   perception (p. 24)
how we interpret information; (3) _____ ____   learning and
_____, which focuses on the ways in which we acquire   memory (p. 24)
and remember information; (4) _____, which studies   cognition (p . 24)
intelligent action; (5) _____ psychology, which focuses   developmental (p. 24)
on changes during the life-span; (6) _____ ____   motivation and
_____, which studies needs and states that activate   emotion (p. 24)
behavior, as well as feelings and moods; (7) _____,   personality (p. 24)
the field that focuses on our consistent ways of behaving;
(8) _____ psychology, the area that studies the influence   social (p. 24)

of others on our behavior, and (9) the area that focuses on ethnic, cultural, and gender issues, _____ psychology.   sociocultural (p. 24)

     The majority of psychologists are _____   applied (p. 24)
psychologists. The major specialties within applied psychology are
(1) _____ psychology, the field concerned with personal   clinical (p. 25)
problems and abnormal behavior; (2) _____ psychology,   counseling (p. 25)
which focuses on personal or school problems and career choices;
(3) _____-_____ psychology, which deals with   industrial-organizational (p. 26)
work-related psychological issues; (4) _____ and school   educational (p. 26)
psychology, which focuses on learning and other school-related
issues; and (5) _____ psychology, which studies the   health (p. 26)
relationship between psychology and health.

     A _____ has completed an M.D., while   psychiatrist (p. 27)
psychologists have been trained in psychology and allied fields. The
specialty within psychology that is most similar to psychiatry is
_____ psychology. Although most states regulate the   clinical (p. 27)
practice of _____ _____, psychiatry, and   clinical psychology (p. 27)
social work, other helping professions are generally not regulated.

Scientific Methods: How We Learn About Behavior

Psychologists gather information by using systematic
_____. The scientific method focuses on the way   observation (p. 28)
information is gathered and hypotheses are _____.   tested (p. 28)
Psychologists believe that behavior is orderly and _____.   lawful (p. 28)

     The simplest of the scientific methods involves
_____. An example of this method involves asking   description (p. 28)
people questions directly; this is the _____ method.   survey (p. 29)
Another descriptive approach, called _____ observation,   naturalistic (p. 30)
involves observing and recording behavior in real-life settings. A
third technique, observing people who are receiving help from a
psychologist, is the _____ method.   clinical (p. 30)

     When psychologists observe factors that can be measured and
whose numerical values can vary, they are studying
_____. To understand the relationship between   variables (p. 31)
variables, psychologists use a technique called the _____   correlational (p. 31)

method. Researchers interested in studying the relationship between two variables, such as intelligence and job performance, would use a mathematical technique called the _____ _____ _____. It's important to remember that, when two variables correlate, it does not necessarily mean that one variable _____ the other.

coefficient
of correlation (p. 31)

causes (p. 31)

The most useful method of observation is the _____ experiment. This approach allows the researcher to draw conclusions about _____-____-_____ relationships. Formal experiments compare quantitative measures of behavior under _____ _____. In formal experiments, the factor that is controlled by the researcher is called the _____ variable. The factor that depends on the effects of the independent variable is the _____ variable. In a study designed to test the effects of caffeine on job performance, caffeine is considered the _____ variable, while job performance is the _____ variable. For simple experiments, two groups of subjects are used. The group that receives the independent variable is called the _____ group, while the group that does not is called the _____ group. Formal experiments allow us to test hypotheses about _____ relationships. Two drawbacks to formal experiments are that they are somewhat _____ and the conclusions are not always _____.

formal (p. 32)

cause-and-effect (p. 32)

different conditions (p. 32)

independent (p. 33)

dependent (p. 33)

independent (p. 33)

dependent (p. 33)

experimental (p. 33)

control (p. 33)

causal (p. 33)

artificial (p. 33)

valid (p. 33)

Ethical Principles of Research with Human Subjects

The following issues are important ethical principles for psychological research with human subjects. Subjects should not be pressured into participating in research; that is, there should be freedom from _____. When a full description of the experiment is made available to potential subjects, the principle being followed is _____ _____. Except under certain circumstances, it is not considered ethical to misrepresent the true purpose of a study. Such misrepresentation is called _____. When subjects are provided with the results of

coercion (p. 33)

informed consent (p. 33)

deception (p. 34)

the study, this is termed _____. Subjects must be   debriefing (p. 34)
assured of their anonymity; that is, their _____ must be   confidentiality (p. 34)
protected.

Ethical Principals of Research with Animals

Psychologists conduct research with animals for several reasons. In
many cases, for example with brain research, it would be unethical
to do the research with _____. Also, using animals   humans (p. 34)
allows psychologists to conduct experiments that are more precisely
_____. Psychologists have also learned much by   controlled (p. 34)
comparing the behavior of animals of different _____.   species (p. 34)
Finally, psychologists are interested in learning about other animal
species. Animal research is considered ethical only when all of the
following conditions are met: _____, health, and   necessity (p. 35)
_____ treatment.   humane (p. 35)

What We Know about Human Behavior: Some Starting Places

Although psychology is a diverse field, most contemporary
psychologists would agree with the following basic ideas:

1. People are influenced to a large extent by factors such as
    heredity and the nervous system; that is, humans are
    _____ creatures.   biological (p. 37)
2. Although every human is unique, we have similar capacities to
    think, feel, etc. Therefore, every person is _____,   different (p. 38)
    yet much the _____.   same (p. 38)
3. As the sociocultural perspective implies, people can be fully
    understood only in the context of their culture,
    _____ identity, and _____ identity.   ethnic (p. 38)/gender (p. 38)
4. Our constant developmental changes and life experiences
    mean that human lives are in a continual process of
    _____.   change (p. 39)
5. People do things for reasons; that is, behavior is
    _____.   motivated (p. 39)
6. People need to have contact with each other; we are
    _____ animals.   social (p. 40)

7. People are not passive; we play an _____ role in creating our experiences.

active (p. 40)

8. Behavior can be influenced by many factors at once; it has _____ causes.

multiple (p. 41)

9. Although we are usually able to adjust to the challenges of life, sometimes we act in harmful ways; behavior can be either _____ or _____.

adaptive (p. 41)/maladaptive (p. 41)

CONCEPT CHECK

Fill in the missing components of the following concept box. The answers are shown below the box.

Contemporary Perspectives

I. Perspective	II. Focus
a. Social learning theory	a. Behavior is learned from others in society.
b. Sociocultural perspective	b.
c.	c. Humans determine their own fates through the decisions they make.
d. Biological perspective	d.
e.	e. Conflicts in the unconscious mind are the main source of psychological problems.
f. Cognitive perspective	f. This perspective emphasizes the processes involving perceiving, believing, thinking, knowing, and so on.

Answers

IIb.   The sociocultural approach emphasizes the importance of culture, ethnic identity, and gender identity.

Ic.   Humanistic perspective

IId.   The biological perspective emphasizes the relationship between the nervous system, hormonal and genetic factors, and behavior.

Ie.   Psychoanalysis

Multiple-Choice Questions

1. The author defines psychology as the science of behavior and
   a. mental processes
   b. overt actions
   c. phenomena
   d. observation
      (p. 6) LO 1

2. Research that is conducted to find out under what circumstances bystanders will help in a crisis is part of which goal of psychology?
   a. describe
   b. predict
   c. understand
   d. influence
      (p. 7) LO 2

3. Which of the four goals of psychology is achieved when we can explain behavior?
   a. describe
   b. predict
   c. understand
   d. influence
      (p. 7) LO 2

4. A tentative explanation about facts or relationships is called a(n)
   a. hypothesis
   b. law
   c. theory
   d. all of the above
      (p. 7) LO 3

5. According to the text, which of the following is correct?
   a. Hypotheses are based on theories.
   b. Theories are based on hypotheses.
   c. A theory can never become a law.
   d. A law can never become a theory.
      (p. 7) LO 3

6. According to William James, psychology should emphasize
   a. what the mind can do
   b. the basic elements of the mind
   c. the factors that have aided our evolution
   d. a and c above
      (p. 11) LO 4

7. If a man wearing a fake beard and a black academic robe asks you to describe the sensations of biting into an apple,
   a. leave the area immediately
   b. he's probably a behaviorist trying to condition you
   c. he's probably a psychoanalyst looking into your unconscious
   d. he's probably a structuralist asking you to do introspection
      (p. 11) LO 4

8. When Pavlov discovered that his dogs associated the sound of the bell with food, he called this
   a. functionalism
   b. conditioning
   c. introspection
   d. the phi phenomenon
      (p. 12) LO 5

9. Which of the following psychologists is known for the development of nonsense syllables?
   a. Pavlov
   b. Wertheimer
   c. Ebbinghaus
   d. Watson
      (p. 12) LO 6

10. The phi phenomenon demonstrates that
    a. the sum of the parts is greater than the whole
    b. the whole is greater than the sum of its parts
    c. some wholes are greater than some parts
    d. none of the above
       (p. 13) LO 7

11. Unconscious motives are the roots of psychological problems according to
    a. psychoanalysts
    b. behaviorists
    c. Gestalt psychologists
    d. humanistic psychologists
       (p. 14) LO 8

12. Two influential women in the early history of psychology are Mary Calkins and
    a. Laurel Furomoto
    b. Elizabeth Loftus
    c. Gilbert Jones
    d. Margaret Floy Washburn
    (p. 15) LO 9

13. Two approaches from early psychology that remain popular today are
    a. structuralism and functionalism
    b. Gestalt psychology and humanistic psychology
    c. psychoanalysis and structuralism
    d. psychoanalysis and behaviorism
    (p. 18) LO 10

14. According to the sociocultural perspective, which of the following must be considered?
    a. culture
    b. ethnic identity
    c. gender identity
    d. all of the above
    (p. 19) LO 10

15. The belief that our behavior and emotions are caused in large part by the way in which we think about things is central to the
    a. humanistic perspective
    b. cognitive perspective
    c. sociocultural perspective
    d. psychoanalytic perspective
    (p. 21) LO 10

16. According to the text, all of the following are examples of applied psychology *except*
    a. clinical psychology
    b. biological psychology
    c. industrial psychology
    d. educational psychology
    (p. 22) LO 11

17. What is the difference between a psychologist and a psychiatrist?
    a. about $25 an hour
    b. a psychiatrist has completed medical school
    c. a psychologist has completed graduate school in psychology
    d. b and c above
    (p. 27) LO 12

18. Each of the following is a key component of the scientific method *except*
    a. testing hypotheses
    b. the belief in an orderly and lawful subject matter
    c. believing that your theory is correct even if the evidence suggests otherwise
    d. systematic observation
    (p. 28) LO 13

19. A psychology student wishes to find out more about test anxiety. She constructs a "Test Anxiety Questionnaire" and gives it to other students. Which technique is she using?
    a. survey method
    b. correlational method
    c. clinical method
    d. formal experiment
    (p. 29) LO 14

20. If you were interested in describing "Happy Hour" behavior among college students, which technique would yield the most accurate data?
    a. survey method
    b. formal experiment
    c. naturalistic observation
    d. clinical method
    (p. 30) LO 14

21. Psychologists seeking to establish a relationship between family income and years of formal education would use which research method?
    a. the clinical method
    b. naturalistic observation
    c. formal experiments
    d. correlational methods
    (p. 30) LO 15

22. Which of the following is an advantage of using formal experimental methods?
    a. Only these methods can establish whether there is any relationship between two variables.
    b. Only these methods allow behavior to be observed as it naturally occurs.
    c. Only these methods allow researchers to determine people's opinions about various issues.
    d. Only these methods allow scientists to determine cause-and-effect relationships.
    (p. 32) LO 16

23. The members of which group receive the independent variable?
    a. the experimental group
    b. the control group
    c. the independent group
    d. depending on the research, any of the above might receive the independent variable.
    (p. 33) LO 16

24. A psychologist is studying the effects that different noise levels have on stress. In the experiment, noise levels are the
    a. correlation
    b. dependent variable
    c. independent variable
    d. control group
    (p. 33) LO 17

25. When a researcher provides the results of her study to all the participants, she is following the ethical principle of
    a. freedom from coercion
    b. informed consent
    c. debriefing
    d. deception
    (p. 34) LO 18

26. Before participating in research, potential subjects must receive a full description of the experiment. This is the ethical principle of
    a. limited deception
    b. confidentiality
    c. debriefing
    d. informed consent
    (p. 33) LO 18

27. To be considered ethical, which of the conditions must researchers using animals meet?
    a. necessity
    b. health
    c. humane treatment
    d. all of the above
    (p. 35) LO 19

28. Psychologists generally agree with all of the following statements *except*
    a. Human beings are biological creatures.
    b. All behavior is predictable.
    c. Every person is different, yet the same.
    d. Behavior is motivated.
    (p. 37) LO 20

29. Each of the following is part of the SQ3R method *except*
    a. read
    b. recognize
    c. recite
    d. review
    (p. 42) LO 21

30. According to the text, each of the following is a good study technique *except*
    a. Consistently study in the same place.
    b. Space out your study time.
    c. Avoid using mnemonic devices.
    d. Use the method of loci, acronym method, and the keyword method.
    (p. 45) LO 21

Multiple-Choice Answers

1. *A* is the answer. Overt actions are of special interest to behavioral psychologists, and all scientists are interested in the observation of phenomena.

2. *B* is the answer because the research is attempting to predict behavior. Description of behavior is often done through the use of questionnaires and surveys; understanding behavior implies an explanation of the behavior, while influencing behavior implies that people's behavior is changed in desirable ways.

3. The answer is *C*. We understand behavior when we can *explain* our knowledge of facts and relationships in psychology, in addition to describing and predicting.

4. The answer is *C*. A hypothesis is a prediction that is based on a theory; a law is a strongly supported and widely accepted theory.

5. *A* is the answer. Hypotheses are derived from theories and then tested in experiments. Those theories that are consistently supported may become laws.

6. The answer is *D* (*A* and *C*). James was interested in studying the functions of the mind, rather than the individual structures of the mind. He was also interested in topics he considered to be evolutionarily important.

7. *D* is the answer. The beard and robe are meant to conjure up the image of Edward Titchener, an influential structuralist. Introspection was the technique that structuralists used to look inward in an effort to isolate the basic elements of the mind.

8. *B* is the answer. Functionalism was a school of thought popularized by William James; the phi phenomenon is a Gestalt psychology term dealing with the perception of movement.

9. *C* is the answer. Ebbinghaus conducted important early research on human memory. Pavlov and Watson were behaviorists and Wertheimer was a Gestalt psychologist. For more practice in associating the names of psychologists with their fields, try the "Who Am I?" matching exercise that follows the key terms exercise.

10. *B* is the answer. The phi phenomenon occurs when individuals perceive movement between two stationary stimuli. This shows that the whole (that is, the perception of movement) is greater than the sum of the parts (two stationary objects).

11. *A* is the answer. Behaviorists tend to focus on observable behavior, Gestalt psychologists focus on perceptual experiences, and humanistic psychologists focus on the capacity of humans to exercise their free will.

12. *D* is the answer. Furomoto researched the role of women in early psychology. Loftus is an influential researcher in the area of eyewitness testimony, and Gilbert Jones, alas, is a male (also the first black psychology professor in the United States).

13. *D* is the answer. The other early approaches have become intermingled; traces of each can be found in today's cognitive perspective.

14. The answer is *D*. As is the case with social learning theory, the sociocultural approach emphasizes that behavior is learned from others. The sociocultural approach, however, emphasizes the cultural, ethnic, and gender context in which behavior is learned.

15. The answer is *B*. The cognitive perspective, with its emphasis on how people think about things, has helped us understand such aspects of psychology as language, intelligence, motivation and emotion, and therapies.

16. The answer is *B*. Applied psychologists apply knowledge acquired by experimental psychologists. Biological psychology is considered to be an experimental field of modern psychology.

17. The answer is *D* (both *B* and *C*). The other choice is an old comedy one-liner (sorry!).

18. The answer is *C*. The scientific method urges its practitioners to remain open to alternative explanations and approaches.

19. The answer is *A*. The correlational method is used to discover the relationship between variables. The clinical method involves observing people who are receiving help for psychological problems. Formal experiments involve manipulation of the independent variable to study its effect on the dependent variable.

20. The answer is *C.* Naturalistic observation allows the researcher to observe behavior as it naturally occurs. Presumably, this approach would allow a researcher more accurate information than merely surveying college students. Formal experiments are not intended to be descriptive, and the clinical method involves observing people while they receive help for psychological problems.

21. The answer is *D.* Correlational methods are used to discover the degree of relationship between variables, such as income and education. See the comments for answer 19.

22. The answer is *D.* Correlational techniques can only suggest that a relationship between variables exists; formal experimental methods can determine whether one variable is the cause of the other. *B* refers to naturalistic observation, while *C* refers to survey methods.

23. The answer is *A.* In conducting formal research, the experimental group receives the independent variable; the control group does not.

24. The answer is *C.* In formal experiments, the variable that is controlled by the experimenter is the independent variable. The variable whose value depends on the independent variable is called the dependent variable. Thus, in this experiment, the amount of stress is the dependent variable.

25. The answer is *C.* Selection *A* refers to the ethical principle of not forcing subjects to participate in research; *B* implies that researchers must fully disclose the nature of the research to potential subjects; and *D* refers to the fact that, except under certain circumstances, subjects must be told the true purpose of the study.

26. The answer is *D.* Informed consent also implies that subjects must be told that they are free to withdraw from the experiment without penalty.

27. The correct answer is *D.*

28. The correct answer is *B.* While most psychologists would probably agree that behavior is *largely* predictable, few would suggest that *all* behavior is predictable.

29. The answer is *B.* SQ3R is composed of survey, question, read, recite, and review.

30. The answer is *C.* The text recommends using mnemonic devices, examples of which are the method of loci, the acronym method, and the keyword method.

Learning Objectives

1. Differentiate among the neuron's cell body, dendrite, and axon.
2. Summarize the processes of neural transmission and synaptic transmission.
3. Compare and contrast excitatory and inhibitory neurotransmitters.
4. Explain the differences among afferent neurons, efferent neurons, and association neurons.
5. List the functions of the autonomic nervous system and describe the roles of the sympathetic and parasympathetic divisions.
6. Describe the following brain-imaging techniques: EEGs, PET scans, and MRIs.
7. Describe the functions of the hindbrain's three main structures (medulla, pons, and cerebellum) and explain the functions of the midbrain.
8. Summarize the functions of the thalamus and hypothalamus.
9. Identify the functions of the limbic system.
10. Explain how the two cerebral hemispheres communicate and describe the changes that occur if the corpus callosum is severed.
11. Identify the location and functions of the four lobes and the association areas of the cerebral cortex.
12. Discuss the role of the cerebral cortex in processing intellectual and emotional information.
13. Describe the functions of the reticular formation.
14. Explain the following statement: "The brain is an interacting system."
15. Describe the functions of the following endocrine glands: pituitary, adrenal, islets of Langerhans, gonads, thyroid, parathyroid, and pineal.
16. Explain the relationship between genes and chromosomes; distinguish between dominant genes and recessive genes.
17. Summarize the role of twin studies and adoption studies in genetics research.
18. Describe the role of inheritance in personality development and in abnormal behavior.
19. (From the "Application" section) Describe the relationship between the brain and such mental disorders as schizophrenia and Alzheimer's disease.

Chapter Overview

The human nervous system is a complex network of neural cells that carry messages and regulate bodily functions and personal behavior. The individual cells of the nervous system are called neurons. Chemical substances transmit electrical messages across the synapse, which separates the axon of one neuron from the dendrite of the next neuron.

The central nervous system is composed of the brain and the spinal cord. The peripheral nervous system carries messages to and from the rest of the body. It is composed of both the somatic and autonomic nervous system. The autonomic nervous system consists of the sympathetic division, which activates internal organs, and the parasympathetic division, which calms internal organs.

The brain has three major parts. The first of these, the hindbrain, contains (a) the medulla, which controls breathing and a variety of reflexes; (b) the pons, which is concerned with balance, hearing, and some parasympathetic functions; and (c) the cerebellum, which is chiefly responsible for maintaining muscle tone and coordinating muscular movements.

A second part of the brain, the midbrain, is a center for reflexes related to vision and hearing.

The forebrain, the third major part of the brain, includes two distinct areas: (a) the thalamus, a switching station that routes sensory information to the appropriate areas of the brain; the hypothalamus, which is involved with our motives and emotions; and most of the limbic system; and (b) the cerebral cortex, which controls conscious experience, intellectual activities, the senses, and voluntary actions. The cortex contains two cerebral hemispheres connected by the corpus callosum. Each hemisphere of the cortex contains four lobes: the frontal lobe is involved with speaking and voluntary movement; the parietal lobe is involved with the sense of touch; the temporal lobe is involved with hearing and understanding language; and the occipital lobe is involved with vision. The cerebral cortex is also important in processing emotions. Each part of the brain interacts with the entire nervous system, and the parts work together in intellectual, physical, and emotional functions.

The endocrine system contains glands that secrete hormones. This system influences emotional arousal, metabolism, sexual functioning, and other bodily processes. The following endocrine glands have important psychological functions. The adrenal glands secrete epinephrine and norepinephrine, which are involved in emotional arousal and which affect the metabolic rate and sexual arousal. The islets of Langerhans secrete glucagon and insulin, which control blood sugar and energy levels. The gonads produce sex cells for human reproduction and also estrogen and testosterone, which are important to sexual functioning and the development of secondary sex characteristics. The thyroid gland secretes thyroxin, which helps control the metabolic rate. The parathyroid glands secrete parathormone, which controls the level of nervous activity. The pineal gland, attached to the top of the thalamus, secretes melatonin. The pituitary gland, often referred to as the master gland, secretes hormones that control the activities of the other endocrine glands and have other important effects on the body.

Human characteristics and behaviors are influenced by genetic inheritance. Characteristics that are inherited are passed on through genes containing DNA. Genes are found in the cell nucleus on strips called chromosomes. Most normal human cells contain 46 chromosomes arranged in 23 pairs. The sex cells, however, each contain only 23 chromosomes and are capable of combining into a new zygote with a unique set of chromosomes.

Although inheritance plays a significant role in influencing human behavior, environmental and other personal factors also play important roles.

Key Terms Exercise

For each of the following exercises, match the key terms on the left with the correct definitions on the right. Page references to the text follow the terms so that you may refer to the text for any items you answer incorrectly or do not understand completely. You may check your responses immediately by referring to the answers that follow each exercise.

The Nervous System (I)

_____ 1. brain (p. 54)
_____ 2. neuron (p. 54)
_____ 3. dendrites (p. 54)
_____ 4. axons (p. 55)
_____ 5. ions (p. 55)
_____ 6. myelin sheath (p. 56)

a. the protective covering around the neuron
b. the mass of neural cells and related cells encased in the skull
c. electrically charged particles
d. neuron endings that transmit messages to other neurons
e. extensions of the cell body that receive messages from other neurons
f. an individual cell of the nervous system

ANSWERS

1. b   4. d
2. f   5. c
3. e   6. a

The Nervous System (II)

_____ 1. synapse (p. 57)
_____ 2. central nervous system (p. 59)
_____ 3. peripheral nervous system (p. 59)
_____ 4. afferent neurons (p. 59)
_____ 5. efferent neurons (p. 59)
_____ 6. association neurons (p. 60)
_____ 7. somatic nervous system (p. 61)
_____ 8. autonomic nervous system (p. 61)

a. the system that receives messages from the sense organs, muscles, joints, and skin and carries messages from the central nervous system to the skeletal muscles

b. the brain and nerve fibers of the spinal cord

c. helps process simple reflexes in the brain and spinal cord

d. the system that controls involuntary action and regulates emotion

e. nerves that branch off from the brain and spinal cord to all parts of the body

f. the space between neurons

g. carry messages from central nervous system to the organs and muscles

h. carry messages from the body to the central nervous system

ANSWERS

1. f	5. g
2. b	6. c
3. e	7. a
4. h	8. d

Structures and Functions of the Brain (I)

_____ 1. medulla (p. 66)
_____ 2. pons (p. 66)
_____ 3. cerebellum (p. 66)
_____ 4. midbrain (p. 66)
_____ 5. thalamus (p. 67)

a. routes messages to appropriate parts of the brain involved in balance, hearing, and some parasympathetic functions

b. involved in balance, hearing, and some parasympathetic functions

c. two structures that are responsible for maintaining muscle tone and muscular conditioning

d. the swelling at the top of the spinal cord, responsible for breathing and a variety of reflexes

e. a small area at the top of the hindbrain that mainly serves as a reflex center for orienting the eyes and ears

ANSWERS

1. d	4. e
2. b	5. a
3. c	

Structures and Functions of the Brain (II)

_____ 1. hypothalamus (p. 67)
_____ 2. limbic system (p. 68)
_____ 3. cerebral cortex (p. 68)
_____ 4. corpus callosum (p. 69)

a. the largest structure of the forebrain, controlling conscious experience and intelligence
b. involved in motivation, emotion, and the functions of the autonomic nervous system
c. the link between the cerebral hemispheres
d. a neural system composed of the amygdala, the hippocampus, the septal area, and the cingulate cortex

ANSWERS

1. b   3. a
2. d   4. c

Structure and Functions of the Brain (III)

_____ 1. frontal lobes (p. 70)
_____ 2. parietal lobes (p. 73)
_____ 3. temporal lobes (p. 73)
_____ 4. occipital lobes (p. 74)
_____ 5. reticular formation (p. 77)

a. contains the somatosensory area
b. contains the visual area
c. contains both Broca's area and the motor area
d. the system of neural structures involved in cortical arousal and attention
e. contains the auditory areas

ANSWERS

1. c   4. b
2. a   5. d
3. e

Endocrine System and Genetic Influences

_____ 1. endocrine system (p. 78)
_____ 2. hormones (p. 78)
_____ 3. gene (p. 83)
_____ 4. chromosome (p. 84)
_____ 5. monozygotic twins (p. 86)
_____ 6. dizygotic twins (p. 86)
_____ 7. dominant gene (p. 85)
_____ 8. recessive gene (p. 85)

a. chemical substances that control internal organs
b. the system of glands that produces hormones
c. the strip in the cell that contains genes
d. the hereditary unit made up of deoxyribonucleic acid
e. formed when two separate egg cells are fertilized by different sperm cells
f. identical twins, formed from a single fertilized egg
g. the gene produces a trait only when paired with the same recessive gene from both parents
h. the gene that produces a trait when paired with another dominant or recessive gene

ANSWERS

1. b   5. f
2. a   6. e
3. d   7. h
4. c   8. g

Guided Review

Nervous System: The Biological Control Center

The complex mass of nerve cells encased in the skull is the

_____. The brain is connected to a bundle of long

nerves running through the spine, called the _____

_____. The most important unit of the nervous system

is the individual nerve cell, or _____. The central part

of the neuron is called the ____ _____; it contains the

cell's control center, or _____. The small branches

extending out from the cell body receive messages from other

neurons and are called _____. The small branches at

the other end of the nerve cell transmit messages to other neurons;

these are _____. The nervous system contains about

____ _____ neurons. Each neuron can receive

messages from or transmit messages to ____ to _____

other neural cells. A bundle of long neurons outside the brain is a

_____.

Neurons, the "wires" of the nervous system, also contain built-

in supplies of _____ power. The fluids inside and

outside the neuron contain electrically charged ____. The overall

ion charge within the cell membrane is _____, while the

fluid outside the cell membrane, which contains sodium ions, is

_____. The cell membrane allows some chemicals to

pass through, but not others; it is _____.

In its normal resting state, with mostly negative ions inside and

mostly positive ions outside, the neuron is electrically

_____. When the membrane is stimulated and positively

charged sodium ions enter the neuron, the process is termed

_____. If sufficient depolarization occurs, the length of

the axon conducts a neural _____. A drug that

interrupts the flow of depolarization is _____.

Axons are insulated by a fatty covering called a

_____ _____. Gaps in the myelin sheath,

called ____ ____ _____, help to speed neural

brain (p. 54)

spinal

cord (p. 54)

neuron (p. 54)

cell body (p. 54)

nucleus (p. 54)

dendrites (p. 54)

axons (p. 55)

100 billion (p. 55)

1,000 (p. 55)/10,000 (p. 55)

nerve (p. 55)

electrical (p. 55)

ions (p. 55)

negative (p. 56)

positive (p. 56)

semipermeable (p. 56)

polarized (p. 56)

depolarization (p. 56)

impulse (p. 56)

Novocain (p. 56)

myelin sheath (p. 56)

nodes of Ranvier (p. 57)

impulses. A disease that destroys the myelin sheath of many

neurons is _____ _____ .   multiple sclerosis (p. 57)

    Although neurons are linked together, there is a small gap

between them called the _____ . Neural messages can be   synapse (p. 57)

transmitted across the synapse if the axon produces

_____ . Neurotransmitters are released into synapses   neurotransmitters (p. 57)

from the synaptic ____ . A drug that blocks the actions of a   knob (p. 57)

neurotransmitter and has been used in treating schizophrenia is

_____ . Neurotransmitters that make it easy for neurons   Thorazine (p. 57)

to fire are called _____ ; those that make it more   excitatory (p. 57)

difficult are called _____ .   inhibitory (p. 57)

    The nervous system consists of two major divisions: (1) the

brain and spinal cord, called the _____ _____   central nervous

_____ , and (2) the nerves that branch off the brain and system (p. 59)

spinal cord to the rest of the body, called the _____   peripheral

_____ _____ . Messages that come from the   nervous system (p. 59)

body into the central nervous system are carried by

_____ _____ . Messages going out from the   afferent neurons (p. 59)

central nervous system are carried by _____ neurons.   efferent (p. 59)

Simple reflexes are processed in the brain and spinal cord by

_____ neurons.   association (p. 60)

    The peripheral nervous system consists of two divisions. The

first is called the _____ _____   somatic nervous

_____ ; it carries messages from the central nervous   system (p. 61)

system to the skeletal muscles and receives messages from the

sense organs, muscles, joints, and skin. The second, the

_____ _____ _____ , carries   autonomic nervous system (p. 61)

messages to and from the glands and visceral organs; it

automatically controls many essential functions of the body,

regulates emotion, and helps to control our motivations. The

autonomic nervous system itself contains two further divisions:

(1) a division that tends to activate the internal organs, called the

_____ division, and (2) a division that generally "calms" sympathetic (p. 61)

the internal organs, called the _____ division. The   parasympathetic (p. 62)

clusters of neural cell bodies, called _____ , are   ganglia (p. 62) organized differently for the sympathetic and parasympathetic divisions.

Structures and Functions of the Brain

One brain-image technique that records the brain's electrical activity is called the _____, or _____. A second technique uses a computer interpretation of an X-ray-like image; this technique is called _____ _____ _____, or _____ _____. A third technique detects and interprets activity from the nuclei of atoms in living cells; this approach is called _____ _____ _____, or _____.

    The lowest part of the brain, responsible for routine functions, is the _____. The hindbrain has three main structures: (1) a part responsible for controlling breathing and a variety of reflexes, called the _____; (2) a structure involved in balance, hearing, and some parasympathetic functions, called the _____; and (3) a part that is mainly responsible for maintaining muscle tone and muscular coordination, called the _____.

    The small area at the top of the hindbrain that serves primarily as a reflex center for orienting the eyes and ears is the _____. The forebrain consists of two main parts. The first contains a structure that primarily routes messages to the appropriate parts of the brain called the _____ and the _____, a tiny structure involved with motives, emotions, and the functions of the autonomic nervous system; the hypothalamus is also involved in aggression and apparently contains _____ centers.

    The hypothalamus influences emotional arousal by working with a complex brain system called the _____ system. A part of the limbic system that is involved in the emotions of fear and rage is the _____. Other limbic structures that process cognitive information in emotions are the hippocampus, _____ area, and the _____ cortex.

electroencephalogram (p. 64)/EEG (p. 64)

positron emission (p. 65)
tomography (p. 65)/PET scan (p. 65)

magnetic resonance
imaging (p. 65)/MRI (p. 65)

hindbrain (p. 66)

medulla (p. 66)

pons (p. 66)

cerebellum (p. 66)

midbrain (p. 66)

thalamus (p. 67)
hypothalamus (p. 67)

pleasure (p. 67)

limbic (p. 68)

amygdala (p. 68)

septal (p. 68) / cingulate (p. 68)

Cerebral Cortex: Sensory, Cognitive, and Motor Functions

The largest structure in the forebrain, called the cerebral cortex, is
involved in _____ experience, language, and   conscious (p. 68)

_____. The cortex is frequently called the   intelligence (p. 68)

"_____" matter of the brain, while the cerebrum is the   gray (p. 69)

_____ matter. The cerebral cortex consists of two   white (p. 69)

cerebral hemispheres joined by the _____   corpus

_____. The corpus callosum allows _____   callosum (p. 69)/communication (p. 69)

between the two hemispheres.

   Patients who have had the corpus callosum surgically severed

are referred to as _____-_____ patients.   split-brain (p. 70)

Research with these patients has revealed the localization of

language expression abilities in the ____ _____.   left hemisphere (p. 70)

   Each hemisphere contains four lobes, and each lobe performs

different cognitive functions. The _____ lobes play an   frontal (p. 70)

important role in organizing behavior and in predicting the

consequence of behavior. The left hemisphere contains

_____ area, which is involved in our ability to speak   Broca's (p. 72)

language. Another area of the frontal lobe, which is involved in the

control of voluntary motor movement, is called the

_____ area. The _____ lobes contain the   motor (p. 72)/parietal (p. 73)

somatosensory area, which is involved in the sense of

_____ and other body senses. The temporal lobes,   touch (p. 73)

extending backward from the temples, are involved with the sense

of _____. In the left temporal lobe, _____   hearing (p. 73)/Wernicke's (p. 74)

area plays an important role in understanding spoken language.

The _____ lobes contain the visual area and play an   occipital (p. 74)

essential role in processing sensory information from the eyes.

Association areas are sometime called the _____   silent

_____ of the cortex.   areas (p. 74)

Cerebral Cortex: Processing Emotional Information

The results of a variety of studies, starting with Broca's research in
1861 and continuing through studies conducted in the nineties,
suggest that the two cerebral hemispheres process different aspects

of _____; that is, positive emotions are processed more in the ____ hemisphere and negative emotions are processed more in the ____ hemisphere.

emotion (p. 75)
left (p. 75)
right (p. 75)

An accident that damaged the _____ _____ lobe of Phineas Gage led to dramatic changes in his personality and cognitive abilities.

left (p. 75)
frontal (p. 76)

A system of neural structures that plays a role in cortical arousal, attention, and the regulation of sleep is the _____ _____.

reticular formation (p. 77)

Endocrine System: Chemical Messengers of the Body

Another system that plays a role in communication and regulation of bodily processes is the _____ system. This system consists of _____ that secrete hormones into the bloodstream. The following glands are the most important psychologically.

endocrine (p. 78)
glands (p. 78)

1. Located near the bottom of the brain and largely controlled by the hypothalamus is the _____ gland. This gland secretes hormones that help regulate the other glands and is frequently referred to as the _____ _____. The pituitary regulates the body's reactions to _____ and resistance to _____.

pituitary (p. 79)

master
gland (p. 79)
stress (p. 79)/disease (p. 79)

2. The glands that sit atop the kidneys and play an important role in emotional arousal are the _____ glands. These glands secrete two hormones that help the body prepare for stress, _____ and _____.

adrenal (p. 79)

epinephrine (p. 79)/norepinephrine (p. 79)

3. The glands that are embedded in the pancreas and regulate the blood sugar level are the _____ ____ _____. These glands secrete _____ and _____.

islets of
Langerhans (p. 80)/glucagon (p. 80)
insulin (p. 80)

4. The glands responsible for sex cell production are the _____. In females the glands are the _____, while in males they are the _____. The most important sex hormones are _____ in females and _____ in males.

gonads (p. 81)
ovaries (p. 81)
testes (p. 81)
estrogen(p. 81)/testosterone (p. 81)

5. The gland that helps regulate metabolism is the

 _____ gland. This gland secretes the hormone   thyroid (p. 81)

 _____, which is necessary for mental development   thyroxin (p. 81)

 in children and for control of weight and level of activity in

 adults. A deficiency of thyroxin can cause a type of mental

 retardation called _____.   cretinism (p. 81)

6. Embedded in the thyroid are four glands called the

 _____ glands. These secrete a hormone called   parathyroid (p. 81)

 _____, which is important in the functioning of the   parathormone (p. 81)

 nervous system.

7. Attached to the top of thalamus is the _____ gland   pineal (p. 81)

 which secretes _____.   melatonin (p. 81)

Genetic Influences on Behavior: Biological Blueprints?

The problem of separating the influence of heredity from that of

the environment is referred to as _____ versus   nature (p. 82)

 _____. In a seabird called the tern, knowing how to   nurture (p. 82)

build a nest is part of the bird's _____ inheritance.   genetic (p. 82)

Among human beings, inheritance seems to _____ much   influence (p. 83)

of our behavior, although we do not inherit specific patterns of

behavior.

 Inherited characteristics are passed on through genetic

material called _____, which are found in the nuclei of   genes (p. 83)

all human cells. Genes provide their instructions through a

complex substance called _____, which stands for _____   DNA (p. 83)/deoxyribonucleic

 _____. Genes are arrayed in the cells on strips called   acid (p. 83)

 _____. All human cells except sex cells have   chromosomes (p. 84)

 _____ chromosomes, arranged in 23 paris, and each chromosome   46 (p. 84)

carries _____ of genes. Sex cells are called   thousands (p. 64)

 _____ and contain _____ unpaired chromosomes. A   gametes (p. 84)/23 (p. 84)

sperm unites with an ovum through the process of

 _____; in this process, a new cell, called a   fertilization (p. 84)

 _____, is formed. Zygotes contain 23 _____   zygote (p. 84)/pairs (p. 84)

of chromosomes, with the mother and father each contributing

half. On the average, brothers and sisters will have about _____   50 (p. 85)

percent of their genes in common; the exception is
_____ twins, who are formed from a single zygote and share all their genes.

identical (monozygotic) (p. 85)

When the gene contributed by one parent conflicts with the gene contributed by the other parent for the same characteristic, the _____ gene will normally reveal its trait. Some traits are revealed only when the same gene has been contributed by both parents; these are _____ genes.

dominant (p. 85)

recessive (p. 85)

A malformation of the 21st chromosome can result in _____ _____.

Down

syndrome (p. 85)

Although researchers have studied genetic influences on animals, selective breeding experiments cannot be carried out with humans for _____ reasons. Instead, researchers have used two descriptive research methods. The first method involves comparing the characteristics of identical or _____ twins with dizygotic twins, formed from the fertilization of two ova by two sperm cells. The second method compares the characteristics of _____ children with those of both their biological parents and their adoptive parents.

ethical (p. 86)

monozygotic (p. 86)

adopted (p. 87)

Research strongly suggests that much of our behavior, both normal and abnormal, is influenced by _____ factors. The research also implies that _____ factors play powerful roles in shaping our personalities.

genetic (p. 88)

environmental (p. 88)

Applications Section

The central feature of schizophrenia is a marked abnormality of _____ _____. MRI images show greatly enlarged ventricles and a smaller _____ in the brains of severe schizophrenics. Brain abnormalities are also reflected in abnormal levels of the neurotransmitter _____. According to Mednick's "double strike" theory, schizophrenia is most likely to occur in those who (1) have a _____ _____ and (2) who suffered some health complication during _____ or _____. Another disease

though processes (p. 88)

hippocampus (p. 91)

dopamine (p. 92)

genetic

predisposition (p. 94)

pregnancy (p. 94)/birth (p. 94)

characterized by brain deterioration is _____   Alzheimer's

_____ .   disease (p. 96)

CONCEPT CHECK

Fill in the missing components of the following concept box. The answers are shown below the box.

Structures and Functions of the Brain

I. Structure	II. Function
a. Hindbrain	a.
b. Hypothalamus	b.
c.	c. This is a neural system composed of the amygdala, hippocampus, septal area, and cingulate cortex. It is also involved in emotional behavior (both arousal and cognitive aspects).
d. Cerebral cortex	d.
e. Lobes of the cerebral cortex	e.
f.	f. This is a neural system involved in helping to arouse the cerebral cortex.

Answers

IIa.   Its main responsibility is general "housekeeping" functions; the medulla controls breathing and other reflexes; the pons helps control balance and hearing; the cerebellum helps maintain muscle tone and coordinates muscular movements.

IIb.   This is the part of the forebrain involved in motivation and emotion, such as eating, drinking, sexuality, pleasure, anger, and fear. It also helps regulate body temperature, endocrine activity, immune system functioning, aggression, and even pleasure.

Ic.   Limbic system
IId.   This is the largest forebrain structure and is involved in conscious experience, voluntary action, language, and intelligence.
IIe.   The frontal lobes help to organize and predict the consequences of our behavior. It is also involved in our ability to speak language; the parietal lobes contain the somatosensory and motor area; the temporal lobes are involved in hearing and in understanding language; the occipital lobes are involved in vision.
If.   Reticular formation

Multiple-Choice Questions

1. The part of the neuron that receives messages from other neurons is called the
   a. dendrite
   b. axon
   c. cell body
   d. synapse
      (p. 54) LO 1

2. The part of the axon responsible for transmitting messages to the next neuron is the
   a. dendrite
   b. myelin sheath
   c. cell body
   d. axon
      (p. 55) LO 1

3. When positively charged ions enter the neuron, the process is called
   a. polarization
   b. depolarization
   c. semipermeability
   d. synaptical transmission
      (p. 56) LO 2

4. A "flowing storm of ions" characterizes
   a. synaptic transmission
   b. neural transmission
   c. neurotransmitters
   d. none of the above
      (p. 57) LO 2

5. Which of the following chemical substances makes it difficult for messages to be transmitted across synapses?
   a. excitatory neurotransmitters
   b. inhibitory neurotransmitters
   c. regulatory neurotransmitters
   d. all of the above
      (p. 57) LO 3

6. Which of the following transmit messages from the body into the nervous system?
   a. afferent neurons
   b. efferent neurons
   c. association neurons
   d. transmittal neurons
      (p. 59) LO 4

7. All of the following are functions of the autonomic nervous system except
   a. breathing
   b. voluntary movements
   c. sweating
   d. sexual arousal
      (p. 61) LO 5

8. Activation of the internal organs is carried out by the
   a. sympathetic nervous system
   b. parasympathetic nervous system
   c. somatic nervous system
   d. all of the above
      (p. 61) LO 5

9. For what purpose are PET scans and MRI used?
   a. observing the process of depolarization
   b. observing images of the brain
   c. measuring the responsiveness of the autonomic nervous system
   d. measuring the sensitivity of the skin's pain receptors
      (p. 65) LO 6

10. The structure responsible for maintaining muscle tone and coordination of muscle movements is the
    a. medulla
    b. pons
    c. cerebellum
    d. thalamus
    (p. 66) LO 7

11. A small area at the top of the hindbrain that helps regulate sensory reflexes is called the
    a. medulla
    b. pons
    c. forebrain
    d. midbrain
    (p. 66) LO 7

12. The hypothalamus plays a role in each of the following *except*
    a. motives and emotions
    b. regulating body temperature
    c. aggression
    d. routing incoming stimuli
    (p. 67) LO 8

13. According to the text, the most dramatic function of the limbic system is carried out by the
    a. hippocampus
    b. cingulate cortex
    c. amygdala
    d. septal area
    (p. 68) LO 9

14. The structure that allows communication between the two cerebral hemispheres is called the
    a. corpus callosum
    b. cingulate cortex
    c. reticular formation
    d. association area
    (p. 69) LO 10

15. People who experience Wernicke's aphasia have had damage to the
    a. frontal lobe
    b. somatosensory area
    c. temporal lobe
    d. occipital lobe
    (p. 73) LO 11

16. Research with split-brain patients has revealed the localization of what types of abilities in the left hemisphere?
    a. emotional expression
    b. recognition of stimuli
    c. abstract thinking
    d. language expression
    (p. 74) LO 10

17. The processing of sensory information from the eyes is carried out in which lobe of the cerebral cortex?
    a. frontal
    b. parietal
    c. temporal
    d. occipital
    (p. 74) LO 11

18. Research suggests that positive emotions are more likely to be processed in the
    a. corpus callosum
    b. left hemisphere
    c. right hemisphere
    d. amygdala
    (p. 75) LO 12

19. One structure that is involved in wakefulness is the
    a. hindbrain
    b. reticular formation
    c. pons
    d. cingulate cortex
    (p. 77) LO 13

20. The reticular formation interacts with
    a. the hindbrain
    b. the forebrain
    c. the midbrain
    d. all of the above
    (p. 77) LO 14

21. The gland that is often considered to be the master gland is the
    a. adrenal
    b. pituitary
    c. gonads
    d. thyroid
    (p. 79) LO 15

22. The gland(s) that produce(s) male and female sex hormones is (are) the
    a. pituitary gland
    b. thyroid gland
    c. adrenal glands
    d. gonads
       (p. 81) LO 15

23. Which of the following statements is *not* correct?
    a. Chromosomes contain genes, which are made of DNA.
    b. A normal human cell contains 46 chromosomes.
    c. A normal gamete contains 23 chromosomes.
    d. DNA is made of genes, which contain chromosomes.
       (p. 83) LO 16

24. How is it possible for two brown-eyed parents to have a blue-eyed child?
    a. if both parents contribute a recessive gene
    b. if both parents contribute a dominant gene
    c. if one parent contributes a recessive gene and one parent contributes a dominant gene
    d. It's impossible for two brown-eyed parents to have a blue-eyed child unless they adopt.
       (p. 85) LO 16

25. Down syndrome
    a. is caused by a malformation in the 21st chromosome pair
    b. can cause mental retardation
    c. causes obvious physical irregularities
    d. all of the above
       (p. 85) LO 16

26. Which of the following characterizes dizygotic twins?
    a. They are formed when two different eggs are fertilized by different sperm cells.
    b. They are formed by a single fertilized egg.
    c. They are identical in appearance
    d. They are identical in genetic structure.
       (p. 86) LO 17

27. To determine the influence of inheritance on behavior, psychologists have used what type of research?
    a. adoption studies
    b. twin studies
    c. formal experiments
    d. a and b above
       (p. 87) LO 17

28. Research on the role of inheritance in personality and abnormal behavior suggests that
    a. personality is inherited
    b. abnormal behavior is inherited
    c. personality and abnormal behavior may be influenced in part by inheritance
    d. none of the above
       (p. 87) LO 18

29. Each of the following has been demonstrated in the brains of schizophrenics *except*
    a. greatly enlarged ventricles
    b. a smaller hippocampus
    c. abnormal levels of acetylcholine
    d. abnormal levels of dopamine
       (p. 91) LO 19

30. According to Mednick, schizophrenia is likely in persons who
    a. have a genetic predisposition
    b. suffer a health complication during pregnancy or birth
    c. live with a schizophrenic parent
    d. a and b above
       (p. 94) LO 19

1. The answer is *A*. While dendrites receive messages, axons help transmit messages to other neurons. The cell body of the neuron contains the nucleus, while the synapse is the area between neurons.

2. The answer is *D*. Remember that the axon "acts on" the next cell.

3. The answer is *B*. The polarized state is the resting state of the neuron, when negative ions are mostly inside and positive ions are mostly outside the cell membrane. Semipermeability refers to the fact that some, but not all, ions can pass through the membrane. When electrical charges reach the synapse, transmission across the gap occurs.

4. The answer is *B*. The process of depolarization along the membrane of a neuron allows for the massive influx of sodium ions.

5. The answer is *B*. Excitatory neurotransmitters increase the likelihood of messages crossing the synapse, and the term regulatory neurotransmitters was made up especially for this question.

6. The answer is *A*. Efferent neurons transmit messages from the central nervous system to the organs and muscles of the body, while association neurons are the neurons in the brain and spinal cord that process the information. Transmittal neurons do not, as far as I know, exist.

7. The answer is *B*. Voluntary movements are higher-order functions and are not processed by the autonomic nervous system.

8. The answer is *A*. The sympathetic nervous system generally activates, while the parasympathetic system is generally involved in calming the organs.

9. The answer is *B*. *PET* stands for positron emission topography and *MRI* stands for magnetic resonance imaging.

10. The answer is *C*. The medulla controls breathing and a variety of reflexes. The pons helps regulate balance, hearing, and some parasympathetic functions. The thalamus helps to route messages to the appropriate parts of the brain.

11. The answer is *D*. The medulla and pons are both part of the hindbrain. The forebrain is the structure that contains the cerebral cortex.

12. The answer is *D*. The routing function is carried out by the thalamus.

13. The answer is *C*. Damage to the amygdala may result in a complete absence of fear or rage, although occasionally the result is uncontrollable rage.

14. The answer is *A*. Severing the corpus callosum results in some unusual problems, discussed in the *Research Report:* "Split Brains."

15. The answer is *C*. Wernicke's aphasia is characterized by an inability to understand language spoken by others, although the person can speak normally. Wernicke's area is located in the left hemisphere.

16. The answer is *D*. When information is presented to the left visual field of each eye, the information reaches the right hemisphere, which has no area controlling verbal expression. As a result, the patient is unable to identify the information.

17. The answer is *D*. Damage to the visual area of the occipital lobe can result in partial or even total blindness.

18. The answer is *B*. Conversely, the right hemisphere is more likely to process negative emotions.

19. The answer is *B*. The reticular formation spans parts of the hindbrain, the midbrain, and the forebrain and helps allow the brain to be an interacting system.

20. The answer is *D*. The reticular formation is an excellent example of the fact that, while structures in the brain carry out specific functions, the brain is an interacting system.

21. The answer is *B*. The hormones of the pituitary help to regulate the activities of the other glands in the endocrine system.

22. The answer is *D*. The adrenals are involved in emotional arousal. The thyroid gland helps to regulate metabolism. The pituitary gland is often called the "master gland" because it helps to regulate the other glands in the endocrine system.

23. The correct answer is *D*. Strands of DNA contain the genetic code to make us who and what we are.

24. The answer is *A*. If both brown-eyed parents possess a recessive gene for blue eyes, and if both contribute this gene to their offspring, their child will have blue eyes.
25. The correct answer is *D*. Down syndrome is one of a variety of chromosomal abnormalities that results in mental retardation.
26. The answer is *A*. Dizygotic twins are no more alike genetically than siblings born at different times; monozygotic twins, however, develop from a single fertilized egg cell and are also called identical twins.
27. The answer is *D*. Both twin studies and adoption studies have allowed psychologists to begin to understand the influence of heredity on behavior. These studies are correlational in nature, however, and not based on formal experiments as described in chapter 1.
28. The answer is *C*. While research has shown that genetic factors are clearly at work, they do not explain all of the differences between people.
29. The answer is *C*. MRI images have revealed many of the dramatic differences between a normal brain and the brains of schizophrenics.
30. The answer is *D*. This hypothesis is referred to as the "double-strike" theory of schizophrenia.

Chapter **3**   **Sensation and Perception**

Learning Objectives

1. Distinguish between sensation and perception.
2. Define transduction.
3. Compare and contrast the absolute threshold and the difference threshold.
4. Explain sensory adaptation.
5. State Weber's Law and discuss its relevance.
6. Explain how the different parts of the eye work together to produce vision.
7. Describe the roles played by the rods and cones in both dark adaptation and light adaptation.
8. Compare and contrast the trichromatic theory and the opponent-process theory; describe the supporting evidence for each theory.
9. Explain how different parts of the ear work together to produce audition (hearing).
10. Describe the roles played by the vestibular organ and the kinesthetic receptors in providing information about orientation and movement.
11. Describe the functions of the skin receptors in detecting pressure, temperature, and pain.
12. Explain the gate control theory of pain and describe the role played by endorphins in "runner's high," acupuncture, and placebos.
13. Discuss the phenomenon of phantom limb pain.
14. List the four basic taste sensations and the seven primary odors; explain the stereochemical theory.
15. Name and explain the five Gestalt principles of perceptual organization.
16. Describe the four kinds of perceptual constancy.
17. Identify the monocular cues and binocular cues of depth perception.
18. Explain how visual illusions are produced.
19. Explain how individual and cultural factors influence perception.
20. (From the "Application" section) Discuss the relationship between visual perception, illusions, and art.

Chapter Overview

Sensation refers to the ability of the sense organs to receive messages from the outside world, while perception refers to the ability to organize and interpret these messages.

We receive external stimuli through specialized sensory receptor cells. First, sense organs receive stimuli. Next, they transduce this sensory energy into neural impulses. The neural impulses are then sent to the brain to be interpreted. The field that studies the relationships between physical stimuli and psychological sensations is called psychophysics.

The sense of sight functions by detecting light energy. The intensity of a light wave determines its brightness, while the wavelength largely determines color. The eye, which works much like a camera, is the primary sense organ for seeing. Light enters the eye through the cornea and lens and then enters the retina. Rods and cones transduce light waves into neural impulses for transportation to the brain. The 100 million rods are located throughout the retina but are not found in the fovea. Although they are active in peripheral vision and vision in dim light, they do not play a role in color vision. The 6 million cones, clustered mainly near the fovea, are involved in color vision. Two theories that explain color vision are trichromatic theory and opponent-process theory.

The sense of hearing functions by detecting sound waves. The frequency of sound waves determines pitch, while their intensity determines loudness. The outer ear collects sound waves, which vibrate the eardrum. The eardrum is connected to a series of movable bones in the middle ear. The inner ear, which contains the cochlea and the organ of Corti, transduces the sound waves' energy into neural impulses. These impulses are transported to the brain.

The sensory system also receives information about internal stimuli. For example, the vestibular organ provides information about body orientation, and the kinesthetic sense reports bodily position and movement. The various skin senses can detect pressure, temperature, and pain.

Humans also possess chemical senses, such as taste and smell. These senses respond to chemicals in the environment rather than to energy.

The interpretation of sensory neural impulses that have been transmitted to the brain is called perception. Perception is an active mental process. Gestalt principles explain many of the ways in which humans tend to organize sensory information. Individual factors, such as motivation and prior learning, also affect perception.

Key Terms Exercise

For each of the following exercises, match the key terms on the left with the correct definitions on the right. Page references to the text follow the terms so that you may refer to the text for any items you answer incorrectly or do not understand completely. You may check your responses immediately by referring to the answers that follow each exercise.

Sensation (I)

_____ 1. sense organs (p. 108)
_____ 2. sensory receptor cells (p. 108)
_____ 3. sensation (p. 108)
_____ 4. perception (p. 108)
_____ 5. stimulus (p. 108)

a. cells that translate messages into neural impulses
b. organs that receive stimuli
c. the process of organizing and interpreting information
d. any aspect of the outside world that influences our behavior
e. the process of receiving, translating, and transmitting messages from the outside world to the brain

ANSWERS

1. b   4. c
2. a   5. d
3. e

Sensation (II)

_____ 1. transduction (p. 108)
_____ 2. absolute threshold (p. 109)
_____ 3. difference threshold (p. 109)
_____ 4. sensory adaptation (p. 109)
_____ 5. psychophysics (p. 109)

a. a weakened sensation resulting from prolonged presentation of the stimulus
b. the smallest magnitude of a stimulus that can be detected half of the time
c. a specialty field that studies sensory limits, sensory adaption, etc.
d. the translation of energy from one form into another
e. the smallest difference between two stimuli that can be detected half of the time

ANSWERS

1. d   4. a
2. b   5. c
3. e

Vision (I)

_____ 1. retina (p. 114)
_____ 2. rods (p. 114)
_____ 3. cones (p. 114)
_____ 4. fovea (p. 114)

a. the central spot of the retina
b. cells located in the center of the retina that code information about light, dark, and color
c. the area that contains the rods and cones
d. cells located outside the center of the retina that code information about light and dark

ANSWERS

1. c   3. b
2. d   4. a

Vision (II)

_____ 1. optic nerve (p. 115)
_____ 2. dark and light adaptation (p. 115)
_____ 3. trichromatic theory (p. 117)
_____ 4. opponent-process theory (p. 117)

a. a theory of color vision that suggests the eye has two kinds of cones
b. changed sensitivity of the eye in response to a change in overall illumination
c. the nerve that carries messages about vision to the brain
d. a theory of color vision that suggests that the eye has three kinds of cones

ANSWERS

1. c   3. d
2. b   4. a

Hearing (I)

_____ 1. audition (p. 120)
_____ 2. eardrum (p. 121)
_____ 3. hammer, anvil, and stirrup (p. 121)
_____ 4. cochlea (p. 122)
_____ 5. basilar membrane (p. 122)
_____ 6. organ of Corti (p. 122)

a. the sense of hearing
b. a membrane in the middle ear
c. a structure of the inner ear that is filled with fluid
d. contains receptor cells that transduce sound waves into neural impulses
e. three bones of the middle ear
f. the organ of Corti rests upon this

ANSWERS

1. a	4. c
2. b	5. f
3. e	6. d

Body Senses, Chemical Senses, and Perception

_____ 1. vestibular organ (p. 125)
_____ 2. kinesthetic receptors (p. 125)
_____ 3. semicircular canals (p. 126)
_____ 4. gustation (p. 136)
_____ 5. olfaction (p. 136)
_____ 6. stereochemical theory (p. 138)
_____ 7. perceptual constancy (p. 142)
_____ 8. monocular and binocular cues (p. 143)

a. the theory that odor receptors are stimulated by specific molecules
b. the sense of taste
c. receptors that provide information about movement, posture, and orientation
d. structures in the inner ear that provide the brain with information about balance and movement
e. three tubes in the vestibular organ that inform the brain about tilts of the head and body
f. the sense of smell
g. visual cues that permit us to perceive distance
h. the tendency to perceive objects as being relatively unchanging

ANSWERS

1. d	5. f
2. c	6. a
3. e	7. h
4. b	8. g

Guided Review

Sensation: Receiving Messages about the World

Humans receive messages through their sense organs. Sense organs operate through _____ _____ _____. These cells allow us to receive, translate, and transmit messages to the brain, a process called _____. We interpret this

sensory receptor cells (p. 108)

sensation (p. 108)

information through a process called _____. Any aspect   perception (p. 108)

of the outside world that directly influences our behavior is a

_____. Stimuli are translated from one form of energy   stimulus (p. 108)

to another through a process called _____. Sensory   transduction (p. 108)

receptor cells transduce sensory energy into _____   neural

_____.   impulses (p. 108)

　　　Not all sensory messages can be detected. The smallest

magnitude of a stimulus that can be detected half the time is the

_____ _____; the smallest difference between   absolute threshold (p. 109)

two stimuli that can be detected half the time is called the

_____ _____. Stimuli that are presented for   difference threshold (p. 109)

prolonged periods may cause weaker sensations due to

_____ _____. The field that studies sensory   sensory adaptation (p. 109)

limits and sensory adaptation is _____. The law stating   psychophysics (p. 109)

that the amount of change in a stimulus needed to detect a

difference is proportional to the intensity of the original stimulus is

called _____ _____.   Weber's law (p. 111)

Vision: Your Human Camera

Visible light is part of a form of energy called _____   electromagnetic (p. 113)

_____, which includes electricity and radio waves. Light   radiation (p. 113)

is composed of waves that have both _____ and   frequency (p. 113)

_____. The intensity of the light determines the   intensity (p. 113)

_____, while the _____ determines the color   brightness (p. 113)/wavelength (p. 113)

we see.

　　　Light first passes through a clear protective coating called the

_____. The colored part of the eye, the   cornea (p. 114)

_____, regulates the light passing through the pupil into   iris (p. 114)

the _____. The lens is held in place by ligaments that   lens (p. 114)

are attached to the _____ _____. This muscle   ciliary muscle (p. 114)

regulates the image that falls on the light-sensitive

_____. Two types of receptor cells in the retina are the   retina (p. 114)

_____ and _____. Each eye has about   rods (p. 114)/cones (p. 114)

_____ _____ cones and about _____ _____ rods.   6 million (p. 114)/125 million (p. 114)

The greatest concentration of cones is in the _____ . In good light, _____ _____ is best for images focused directly on the fovea. The rods are located throughout the retina except in the center. There are four differences between rods and cones: (1) rods are largely responsible for _____ vision; (2) rods are much more sensitive to _____ than the cones; (3) rods produce images that are perceived with less _____ _____ ; and (4) only cones code information about _____ . An area near the center of the retina contains no rods or cones and is called the _____ _____ . Information in the optic nerve crosses over at the _____ _____ .

fovea (p. 114)
visual acuity (p. 114)

peripheral (p. 114)
light (p. 114)
visual acuity (p. 114)
color (p. 115)

blind spot (p. 115)
optic chiasm (p. 115)

The processes by which the eyes change their sensitivity to darkness or light are referred to as _____ ____ _____ _____ . The following two theories of color vision have received attention from psychologists: (1) the theory that there are three kinds of cones in the retina, responding to either the red, green, or blue range of wavelength, referred to as _____ _____ ; and (2) the theory that there are two kinds of cones that respond to light in either the red-green or yellow-blue ranges of wavelength, called the _____- _____ _____ . The opponent-process theory successfully explains four phenomena: _____ colors, color _____ , color _____ , and _____ responses.

dark and
light adaptation (p. 115–116)

trichromatic theory (p. 117)

opponent-
process theory (p. 117)
complementary (p. 117)
afterimages (p. 118)/blindness (p. 118)
neuron (p. 118)

Total color blindness is a rare condition called _____ . A type of color blindness in which the individual is unable to distinguish red from green or yellow from blue is called _____ .

monochromacy (p. 118)

dichromacy (p. 118)

Hearing: Sensing Sound Waves

The sense of hearing is called _____ . Audition occurs when there are vibratory changes in the air known as _____ _____ . The rate of vibration of sound waves is termed the _____ ____ _____ ; its

audition (p. 120)

sound waves (p. 120)
frequency of cycles (p. 120)

unit of measurement is called _____. Our experience of
these sound vibrations is called _____. The loudness of
a sound is determined by its _____. Intensity is
measured in units called _____. The complexity of a
sound wave determines the _____ of a sound.

hertz (p. 120)

pitch (p. 121)

intensity (p. 120)

decibels (p. 121)

timbre (p. 121)

    The external part of the ear, which helps to collect sound, is
the _____. The pinna is connected to the middle ear by
the _____ _____ _____. The first
structure of the middle ear is the _____. Sound waves
vibrate the eardrum; this sets into movement the three bones of
the middle ear, called the _____, _____, and
_____. In the inner ear, a membrane called the ____
_____ is set into motion. The vibration of the oval
window creates waves in the fluid-filled _____. The
pressure of these waves is relieved by the _____
_____. The ear's sensory receptors, located in the
_____ ____ _____, are stimulated by a
membrane in the cochlea called the _____
_____. The organ of Corti then codes the messages to
the brain, based on the _____ and the _____
of the sound waves. Not all sounds are transmitted from the outer
ear to the cochlea; for example, we hear ourselves speak largely
through _____ _____ hearing. The existence
of two ears helps us to _____ the origin of sounds.

pinna (p. 121)

external auditory canal (p. 121)

eardrum (p. 121)

hammer (p. 121)/anvil (p. 121)

stirrup (p. 121)/oval

window (p. 122)

cochlea (p. 122)

round

window (p. 122)

organ of Corti (p. 122)

basilar

membrane (p. 122)

intensity (p. 122)/frequency (p. 122)

bone conduction (p. 122)

locate (p. 123–124)

Body Senses: Messages from Myself

Messages about the orientation and movement of the body come
from two kinds of sense organs. The first, located in the inner ear,
is the _____ _____. This organ is composed
of (1) fluid-filled sacs called the _____ and
_____, which tell the brain about the body's orientation,
and (2) three nearly circular tubes that inform the brain about tilts
of the head and body, called the _____
_____. The sensory receptors of each canal are located
in the _____.

vestibular organ (p. 125)

saccule (p. 126)

utricle (p. 126)

semicircular

canals (p. 126)

cupula (p. 126)

The _____ _____ consists of individual
receptors located in the skin, muscles, joints, and tendons. The skin
can detect _____, _____, and
_____. It contains four types of receptors:
_____ nerve endings, _____ cells, tactile
_____, and specialized _____ bulbs.
Apparently, all four types play a role in detecting _____,
while the free nerve endings are also the primary receptors for
temperature and _____.

The sensitivity of the skin differs from one region to the next.
The most sensitive regions are the _____, the
_____, and the _____. One set of spots on
the skin detects _____ and one set detects
_____, but the sensation of _____
_____ is created by both warm and cold spots.

Psychologists know that pain is conducted by _____
_____ _____. We often experience "first and
second pain" due to the existence of _____ and
_____ neural pathways. No direct relationship exists
between the pain stimulus and the amount of pain a person
experiences. Sometimes circumstances can block pain. One theory
that explains these phenomena is called the _____
_____ _____ _____ _____. This
theory proposes that pain signals are allowed in or blocked from
the brain by neural "gates."

The pain gates appear to be operated by specialized neurons
called _____ neurons. These neurons inhibit the pain
neurons by using substances called _____, which inhibit
the firing of axons. Recent evidence suggests that women have a
second pain-gate mechanism, based on the hormone
_____. The opiate morphine duplicates the effects of
_____. Additionally, "runner's high" appears to be the
result of the release of high levels of _____. Research
also suggests that the pain-reducing effects of _____ and
placebo medications may be due to stimulating the body's

kinesthetic sense (p. 126)

pressure (p. 127)/temperature (p. 127)

pain (p. 127)

free (p. 127)/basket (p. 127)

discs (p. 127)/end (p. 127)

pressure (p. 128)

pain (p. 129)

fingertips (p. 128)

lips (p. 128)/genitals (p. 128)

warmth (p. 128)

coldness (p. 128)/intense

heat (p. 129)

free

nerve endings (p. 129)

rapid (p. 129)

slow (p. 129)

gate

control theory of pain (p. 129)

gate (p. 130)

endorphins (p. 130)

estrogen (p. 130)

endorphins (p. 130)

endorphins (p. 130)

acupuncture (p. 130)

endorphins. Endorphins may have a negative effect on the body's

_____ system. According to Melzack, pain sensations   immune (p. 130)

from a phantom limb may arise from spontaneous neural firing in

the _____ .   brain (p. 133)

Chemical Senses: The Flavors and Aromas of Life

The sense of taste, called _____ , and the sense of smell,   gustation (p. 136)

called _____ , respond to chemicals rather than to   olfaction (p. 136)

energy. There are approximately _____ taste buds on   10,000 (p. 136)

the tongue, each containing approximately a dozen sensory

receptors called _____ . The taste buds are clustered   taste cells (p. 136)

together in bumps called _____ . All of our sensations of   papillae (p. 136)

taste result from the four basic sensations: _____ ,   sweetness (p. 137)

sourness, _____ , and bitterness.   saltiness (p. 137)

Olfactory receptor cells are located in the nasal cavity in a

mucous-coated sheet called the _____ _____ .   olfactory epithelium (p. 137)

One system of classifying odors suggests that all of the complex

odors and aromas of life are combinations of _____   seven (p. 137)

primary qualities. Professionals who create perfumes and other

aromas, however, distinguish _____ different types of   146 (p. 137)

odors. Nearly all of the odors that humans can detect are

_____ compounds. The theory that odor receptors can   organic (p. 137)

only be stimulated by molecules of a specific size and shape is

called the _____ theory.   stereochemical (p. 138)

Perception: Interpreting Sensory Messages

The process of organizing and interpreting neural energy is

_____ . Gestalt psychologists have described the   perception (p. 138)

following ways in which we organize our visual perception: (1) the

center of attention and the background, called _____ -   figure-

_____ , can be reversed; (2) things that are close   ground (p. 140)

together are perceived as belonging together, according to the

principle of _____ ; (3) we tend to perceive   proximity (p. 140)

_____ in lines and patterns; (4) similar things tend to be   continuity (p. 140)

perceived together, according to the principle of _____ ;   similarity (p. 140) and (5) incomplete figures are perceived as wholes, according to the concept of _____.   closure (p. 140)

Although raw sensations are constantly changing, we tend to perceive objects as being fairly constant and unchanging. This tendency is called _____ _____ and relates to   perceptual constancy (p. 142)
the brightness, color, size, and shape of objects.

We are able to perceive a three-dimensional world with a two-dimensional retina because we use _____ in depth   cues (p. 143)
perception. Those cues that can be seen by one eye are

_____ cues, while those that require both eyes are   monocular (p. 143)
called _____ cues. The monocular cues are texture   binocular (p. 143)
_____, linear _____, superposition,   gradient (p. 143)/perspective (p. 143)
shadowing, speed of _____, aerial _____, and   movement (p. 143)/perspective (p. 143)
accommodation. The binocular cues are convergence and retinal

_____.   disparity (p. 144)

Intentional manipulations of cues to create a perception of something that is not real are referred to as _____   visual

_____.   illusions (p. 145)

There is evidence that _____ and _____   individual (p. 148)/cultural (p. 148)
factors play an important role in perception.

Painters often use _____ cues of depth perception   monocular (p. 151)
to create the illusion of a _____-dimensional object.   three (p. 151)

CONCEPT CHECK

Fill in the missing components of the following concept box. The answers are shown below the box.

Structures and Functions of the Eyes and Ears

I. Structure	II. Function
a. Iris	a.
b.	b. This is the light-sensitive area at the back of the eye.
c. Rods	c.
d.	d. These are concentrated in the fovea and code information light, dark, and color.
e. Optic nerve	e.
f. Pinna	f.
g.	g. This is a thin membrane in the middle ear that vibrates in response to sound waves.
h. Cochlea	h.
i.	i. This contains the receptor cells that transduce the sound waves of the cochlear fluid into neural impulses.

Answers

a. The iris opens and closes to control the amount of light that passes through the pupil into the lens.
b. Retina
c. The rods are located throughout the retina except in the fovea. They are largely responsible for peripheral vision and are highly sensitive to light. They cannot code information about color.
d. Cones
e. This carries neural messages to the brain.

f. This is the outer ear, which is responsible for collecting sound waves.
g. Eardrum
h. This is a long, curled structure, filled with fluid. It is set into motion by the oval window.
i. Organ of Corti

Multiple-Choice Questions

1. Each of the following is part of the process of sensation *except*
    a. receiving messages
    b. translating messages
    c. transmitting messages
    d. interpreting messages
        (p. 108) LO 1

2. Which of the following describes the process of transduction?
    a. when a friend plays the radio below your absolute threshold
    b. when light waves are converted to neural impulses
    c. when stimuli occur that are not attended to
    d. none of the above
        (p. 108) LO 2

3. After repeatedly asking your roommate to turn down the stereo so that you can study your psychology, you lose your temper. You rush into the living room, where your roommate indicates that the stereo *was* turned down! The amount by which the stereo was turned down was below your
    a. difference threshold
    b. absolute threshold
    c. sensory adaption level
    d. in-between threshold
        (p. 109) LO 3

4. The smallest magnitude of a stimulus that can be detected is called the
    a. absolute threshold
    b. difference threshold
    c. minimum threshold
    d. transduction threshold
        (p. 108) LO 3

5. Joe was upset when he started his car because the radio blared out loudly. Then he realized that he was the one who last played the car radio. "I didn't think I had the volume turned up so high," he thought. What phenomenon is occurring here?
    a. the absolute threshold
    b. the difference threshold
    c. sensory adaptation
    d. transduction
        (p. 109) LO 4

6. Weber's law
    a. refers to the ability to detect changes in the intensity of various stimuli
    b. helps to explain the process of sensory adaptation
    c. is useful in predicting the absolute threshold
    d. a and b above
        (p. 111) LO 5

7. In the eye, light waves are transduced into neural impulses by
    a. the cornea and the iris
    b. the pupil and the lens
    c. the rods and the cones
    d. none of the above
        (p. 114) LO 6

8. The amount of light entering the eye is controlled by the
    a. pupil
    b. lens
    c. iris
    d. fovea
        (p. 114) LO 6

9. When compared with cones, rods
   a. are responsible for peripheral vision
   b. are less sensitive to light
   c. produce images perceived with good visual acuity
   d. can code information about color
   (p. 114) LO 7

10. Rods and cones stop firing almost completely during the process of
   a. dark adaptation
   b. light adaptation
   c. color vision
   d. monochromacy
   (p. 115) LO 7

11. Which of the following events is explained by the opponent-process theory of color vision?
   a. complementary colors
   b. color afterimages
   c. neuron responses
   d. all of the above
   (p. 117) LO 8

12. The inability to distinguish the color red from the color green is called
   a. monochromacy
   b. dichromacy
   c. trichromatic theory
   d. opponent-process
   (p. 118) LO 8

13. The eardrum, hammer, anvil, and stirrup are located in the
   a. inner ear
   b. middle ear
   c. outer ear
   d. external auditory canal
   (p. 121) LO 9

14. The organ of Corti codes neural messages for the brain based on
   a. the intensity of a sound wave
   b. the frequency of a sound wave
   c. the pitch of a sound wave
   d. a and b above
   (p. 122) LO 9

15. In the car, sound waves are transduced into neural messages by receptors located in the
   a. organ of Corti
   b. hammer, anvil, and stirrup
   c. middle ear
   d. pinna
   (p. 122) LO 9

16. Information about the location and movement of skin, muscles, joints, and tendons is provided by
   a. basket cells
   b. kinesthetic receptors
   c. tactile discs
   d. specialized end bulbs
   (p. 125) LO 10

17. If you were to touch an extremely hot surface, which types of skin receptors would be likely to fire?
   a. heat receptors
   b. cold receptors
   c. pain receptors
   d. all of the above
   (p. 127) LO 11

18. Each of the following phenomena may be explained by endorphins *except*
   a. visual acuity
   b. "runner's high"
   c. acupuncture
   d. placebos
   (p. 130) LO 12

19. Pain gates appear to use
   a. endorphins
   b. estrogen in women
   c. placebos
   d. a and b above
   (p. 130) LO 12

20. According to Melzack, phantom pain messages arise from
   a. the severed nerves from the missing limb
   b. the spinal cord continuing to fire
   c. spontaneous firing of neural networks in the brain
   d. all of the above
   (p. 132) LO 13

21. Each of the following is a basic taste sensation *except*
    a. spicy
    b. sweet
    c. sour
    d. bitter
       (p. 137) LO 14

22. Molecules responsible for each of the primary odors have a specific shape that will "fit" only one type of receptor, according to the
    a. olfactory epithelium approach
    b. opponent-process theory of smell
    c. integrated-key theory
    d. stereochemical theory
       (p. 138) LO 14

23. The tendency to mentally "fill in" incomplete figures is the Gestalt principle of perception called
    a. figure-ground
    b. proximity
    c. dissimilarity
    d. closure
       (p. 140) LO 15

24. The perception of items as containing a center and a background is referred to as the Gestalt principle of
    a. proximity
    b. figure-ground
    c. continuity
    d. similarity
       (p. 140) LO 15

25. We continue to perceive that a penny is round, regardless of the angle from which it is viewed. This is an example of a process called
    a. perceptual constancy
    b. light adaptation
    c. figure-grounding
    d. proximity
       (p. 142) LO 16

26. Each of the following is a monocular cue *except*
    a. texture gradient
    b. aerial perspective
    c. accommodation
    d. convergence
       (p. 144) LO 17

27. According to the text, which illusion may help to explain some airplane crashes?
    a. the Ames room
    b. the Müller-Lyer illusion
    c. the Ponzo illusion
    d. the Poggendorf illusion
       (p. 148) LO 18

28. The Ames room demonstrates
    a. convergence
    b. retinal disparity
    c. a visual illusion
    d. all of the above
       (p. 146) LO 18

29. According to the text, the hook-swinging ceremony is proof of
    a. the influence of motivation on perception
    b. individual influences on perception
    c. cultural influences on perception
    d. none of the above
       (p. 149) LO 19

30. According to the text, effective painters, drawers, and sculptors make good use of
    a. depth perception cues
    b. visual illusions
    c. perceptual constancy cues
    d. all of the above
       (p. 151) LO 20

Multiple-Choice Answers

1. The answer is *D*. While choices *A, B,* and *C* are all part of the process of sensation, the process of interpreting messages is called perception.
2. The answer is *B*. The process of transduction refers to translating one form of energy to another. Thus, in order for people to see, light waves must be transduced into neural impulses.

3. The answer is *A*. The difference threshold is the smallest difference between two stimuli that can be detected half the time. Your roommate did, in fact, turn down the volume of the stereo, but the difference was small enough so that you could not detect it. Now, aren't you sorry that you yelled at your roomie?

4. The answer is *A*. While the absolute threshold refers to the smallest magnitude of a stimulus that can be detected, the difference threshold is the smallest difference between two stimuli that can be detected half the time.

5. The answer is *C*. Sensory adaptation refers to the weakened magnitude of a sensation resulting from prolonged presentation of a stimulus. Other examples include "getting used to" the cool water in a swimming pool and "getting used to" loud rock music.

6. The answer is *A*. Weber's law states that the *difference* threshold is in direct proportion to the intensity of the original stimulus. This helps to predict our ability to detect changes in stimuli. The *absolute* threshold refers to the smallest magnitude of a stimulus that can be detected.

7. The answer is *C*. The rods and cones are receptor cells that are found in the retina. The cornea is a protective covering on the eye's surface. The iris regulates the amount of light that enters the eye. The pupil is the opening of the iris, while the lens focuses light on the retina.

8. The answer is *C*. The colored part of the eye, the iris, opens and closes to regulate the amount of light passing through the pupil into the lens.

9. The answer is *A*. Each of the other alternatives is true of cones.

10. The answer is *A*. When we enter a dark room after being in sunlight, the rods and cones are not sensitive enough to be stimulated by the low-intensity light. The receptors thus get to rest before regaining their sensitivity to light. In light adaptation, on the other hand, the rods and cones that have been "in the dark" for a while are extremely sensitive to light.

11. The answer is *D*. According to the opponent-process theory, there are two kinds of cones in the retina that respond to light in either the red-green or yellow-blue ranges of wavelength.

12. The answer is *B*. While dichromats are unable to distinguish red from green (or yellow from blue), monochromats cannot see in color at all.

13. The answer is *B*. The middle ear transduces sound waves into mechanical energy and passes the energy on to the inner ear.

14. The answer is *D*. The intensity is coded by the number of receptors that fire, while the frequency is coded according to location in the organ of Corti and the firing of volleys of impulses by different groups of neurons.

15. The answer is *A*. The organ of Corti is located in the cochlea of the inner ear. The outer ear, called the pinna, helps to collect sound waves. The middle ear transduces sound waves into mechanical energy. The hammer, anvil, and stirrup are small bones located in the middle ear.

16. The answer is *B*. Kinesthetic receptors are individual sensory receptors located in the skin, muscles, joints, and tendons. Basket cells, tactile discs, and specialized end bulbs are different receptors found in the skin.

17. The answer is *D*. The sensation of intense heat is created by both heat and cold receptors. At extremely high temperatures, the pain receptors also fire.

18. The answer is *A*. Endorphins have been implicated in everything from the gate control theory of pain to the experience of "runner's high," the pain-reducing effects of acupuncture, and the effects of placebos.

19. The answer is *D*. While the effect of endorphins on gate neurons has been known for some time, recent research has pointed to the importance of estrogen in helping block pain for women.

20. The answer is *C*. According to Melzack, the cerebral cortex has formed a "map" of the body; spontaneous firing of neurons is interpreted as phantom limb pain.

21. The answer is *A*. The missing basic taste sensation is saltiness.

22. The answer is *D*. All of the other choices are flights of whimsy.

23. The answer is *D*. Figure-ground refers to the tendency to focus on figure, while the remainder of a stimulus is indistinct background. The principle of proximity suggests that things that are close together are usually perceived as belonging together. Dissimilarity is not a Gestalt principle.

24. The answer is *B*. The center of our attention is the figure and the rest is background, as demonstrated by the vase figure.
25. The answer is *A*. The principle of perceptual constancy in this particular example is called shape constancy. Other examples of perceptual constancy are brightness constancy, color constancy, and size constancy.
26. The answer is *D*. Both monocular and binocular cues allow us to perceive depth. Monocular cues are those that can be seen using one eye. Binocular cues require both eyes for depth perception. Convergence is an example of a binocular cue.
27. The answer is *D*. The Poggendorf illusion, in which lines appear to "move over" after they pass through solid objects, has been suggested as the cause of at least one tragic airplane crash.
28. The answer is *C*. Visual illusions are astounding because they intentionally manipulate the perceptual cues we use in order to create a perception of something that is not real.
29. The answer is *C*. The hook-swinging ceremony, a practice in which an individual perceives no pain in spite of the fact that two metal hooks are pushed through his or her back, indicates the powerful influence of culture on individual perception.
30. The answer is *D*. Artists use monocular cues of depth perception to create the illusion of three-dimensional objects.

Learning Objectives

1. Define consciousness and compare directed consciousness, flowing consciousness, and daydreams.
2. Explain Hilgard's concept of divided consciousness.
3. Identify the characteristics of the unconscious mind.
4. List and describe the stages of sleep.
5. Describe the relationship between dream sleep and REM sleep.
6. Compare and contrast REM sleep and non-REM sleep features.
7. Describe the theories that seek to explain why we sleep and dream.
8. Discuss Sigmund Freud's ideas about dream content and meaning.
9. Describe the following sleep phenomena: nightmares, night terrors, sleepwalking, and sleeptalking.
10. Distinguish among insomnia, narcolepsy, and sleep apnea.
11. Explain circadian and other rhythms; describe the consequences of interrupting circadian rhythms.
12. List the characteristics of altered states of consciousness.
13. Describe the meditation process and discuss the controversy regarding the benefits of meditation.
14. Identify the characteristics of the hypnotic state.
15. Describe depersonalization and astral projection.
16. Describe the reports of individuals who have had near-death experiences.
17. List variables that influence individual responses to drugs.
18. Distinguish between psychological dependence and physiological addiction.
19. Explain the effects of stimulants and compare the effects of amphetamines and cocaine.
20. Describe the effects of sedatives, tranquilizers, and narcotics.
21. Describe the effects of inhalants, hallucinogens, and marijuana.
22. Differentiate between act-alike drugs and designer drugs.
23. Explain why polydrug abuse is a societal problem.
24. (From the "Application" section) Discuss the issues regarding legal consciousness-altering drugs.

Chapter Overview

Consciousness is a state of awareness. Directed consciousness occurs when our awareness is directed toward a single focus. In the state of flowing consciousness, awareness drifts from one thought to another. Daydreams combine the features of directed consciousness and dreamlike fantasies. Divided consciousness refers to the splitting off of two conscious activities that occur simultaneously. The unconscious mind processes information without our being consciously aware.

Sleep begins as we enter a semiwakeful hypnagogic state and becomes progressively deeper as we enter dreaming or REM sleep. WE typically enter dream sleep four to six times each night. Dreams include alterations of reality, which Freudian psychologists believe provide information about the unconscious mind. Sleeping and dreaming seem essential to physical and physiological health; sleep deprivation brings on fatigue, inefficiency, and irritability. Nightmares, night terrors, sleepwalking, and sleeptalking are fairly common sleep phenomena. Three types of sleep disorders are insomnia, narcolepsy, and sleep apnea. Sleep cycles follow a pattern called the circadian rhythm.

Altered states of consciousness share several common characteristics, including distortions of perception, intense positive emotions, a sense of unity, and others. Many persons achieve a very relaxed state by a process called meditation. Hypnosis is sometimes used to alter consciousness and to relieve pain.

Depersonalization is the experience of one's body or surroundings becoming distorted or "unreal" in some way.

Consciousness can be altered through the use of various psychotropic drugs. These may be classified as stimulants, depressants, inhalants, and hallucinogens. Although risks differ from drug to drug, all drug users run the risk of abuse, dependence, addiction, and direct or indirect side effects.

Stimulants are drugs that activate the central nervous system. Even mild stimulants like caffeine and nicotine are physiologically addictive. Amphetamines and cocaine are other highly addictive stimulants. Depressants influence conscious activity by depressing pats of the central nervous system. Alcohol, tranquilizers, sedatives, and narcotics are all depressant drugs. Inhalants are usually toxic and often cause brain damage. Hallucinogens alter perceptions, cause hallucinations, and are often associated with bizarre or violent behavior. Psychological dependence is common with hallucinogens. Marijuana is a popular although illegal drug that produces a sense of well-being and sometimes alters perception. Polydrug abuse refers to the abuse of many drugs at the same time. The four stages of classic alcoholism are (1) the prealcoholic stage, (2) the prodromal stage, (3) the crucial stage, and (4) the chronic stage.

Key Terms Exercise

Wide Awake

_____ 1. consciousness (p. 164)
_____ 2. directed consciousness (p. 164)
_____ 3. flowing consciousness (p. 164)
_____ 4. daydreams (p. 165)
_____ 5. divided consciousness (p. 166)
_____ 6. unconscious mind (p. 166)

a. mental processes that occur without conscious awareness
b. focused, orderly awareness
c. drifting, unfocused awareness
d. a state of awareness
e. focused thinking about fantasies
f. occurs when two conscious activities that occur simultaneously are split

ANSWERS

1. d   4. e
2. b   5. f
3. c   6. a

Sleeping and Dreaming

_____ 1. hypnagogic state (p. 168)
_____ 2. myoclonia (p. 168)
_____ 3. REM sleep (p. 170)
_____ 4. manifest content of dreams (p. 172)
_____ 5. latent content of dreams (p. 172)
_____ 6. night terror (p. 174)
_____ 7. sleepwalking (p. 174)

a. rapid eye movement sleep, often during dreaming
b. a falling sensation that occurs during the hypnagogic state
c. a twilight state between wakefulness and sleep
d. the events that happen in a dream
e. the symbolic meaning of a dream
f. walking and carrying on activities during non-REM sleep
g. an upsetting experience that occurs during deep non-REM sleep

ANSWERS

1. c   5. e
2. b   6. g
3. a   7. f
4. d

Altered States of Consciousness

_____ 1. meditation (p. 179)
_____ 2. transcendental state (p. 179)
_____ 3. hypnosis (p. 180)
_____ 4. depersonalization (p. 181)

a. an altered state of consciousness that transcends normal human experience
b. methods of focusing attention away from thoughts and producing relaxation
c. an altered state in which the individual is susceptible to suggestion
d. the perception that one's body or surroundings are unreal

ANSWERS

1. b   3. c
2. a   4. d

Altering Consciousness with Drugs

_____ 1. psychotropic drugs (p. 183)
_____ 2. stimulants (p. 185)
_____ 3. depressants (p. 188)
_____ 4. opiates (p. 189)
_____ 5. inhalants (p. 189)
_____ 6. hallucinogens (p. 189)
_____ 7. alcoholism (p. 196)

a. drugs that increase the activity of the central nervous system
b. drugs that alter perceptions
c. narcotic drugs derived from the opium poppy
d. drugs that reduce the activity of the central nervous system
e. addiction to alcohol
f. substances that produce intoxication when inhaled
g. drugs that alter conscious experience

ANSWERS

1. g   5. f
2. a   6. b
3. d   7. e
4. c

Guided Review

Wide Awake: Normal Waking Consciousness

Consciousness is a state of _____. We assume that the   awareness (p. 164)

"real" consciousness is _____ consciousness. Waking   waking (p. 164)

consciousness includes three types: (1) a focused, orderly type,

called _____ consciousness; (2) a type in which   directed (p. 164)

awareness drifts, called _____ consciousness; and   flowing (p. 164)

(3) focused thinking that involves fantasies, called

_____. Freud believed that daydreams reduce the   daydreams (p. 164)

tension left by unfulfilled _____. Some researchers have   needs (p. 165)

found, however, that daydreams may actually _____ tension.   create (p. 166)

   When our conscious awareness becomes "split" and we

perform two activities that require conscious awareness at the

same time, this is called _____ consciousness.   divided (p. 166)

   Today a number of psychologists are attempting to

scientifically investigate the unconscious. For example,

psychologists have studied what happens when we "tune out" one

voice we hear and pay attention to a second voice, an experience

called the _____ _____ phenomenon.   cocktail party (p. 166)

Researchers have found that we are able to process words we hear

without being _____ aware of them.   consciously (p. 166)

Sleeping and Dreaming: Conscious While Asleep

The sleep cycle contains several stages. After daydreaming, we

generally pass into a relaxed "twilight" state called the

_____ state. Occasionally we experience a sense of   hypnagogic (p. 168)

falling, and our body experiences a sudden jerk called a

_____. Sleep researchers have distinguished _____ levels   myoclonia (p. 168)/four (p. 169)

of sleep on the basis of electroencephalogram (EEG) recordings.

We pass through these levels, upward and downward, many times

during the night. Several times per night the sleeper enters a stage

called _____ sleep. Because of eye movements during   dream (p. 169)

dreaming, dream sleep is often called rapid eye movement or

_____ sleep. Other important physical changes also   REM (p. 170) occur during sleep. One researcher has likened dream sleep to an

"_____ _____."   autonomic storm (p. 170)

When we miss sleep, we apparently create a "_____   sleep

_____" that needs to be made up. In one experiment,   debt (p. 171)

no detrimental effects occurred when sleep was gradually reduced

from eight to four hours per night. However, irritability and fatigue

occurred when the amount of nightly sleep was _____   abruptly (p. 171)

reduced. According to Hobson, sleep helps to restore the sleep-

_____ system in the brain stem. According to Webb,   inhibiting (p. 172)

sleep serves a _____ role.   protective (p. 172)

Subjects who were awakened whenever they entered REM

sleep became irritable and fatigued, and on subsequent nights they

showed an increase in _____ sleep.   REM (p. 172)

According to Freud, the events that happen in a dream are the

_____ content, while the symbolic meaning of the   manifest (p. 172)

dream is the _____ content. The emotional content of   latent (p. 172)

dreams is mostly _____.   negative (p. 173)

The terrifying dreams that occur during REM sleep are called

_____. An experience that occurs during non-REM   nightmares (p. 174)

sleep that leaves the individual in a state of panic is called a

_____ _____. Walking and carrying on   night terror (p. 174)

complicated activities during the deepest part of non-REM sleep is

called _____, while talking during any phase of the sleep sleepwalking (p. 174)

cycle is _____.   sleeptalking (p. 174)

Sleep Disorders

The troublesome but highly treatable disorders of the sleep process

are called sleep _____. Individuals who sleep less than   disorders (p. 174)

they wish are experiencing _____. Individuals who have   insomnia (p. 174)

difficulty falling asleep when they wish are experiencing

_____-_____ insomnia, while those who wake   sleep-onset (p. 174)

up earlier than they wish experience _____-   early-

_____ insomnia. While these disorders are found in   awakening (p. 174)

individuals experiencing no other psychological problems, they are

more common in individuals experiencing _____,   stress (p. 174) anxiety, or _____. A rare sleep disorder in which   depression (p. 174)

individuals fall deeply asleep while at work or even while in

conversation with others is called _____. The sudden   narcolepsy (p. 174)

interruption of breathing during sleep is called _____   sleep

_____.   apnea (p. 174)

Circadian and Other Rhythms

A cycle of waking and sleeping that regulates our pattern of sleep

is called the _____ _____. A hormone called   circadian rhythm (p. 175)

_____ and the pineal gland appear to be key factors in   melatonin (p. 175)

regulating sleepfulness. The body has other circadian rhythms

which are linked to the sleep-awake cycle. For example, the largest

amount of growth hormone is secreted by the _____   pituitary

_____ during the first two hours of sleep. Two other   gland (p. 175)

examples of circadian rhythm linked to the sleep cycle are body

temperature and the production of _____. Subjects who   cortisol (p. 175)

were isolated in chambers that were always kept lighted evidenced

a _____-_____ cycle. The disruption of   25-hour (p. 176)

circadian rhythms that results from long airline flights is called

"_____ _____." Similar circadian rhythm   jet lag (p. 176)

disruptions occur with individuals whose work is subject to

_____-_____ rotations. Evidence also exists   work-shift (p. 176)

that some individuals are influenced by annual and weekly mood

cycles in addition to the 28-day _____ cycle.   menstrual (p. 176)

Altered States of Consciousness

Among the common characteristics of altered states of

consciousness are distortions of _____, intense positive   perception (p. 178)

_____, and self-evident _____.   emotions (p. 178)/reality (p. 179)

Assuming a relaxed position, breathing deeply and slowly, and

directing all attention toward breathing describe the process of

_____. Some experienced meditators achieve an altered   meditation (p. 179)

state of consciousness called the _____ state.   transcendental (p. 179)

The hypnotic state usually has the following qualities: (1) a

sense of deep _____, (2) distortions referred to as   relaxation (p. 180)

_____ hallucinations, (3) a loss of the sense of touch or pain referred to as hypnotic _____, (4) a sense of passing back in time called hypnotic ____ _____, and (5) hypnotic _____.

hypnotic (p. 180)
analgesia (p. 180)
age regression (p. 180)
control (p. 180)

A physician practicing in the 1700s who treated patients with "magnetic seances" was Franz Anton _____. The process of putting people into trances was for many years called _____. In recent years, some doctors and dentists have found hypnosis to be an effective way to relieve _____.

Mesmer (p. 180)

mesmerism (p. 181)
pain (p. 181)

An altered state of consciousness in which the body is perceived as being distorted or unreal is called _____. The illusion that the mind has left the body is called _____ _____. Many individuals who have had near-_____ experiences have reported similar occurrences.

depersonalization (p. 181)

astral projection (p. 182)
death (p. 182)

Altering Consciousness with Drugs

Drugs that alter conscious experience are called _____ drugs. The categories of psychotropic drugs are (1) drugs that increase the activity of the central nervous system, _____; (2) those that reduce the activity of the central nervous system, _____; (3) those that produce alterations in perceptual experience, _____; and (4) those that produce a sense of intoxication when inhaled, _____.

psychotropic (p. 183)

stimulants (p. 183)
depressants (p. 183)
hallucinogens (p. 183)

inhalants (p. 183)

Some factors that influence an individual's response to a drug include (1) dose and _____, (2) personal _____, (3) _____, (4) the _____ situation, and (5) _____. The risks associated with drug use include (1) the potential to cause damage or impair psychological functioning, called _____ _____; (2) a need to use the drug regularly in order to feel comfortable psychologically, called psychological _____; (3) a chemical need for the drug, called physiological _____; (4) powerful and potentially

purity (p. 184)
characteristics/expectations/social (p. 184)
moods (p. 184)

drug
abuse (p. 185)

dependence (p. 185)
addiction (p. 185)

dangerous _____ side effects; and (5) the risk of   direct (p. 185)
infection or other _____ side effects.   indirect (p. 185)

Drugs that activate the central nervous system are called
_____ (uppers). Among the most widely used stimulants   stimulants (p. 185)
are (1) the drug found in coffee, tea, and cola, _____;   caffeine (p. 185)
and (2) the drug found in tobacco, _____. Other   nicotine (p. 185)
stimulants that produce a sense of increased energy and a euphoric
high are called _____. Prolonged excessive use of   amphetamines (p. 185)
amphetamines may lead to amphetamine _____. A   psychosis (p. 185)
widely abused stimulant made from the leaves of the coca plant is
_____. Repeated use of cocaine rapidly leads to   cocaine (p. 187)
_____.   addiction (p. 187)

After the prolonged use of cocaine, the user experiences a
cocaine crash, marked by _____, agitation, confusion,   depression (p. 187)
and exhaustion. Cocaine produces its effect by interfering with the
reuptake of neurotransmitters called _____. Withdrawal   catecholamines (p. 187)
from cocaine addiction is marked by intense depression,
_____, and craving for cocaine.   agitation (p. 188)

Drugs that depress parts of the central nervous system are
called _____.   depressants (p. 188)

A state of relaxation is produced by the highly addictive group
of depressants called _____. A sense of relaxation for a   sedatives (p. 188)
briefer period is provided by _____.   tranquilizers (p. 188)

Powerful and highly addictive depressants are called
_____. Narcotics such as morphine and heroin are   narcotics (p. 188)
derived from the opium poppy and are called _____.   opiates (p. 189)
Substances that are inhaled to produce a sense of intoxication, such
as glue and paint, are called _____.   inhalants (p. 189)

Drugs that powerfully alter consciousness, such as LSD and
mescaline, are called _____. One highly dangerous   hallucinogens (p. 189)
hallucinogen, originally developed as an animal tranquilizer, is
_____.   phencyclidine (PCP) (p. 189)

A powerful although illegal drug that generally produces a
sense of relaxation and well-being is _____. Although   marijuana (p. 189)
not physically addictive, psychological _____ is possible.   dependence (p. 190)

Two special drug-related concerns involve _____ - _____ and _____ drugs. A condition in which a person abuses many drugs at the same time is _____ _____.

Coffee, tea, and cola contain the powerful stimulant _____. Prolonged use of caffeine, even at moderate levels, can produce physiological _____. Caffeine also produces marked increases in blood pressure, especially during times of _____. Although technically a stimulant, the drug found in tobacco, _____, can produce relaxation at times. In spite of a variety of health risks, people continue to smoke tobacco. Smokers rapidly develop a psychological _____ and a physiological _____. Smokers then continue smoking to avoid the _____ of not smoking.

A widely abused addictive depressant drug is _____. The amount of alcohol consumption that can be harmful depends on the person and the _____. Also, the potential harmful effects can affect job performance, relationships, and personal _____. Drinking during pregnancy has been linked to _____ _____ syndrome in infants. About one-third of all individuals addicted to alcohol experience a series of changes called _____ _____. The stages of classic alcoholism are (1) the _____ stage, in which drinking helps relieve tension, and tolerance for alcohol increases; (2) the _____ stage, in which the drinking is excessive and blackouts occur; (3) the _____ stage in which deterioration of self-esteem and blackouts occur; and (4) the _____ stage, in which drinking is almost constant with little or no control. A variety of techniques exist for individuals who wish to quit using these legal consciousness-altering drugs.

act

alike (p. 190)/designer (p. 190)

polydrug

abuse (p. 190)

caffeine (p. 192)

addiction (p. 192)

stress (p. 193)

nicotine (p. 193)

dependence (p. 194)/addiction (p. 194)

discomforts (p. 194)

alcohol (p. 194)

situation (p. 195)

health (p. 195)

fetal alcohol (p. 195)

classic alcoholism (p. 196)

prealcoholic (p. 196)

prodromal (p. 196)

crucial (p. 196)

chronic (p. 196)

CONCEPT CHECK

Fill in the missing components of the following concept box. Answers are below the box.

Psychoactive Drugs

I. Type of drug	II. Effect	III. Examples
a. Stimulants	a. Activate the CNS.	a. Amphetamines and cocaine.
b. Depressants	b. Depress parts of the CNS.	b.
c. Inhalants	c.	c. Glue, cleaning fluid, and paint.
d.	d. Powerfully alter consciousness by altering perceptual experiences.	d. LSD and mescaline.
e. Designer drugs	e. Produce a dreamlike high.	e.

Answers

IIIb.   Sedatives, tranquilizers, and narcotics.
IIc.   Produce a sense of intoxication when inhaled.
Id.   Hallucinogens.
IIIe.   MDA and MDMA (ecstasy).

Multiple-Choice Questions

1. Which of the following is characterized by an awareness that drifts from one thought to another?
    a. directed consciousness
    b. flowing consciousness
    c. daydreaming
    d. all of the above
        (p. 164) LO 1

2. According to Freud, which state of consciousness helps to reduce the tension of unmet needs and wishes?
    a. directed consciousness
    b. divided consciousness
    c. daydreaming
    d. flowing consciousness
        (p. 165) LO 1

3. Driving long distances while thinking about other events is an example of
   a. REM sleep
   b. the unconscious mind
   c. myoclonia
   d. divided consciousness
      (p. 166) LO 2

4. The ability to focus on one voice and tune out other voices has been labeled
   a. the cocktail party phenomenon
   b. divided consciousness
   c. the hypnagogic state
   d. depersonalization
      (p. 166) LO 3

5. According to researchers, voices that we "tune out" may nevertheless be processed
   _____.
   a. consciously
   b. unconsciously
   c. in a hypnagogic state
   d. in a state of flowing consciousness
      (p. 106) LO 3

6. Myoclonia is experienced in which stage of sleep?
   a. hypnagogic stage
   b. light sleep
   c. deep sleep
   d. REM sleep
      (p. 168) LO 4

7. How many hours per night does the average college student spend dreaming?
   a. 1
   b. 2
   c. 4
   d. 6
      (p. 169) LO 5

8. Which of the following may occur during REM sleep?
   a. movement of the eyes
   b. increased blood flow to the brain
   c. irregular breathing
   d. all of the above
      (p. 170) LO 6

9. The important missing element when we do not get enough sleep appears to be
   a. the hypnagogic stage
   b. light sleep
   c. REM sleep
   d. all of the above
      (p. 170) LO 7

10. According to sleep researcher Hobson, the purpose of sleep and dreaming is to
    a. keep us from functioning during nighttime hours, for which we are ill-prepared
    b. allow the sleep-inhibiting system a chance to rest
    c. allow the sleep-promoting areas a chance to rest
    d. b and c above
       (p. 172) LO 7

11. According to Freud, the symbolic meaning of dreams is called the
    a. manifest content
    b. latent content
    c. hypnagogic content
    d. reality content
       (p. 172) LO 8

12. The upsetting nocturnal experiences that occur during non-REM sleep are
    a. sleepwalking
    b. nightmares
    c. night terrors
    d. sleeptalking
       (p. 174) LO 9

13. A sleep disorder characterized by the sudden interruption of breathing is called
    a. narcolepsy
    b. sleep apnea
    c. insomnia
    d. myoclonia
       (p. 174) LO 10

14. Which of the following appears to be regulated by the circadian rhythm?
    a. the secretion of growth hormone
    b. body temperature
    c. sleep-awake cycles
    d. all of the above
       (p. 175) LO 11

15. If you are a manager of a manufacturing plant where workers are required to work in rotating shifts, which rotation would be least disruptive to the workers?
    a. from day shift to night shift
    b. from swing shift to day shift
    c. from night shift to day shift
    d. from day shift to swing shift
    (p. 176) LO 11

16. All of the following characterize altered states of consciousness *except*
    a. distortions of reality
    b. intense positive emotions
    c. self-evident reality
    d. logical experiences
    (p. 178) LO 12

17. Which of the following is true of meditators?
    a. Mantras are often used.
    b. Meditation generally produces a relaxed state.
    c. Some meditators reach a transcendental state.
    d. all of the above
    (p. 179) LO 13

18. Which of the following is *not* a characteristic of the hypnotic experience?
    a. hypnotic hallucinations
    b. hypnotic analgesia
    c. hypnotic control
    d. hypnotic repression
    (p. 180) LO 14

19. Each of the following is a characteristic of depersonalization *except*
    a. they may occur spontaneously
    b. they are not unusual among young adults
    c. they may include astral projection
    d. they are an indication of insanity
    (p. 181) LO 15

20. According to Raymond Moody, individuals who died and then were brought back to life experienced
    a. a pleasant sound
    b. a sense that their minds and bodies were separating
    c. movement through a tunnel
    d. all of the above
    (p. 182) LO 16

21. An individual's response to a drug can be affected by
    a. dose and purity of the drug
    b. the individual's personal characteristics
    c. the social situation
    d. all of the above
    (p. 184) LO 17

22. Richard finds that he feels comfortable psychologically only when he can smoke marijuana daily. He shows evidence of
    a. drug abuse
    b. psychological dependence
    c. physiological addiction
    d. severe emotional problems
    (p. 185) LO 18

23. Each of the following is a stimulant *except*
    a. alcohol
    b. caffeine
    c. amphetamines
    d. cocaine
    (p. 185) LO 19

24. Each of the following activates the central nervous system *except*
    a. stimulants
    b. amphetamines
    c. cocaine
    d. opiates
    (p. 185) LO 19

25. Each of the following is considered to be addictive *except*
    a. sedatives
    b. tranquilizers
    c. narcotics
    d. hallucinogens
    (p. 189) LO 20

26. Each of the following is a potential side effect of prolonged marijuana use *except*
   a. damage to the chromosomes of reproductive cells
   b. reverse tolerance
   c. a decrease in the efficiency of cognitive processing
   d. a decrease in the action of male sex hormones
      (p. 190) LO 21

27. Drugs such as MDA and MDMA (ecstasy) are considered to be
   a. look-alike drugs
   b. act-alike drugs
   c. designer drugs
   d. depressants
      (p. 190) LO 22

28. Which of the following is a risk associated with polydrug abuse?
   a. the increased possibility of addiction and dependence
   b. the increased chance that drug use will interfere with an individual's adjustment to life
   c. the potential for the drugs to chemically interact to produce toxic effects
   d. all of the above
      (pp. 190–191) LO 23

29. Alcohol is considered to be
   a. a depressant, because it frequently leaves drinkers feeling depressed
   b. a stimulant, because it makes the drinker less inhibited
   c. a depressant, because it depresses inhibitory mechanisms in the brain
   d. both a stimulant and a depressant
      (p. 194) LO 24

30. In classic alcoholism, binging begins in the
   a. prealcoholic stage
   b. prodromal stage
   c. crucial stage
   d. chronic stage
      (p. 196) LO 24

Multiple-Choice Answers

1. The answer is *B*. Directed consciousness refers to a state in which we are focused. Flowing consciousness, a state we find ourselves in most of the day, is characterized by drifting, unfocused awareness. While daydreams are relatively focused, the focus is on fantasies.
2. The answer is *C*. Freud's explanation of daydreaming, however, fails to explain the fact that many daydreams *create* rather than release tension.
3. The answer is *D*. According to Hilgard, our conscious awareness becomes split, and we simultaneously perform two activities requiring conscious awareness.
4. The answer is *A*. The label results from the fact that this phenomenon often occurs at parties.
5. The answer is *B*. Researchers have found that even words that were "ignored" can be processed without conscious awareness.
6. The answer is *A*. The hypnagogic stage is the relaxed "twilight" state between wakefulness and sleep. Occasionally, while in this state, we suddenly feel as though we are falling and our body experiences a sudden jerking movement called a myoclonia.
7. The answer is *B*. While the length of the dreams vary, the longest is usually about an hour and typically occurs during the last part of the sleep cycle.

8. The answer is *D*. REM sleep, which occurs while we dream, occurs during an "autonomic storm." Dreams also occur during non-REM sleep.

9. The answer is *C*. Researchers have demonstrated the REM-deprived subjects are irritable and fatigued, and, on subsequent nights, show an increase in the amount of REM sleep.

10. The answer is *B*. According to Hobson, the sleep-inhibiting system, located in the brain stem, is active when we are awake and needs sleep to replenish itself.

11. The answer is *B*. Freud believed that the latent content contained the true meaning of a dream. The manifest content was the obvious, but superficial, meaning of the dream.

12. The answer is *C*. Night terrors occur in the deepest phases of non-REM sleep and are most common in preschool-age children. Nightmares, on the other hand, occur during REM sleep.

13. The answer is *B*. Sleep apnea is particularly common in older adults who snore. Narcolepsy is a rare sleep disorder in which the person suddenly falls into a deep sleep during the middle of the day. Insomnia refers to a variety of difficulties in which individuals sleep less than they wish.

14. The answer is *D*. The circadian rhythm is just one of several rhythms that influence our behavior.

15. The answer is *C*. When rotating from the night shift to the day shift, you stay awake longer on the first day of the rotation. This is consistent with the natural tendency to lengthen our circadian rhythms.

16. The answer is *D*. In fact, many of the experiences that occur in altered states are illogical.

17. The answer is *D*. Although mantras contain religious meaning, researchers have found that any pleasant sound can produce the same effect.

18. The answer is *D*. While hypnotic repression does not exist, hypnotic age regression (in which a subject feels that he is experiencing an earlier time in his life) does exist.

19. The answer is *D*. While recurrent depersonalization experiences may be an indication of psychological problems, they are not, by themselves, an indication of insanity.

20. The answer is *D*. Although more recent data suggest that near-death experiences are less uniform than Moody's findings, this area of research remains fascinating.

21. The answer is *D*. In addition to the factors listed in the question, the expectations that we have of the drug's effects and the mood at the time of taking the drug can also affect the response to the drug.

22. The answer is *B*. Psychological dependence occurs when the individual needs to use the drug to feel comfortable psychologically. Drug abuse occurs when it causes biological damage or impaired psychological or social functioning. Physiological addiction occurs when the body begins to require the presence of the drug and the user begins to experience withdrawal symptoms in the drug's absence.

23. The answer is *A*. While choices *B, C,* and *D,* are stimulants, that is, drugs that activate the nervous system, alcohol is a depressant.

24. The answer is *D*. Opiates are considered to be depressants.

25. The answer is *D*. Sedatives, tranquilizers, and narcotics are recognized as highly addictive drugs. Hallucinogens can alter perceptual experiences but are not generally considered to be addictive.

26. The answer is *A*. Among other problems created by the prolonged use of marijuana are a weakening of the body's immune system and an increased risk of lung cancer.

27. The answer is *C*. Designer drugs are those that have been designed by chemists so recently that they have not yet been classified as illegal.

28. The answer is *D*. According to the text, polydrug abusers have a high rate of previous emotional difficulties.

29. The answer is *C*. Although alcohol does make drinkers less inhibited, and it can reduce tension and anxiety, its classification as a depressant refers to its effect on the nervous system.

30. The answer is *C*. This stage is also characterized by deterioration in self-esteem and general social functioning.

Chapter **5**   **Basic Principles of Learning**

Learning Objectives

1. Identify the key features of the definition of learning.
2. Define the key components of classical conditioning (UCS, UCR, CS, and CR) and describe the process of classical conditioning.
3. Describe contemporary research and applications of classical conditioning.
4. Describe the process of operant conditioning.
5. Explain how positive reinforcement is influenced by timing, consistency, and individual preferences.
6. Distinguish between primary reinforcement and secondary reinforcement.
7. Compare and contrast the four schedules of reinforcement: fixed ratio, variable ratio, fixed interval, and variable ratio.
8. Explain the process of shaping.
9. Define negative reinforcement, and compare escape conditioning and avoidance conditioning.
10. List the dangers of using punishment and give guidelines for the appropriate use of punishment.
11. Discuss the differences between classical and operant conditioning.
12. Distinguish between stimulus discrimination and stimulus generalization.
13. Explain the phenomenon of extinction.
14. Explain spontaneous recovery and external disinhibition.
15. Compare the cognitive and connectionist theoretical interpretations of learning.
16. Describe the characteristics of place learning, latent learning, and insight learning.
17. Describe modeling and explain the roles of vicarious reinforcement and vicarious punishment in learning.
18. Describe biological factors in learning, including learned taste aversions.
19. (From the "Application" section) Describe the role of superstitious behavior and learned helplessness in "learning the wrong things."

Chapter Overview

Learning refers to any relatively permanent change in behavior brought about through experience. One type of learning is called classical conditioning. In this type of learning, a previously neutral stimulus called a conditioned stimulus (CS) is paired with an unconditioned stimulus (UCS) that elicits an unlearned or unconditioned response (UCR). Eventually, the CS comes to elicit a conditioned response (CR) that is identical or very similar to the UCR. Classical conditioning occurs because of the association in time of a neutral stimulus and a stimulus that already elicits the response. Contemporary research indicates that classical conditioning may play a role in resistance to disease, increases in pain tolerance, and sexual arousal.

Operant conditioning is a form of learning in which the consequences of behavior lead to changes in the probability of its occurrence. Positive reinforcements increase the probability of a response. Three important issues involving the use of positive reinforcement are timing, consistency, and the selection of an appropriate positive reinforcer.

Primary reinforcers, such as food and water, are innately reinforcing; secondary reinforcers are learned. There are four different schedules of reinforcement, each resulting in different patterns of behavior. The schedules are fixed ratio, variable ratio, fixed interval, and variable interval. Shaping refers to the process of reinforcing behaviors that are progressively more similar to the target response. Negative reinforcement occurs when the reinforcing consequence is (1) the removal of a negative event, also called escape conditioning, or (2) the avoidance of a negative event, also called avoidance conditioning. Punishment is a negative consequence of a behavior that reduces the frequency of the behavior. Stimulus discrimination occurs when a response is more likely in the presence of a specific stimulus than in the presence of other stimuli. Stimulus generalization has occurred when an individual responds to similar but different stimuli.

Extinction is the process of unlearning a learned response when the original source of learning is removed. Extinction is often slowed because of spontaneous recovery and external disinhibition.

Psychologists disagree about whether learning results from neural connections between specific stimuli and specific responses or whether learning is a change in cognition. Research that supports the cognitive view includes Tolman's studies of place learning and latent learning, Köhler's studies of insight learning, and Bandura's work on modeling.

The ability of humans to learn from experience is not limitless; it is influenced in a number of ways by biological factors.

Key Terms Exercise

For each of the following exercises, match the key terms on the left with the correct definitions on the right. Page references to the text follow the terms so that you may refer to the text for any items you answer incorrectly or do not understand completely. You may check your responses immediately by referring to the answers that follow each exercise.

Classical Conditioning

_____ 1. learning (p. 204)
_____ 2. unconditioned stimulus (UCS) (p. 207)
_____ 3. unconditioned response (UCR) (p. 207)
_____ 4. conditioned stimulus (CS) (p. 207)
_____ 5. conditioned response (CR) (p. 207)
_____ 6. classical conditioning (p. 209)

a. an unlearned, inborn reaction to an unconditioned stimulus
b. any relatively permanent change in behavior brought about through experience
c. a stimulus that comes to elicit responses as a result of learning
d. a response that comes to be elicited by a conditioned stimulus
e. a stimulus that can elicit a response without any learning
f. a form of learning in which a previously neutral stimulus is paired with an unconditioned stimulus to elicit a conditioned response that is very similar to the unconditioned response

ANSWERS

1. b   4. c
2. e   5. d
3. a   6. f

Operant Conditioning (I)

_____ 1. operant conditioning (p. 212)
_____ 2. positive reinforcement (p. 212)
_____ 3. primary reinforcement (p. 214)
_____ 4. secondary reinforcement (p. 214)
_____ 5. fixed ratio schedule (p. 215)
_____ 6. variable ratio schedule (p. 215)
_____ 7. fixed interval schedule (p. 215)
_____ 8. variable interval schedule (p. 216)

a. a schedule in which the reinforcer is given following the first response after a predetermined amount of time
b. learning in which the consequences of behavior lead to changes in the probability of its occurrence
c. a schedule in which the reinforcer is given following the first response after a variable amount of time
d. a schedule in which the reinforcer is given after a varying number of responses have been made
e. any consequence of a behavior that leads to an increase in the probability of its occurrence
f. reinforcement that does not have to be learned
g. a schedule in which the reinforcer is given only after a specified number of responses
h. learned reinforcers

ANSWERS

1. b	5. g
2. e	6. d
3. f	7. a
4. h	8. c

Operant Conditioning (II)

_____ 1. shaping (p. 217)
_____ 2. negative reinforcement (p. 218)
_____ 3. escape conditioning (p. 218)
_____ 4. avoidance conditioning (p. 218)
_____ 5. punishment (p. 219)
_____ 6. stimulus discrimination (p. 222)
_____ 7. stimulus generalization (p. 223)

a. behavior reinforcement that causes a negative event to cease
b. positively reinforcing behaviors that successively become more similar to desired behaviors
c. behavior reinforcement that prevents something negative from happening
d. the tendency for similar stimuli to elicit the same response
e. a negative consequence that leads to a reduction in the frequency of the behavior that produced it
f. reinforcement that comes from the removal or avoidance of a negative event as a consequence of a behavior
g. the tendency for responses to occur more often in the presence of one stimulus than with others

ANSWERS

1. b	5. e
2. f	6. g
3. a	7. d
4. c	

Extinction and Theoretical Interpretations of Learning

_____ 1. extinction (p. 225)
_____ 2. partial reinforcement effect (p. 226)
_____ 3. spontaneous recovery (p. 226)
_____ 4. external disinhibition (p. 226)
_____ 5. insight (p. 232)
_____ 6. modeling (p. 234)
_____ 7. vicarious reinforcement (p. 235)
_____ 8. vicarious punishment (p. 235)
_____ 9. superstitious behavior (p. 239)
_____ 10. learned helplessness (p. 241)

a. a form of cognitive change involving recognition of previously unseen relationships

b. observed reinforcement in a model that also increases the probability of the same behavior in the observer

c. observed punishment in a model that decreases the probability of the same behavior in the observer

d. a temporary increase in the strength of a response that may occur during extinction and after the passage of time

e. unlearning a learned response because the original source of learning is removed

f. learning based on observing the behavior of others

g. a temporary increase in the strength of an extinguished response caused by an unrelated stimulus event

h. responses that have been reinforced on a variable schedule are more difficult to extinguish than those that have been continuously reinforced

i. behavior that is reinforced when a reinforcing stimulus accidentally follows a response

j. a learned pattern of not trying to avoid negative events

ANSWERS

1. e	6. f
2. h	7. b
3. d	8. c
4. g	9. i
5. a	10. j

Who Am I?

Match the psychologists on the left with their contributions to the field of psychology on the right. Page references to the text follow the names of the psychologists so that you may refer to the text for further review of these psychologists and their contributions. You may check your responses immediately by referring to the answers that follow each exercise.

_____ 1. Ivan Pavlov (p. 204)
_____ 2. John B. Watson (p. 209)
_____ 3. B. F. Skinner (p. 216)
_____ 4. Edward C. Tolman (p. 229)
_____ 5. Wolfgang Köhler (p. 231)
_____ 6. Albert Bandura (p. 234)

a. I believe that modeling is an important aspect of learning.
b. I observed insight learning in my friend Sultan.
c. I was an American behaviorist who taught little Albert to fear white rats.
d. I believed that rats were capable of place learning and latent learning and could form cognitive maps.
e. I was a Russian physiologist who believed that conditioning was a form of learning through association.
f. My name is associated with superstitious reinforcement, schedules of reinforcement, and a learning apparatus.

ANSWERS

1. e   4. d
2. c   5. b
3. f   6. a

Guided Review

Definition of Learning

In psychology, any relatively permanent change in behavior brought about by experience is referred to as _____ .

learning (p. 204)

Classical Conditioning: Learning by Association

The scientific study of classical conditioning began around the turn of the century with an accidental discovery made by a Russian physiologist named Ivan _____ . While studying the role of saliva in digestion, Pavlov observed that his laboratory dogs

Pavlov (p. 204)

began to _____ even before an attendant placed food in their mouths. The sight of the attendant had come to elicit the

salivate (p. 205)

same _____ _____ to food. Pavlov

reflexive response (p. 205)

considered _____ _____ to be the association

classical conditioning (p. 206)

in time of a neutral stimulus and a stimulus that elicits the response.

A stimulus that can elicit a response without any learning is called a ____ , or _____ _____ . An

UCS/unconditioned stimulus (p. 207)

unlearned, inborn reaction to the unconditioned stimulus is

referred to as a ____, or _____ _____. A UCR/unconditioned response (p. 207)
stimulus that is originally unable to elicit a response but acquires
the ability to do so through classical conditioning is a ____, or CS (p. 207)
_____ _____. When the previously conditioned stimulus (p. 207)
unconditioned response can be elicited by the conditioned stimulus,
it is called a ____, or _____ _____. CR/conditioned response (p. 207)

     Responding to the mere sight of a needle as if you were
actually being injected is brought about by _____ classical
_____. Classical conditioning is defined as a form of conditioning (p. 209)
learning in which a previously _____ stimulus (CS) is neutral (p. 209)
followed by a stimulus (UCS) that elicits an _____ unlearned (p. 209)
response (UCR). As a result, the _____ stimulus comes conditioned (p. 209)
to elicit a response similar to the UCR. Classical conditioning is
considered a form of learning because an old behavior can be
elicited by a new _____. stimulus (p. 209)

     The experiment conducted by _____ and Rayner on Watson (p. 209)
"Little Albert" demonstrated the classical conditioning of
_____. Research suggests that classical conditioning fear (p. 209)
plays a role in allergic reactions and in the functioning of the
body's _____ system. Other researchers, investigating immune (p. 210)
stress-induced analgesia, have found that increases in pain
tolerance can be _____ conditioned. Still other classically (p. 210)
researchers have explored the role of classical conditioning in
_____ _____. sexual arousal (p. 210)

Operant Conditioning: Learning from the Consequences of Your Behavior
People often change the frequency with which they do things based
on the consequences of their actions. Learning from the
consequences of behavior is called _____ operant
_____. When the consequences of a behavior tend to conditioning (p. 212)
increase its occurrence, this is called _____ positive
_____. Researchers helped a girl overcome her shyness reinforcement (p. 212)
by praising her only when she played with another child. In this
case, the consequence of playing with other children was positive,
and the frequency of her behavior _____. increased (p. 212)

There are three important issues in the use of reinforcement: (1) The greater the delay between the response and the reinforcer, the slower the learning; this is called _____ _____ _____. (2) For learning to take place, positive reinforcement should be given _____. (3) The positive reinforcer should, in fact, be _____ to the learner.

delay of

reinforcement (p. 213)

consistently (p. 213)

reinforcing (p. 213)

Reinforcers that do not have to be acquired through learning, such as food, water, and physical activity, are called _____ _____. In contrast, reinforcers that are learned are _____ _____.

primary reinforcers (p. 214)

secondary reinforcers (p. 214)

Positive reinforcers may not always follow every response but may occur on a variety of _____. Two schedules are based on the number of _____. When a reinforcer is given only after a specified number of responses, it is called a _____ _____ schedule. If a reinforcer is given after a varying number of responses has been made, it is a _____ _____ schedule. Two additional schedules are based on the passage of _____. When a reinforcer follows the first response occurring after a predetermined amount of time, it is termed a _____ _____ schedule. Finally, when reinforcement is given to the first response after a varying amount of time, it is a _____ _____ schedule.

schedules (p. 214)

responses (p. 215)

fixed ratio (p. 215)

variable ratio (p. 215)

time (p. 215)

fixed

interval (p. 215)

variable interval (p. 216)

If the response to be reinforced is not likely to occur, a technique can be used that reinforces responses that are progressively more similar to the desired response. This is called the method of _____ _____, or _____.

successive approximations (p. 217)

shaping (p. 217)

Sometimes the reinforcing consequence removes or avoids a negative event. This situation is called _____ _____. One form of negative reinforcement occurs when the behavior causes a negative event to stop; this is referred to as _____ _____. Another form of negative reinforcement occurs when the behavior causes something not to

negative

reinforcement (p. 218)

escape conditioning (p. 218)

happen when it otherwise would have happened; this is called

_____ _____.

If the consequence of a behavior is negative and, as a result, the frequency of a behavior decreases, the behavior has been

_____. Although punishment can be an effective method

of reducing the frequency of the behavior, there are several dangers in using punishment. For example, punishment is often

_____ to the punisher. Punishment also may have a

generalized _____ effect on the individual. Punishment

is often painful and may lead the person who is punished to dislike

or to act _____ toward the punisher. Punishers may find

an increase in the behavior they are trying to punish, a result

known as the _____ _____. Finally, even

when punishment is effective in suppressing inappropriate

behavior, it does not teach the individual how to act more

_____ instead.

The following guidelines are suggested for the use of

punishment: (1) Use the least _____ punishment that

will still be effective. (2) Reinforce _____ behavior to

take the place of the inappropriate behavior you are trying to

eliminate. (3) Do not punish people; punish specific

_____ instead. (4) Do not mix punishment with

_____. (5) Once you have begun to punish, do not

_____ _____.

Classical and operant conditioning differ in three primary

ways: (1) classical conditioning involves an _____

between two stimuli, while operant conditioning involves an

association between a response and the resulting _____;

(2) classical conditioning usually involves _____

involuntary behavior, while operant conditioning usually involves

more complicated _____ behaviors; and (3) in classical

conditioning the individual does not have to do anything for the CS

or the UCS to be presented, but in operant conditioning the

reinforcement is _____ on the response.

As part of adapting to the world, most responses are more likely to occur in the presence of some stimuli than in the presence of others; this is called stimulus _____. The stimulus in which the response is reinforced is referred to as the

_____ _____, while the stimulus in which the response is never reinforced is called _____. The opposite of stimulus discrimination is stimulus _____, which refers to the fact that similar stimuli tend to elicit the same response.

discrimination (p. 222)

discriminative stimulus (p. 222)
S^{delta} (p. 222)
generalization (p. 223)

Extinction: The Process of Unlearning

The process of unlearning a learned response because of a change in the part of the environment that originally caused the learning is termed _____. In operant conditioning, extinction results from a change in the _____ of behavior. The extinction of operantly conditioned behavior is affected by the reinforcement schedule and the type of reinforcement, according to the _____ _____ effect. Responses learned through _____ _____ are the most difficult responses to extinguish.

extinction (p. 225)

consequences p. 225)

partial reinforcement (p. 226)

avoidance learning (p. 226)

Extinction often proceeds irregularly. If there is a long time between presentations of the CS, the response being extinguished can undergo _____ _____. If some intense but unrelated stimulus occurs, the extinguished response may temporarily return; this is termed _____

_____.

spontaneous recovery (p. 226)

external

disinhibition (p. 227)

Theoretical Interpretations of Learning

One view of learning suggests that during the learning process _____ connections are made between specific stimuli and specific responses. Another view holds that learning involves changes in _____. Edward C. Tolman concluded that laboratory rats who chose to take a shortcut to reach a goal had actually learned a _____ _____ of the location of the goal. In another experiment, Tolman concluded that

neural (p. 227)

cognition (p. 228)

cognitive map (p. 229)

a group of unreinforced rats had learned as much about the location of a goal as a reinforced group. This type of unreinforced learning is called _____ _____. Wolfgang Köhler provided additional evidence for the cognitive view with his research on apes. When presented with a problem, the apes would not make any progress in reach a solution until they developed a cognitive change called _____. According to Harlow, the monkeys were successful at solving problems because they had acquired a _____ _____. Albert Bandura has demonstrated the importance of learning by observation, referred to as _____. We are more likely to imitate a model whose behavior we see reinforced; this is called _____ _____. On the other hand, we are less likely to imitate a model whose behavior we see punished; this is termed

_____ _____.

latent learning (p. 230)

insight (p. 232)

learning set (p. 232)

modeling (p. 234)
vicarious
reinforcement (p. 236)

vicarious punishment (p. 236)

Biological Factors in Learning

Learning is influenced in a number of ways by _____ factors. Apparently, people are biologically prepared to learn some kinds of _____ more readily than others. Also, people seem to be highly prepared to learn to avoid certain kinds of foods; this is called _____ _____ _____. Researchers have shown learned taste aversion in the foods eaten by cancer patients just prior to undergoing nausea-producing _____.

Skinner has suggested that _____ are learned through flukes in positive reinforcement. Research conducted with schizophrenics has demonstrated that the frequency of their _____ statements is subject to reinforcement contingencies. According to Seligman, an individual's depression may be caused by _____ _____, a pattern of no longer trying to avoid negative events.

biological (p. 236)

fears (p. 236)

learned taste
aversion (p. 236)

chemotherapy (p. 237)
superstitions (p. 239)

delusional (p. 240)

learned helplessness (p. 241)

CONCEPT CHECK

Fill in and explain the missing components to the classical conditioning paradigm below. Answers are shown below the box.

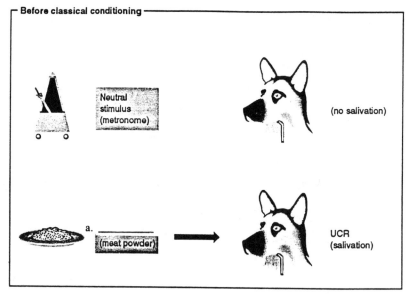

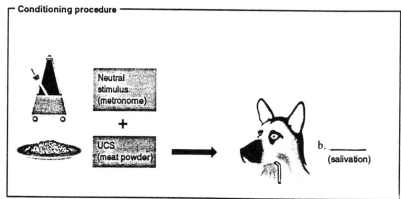

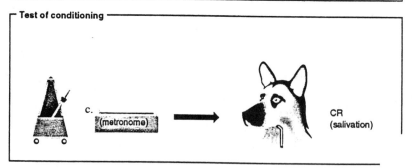

Answers

a. UCS (unconditioned stimulus)
b. UCR (unconditioned response)
c. CS (conditioned stimulus)

Multiple-Choice Questions

1. Which of the following is/are part of the definition of learning?
   a. change in behavior
   b. relatively permanent
   c. brought about by experience
   d. all of the above
      (p. 204) LO 1

2. Pavlov's initial interest in classical conditioning was stimulated when he observed his research dogs salivating at the sight of
   a. food
   b. the attendants
   c. saliva
   d. the food dish
      (p. 205) LO 2

3. In classical conditioning, an unlearned, inborn reaction to an unconditioned stimulus is a(n)
   a. unconditioned stimulus
   b. conditioned stimulus
   c. unconditioned response
   d. conditioned response
      (p. 207) LO 2

4. In Pavlov's classic experiment, meat powder was the
   a. unconditioned stimulus
   b. unconditioned response
   c. conditioned stimulus
   d. conditioned response
      (p. 207) LO 2

5. Classical conditioning apparently plays a role in the development of
   a. resistance to disease
   b. allergic reactions
   c. sexual arousal
   d. all of the above
      (p. 210) LO 3

6. Learning that results from the consequences of behaviors is called
   a. extinguished conditioning
   b. operant conditioning
   c. classical conditioning
   d. positive conditioning
      (p. 212) LO 4

7. If positive reinforcement is not given within a short time following the response, learning will proceed slowly. This phenomenon is called
   a. delay of reinforcement
   b. extinction
   c. conditioned response
   d. consistency
      (p. 213) LO 5

8. Reinforcers that are innately reinforcing, such as food, water, and warmth are called
   a. primary reinforcers
   b. secondary reinforcers
   c. extinguished reinforcers
   d. superstitious reinforcers
      (p. 214) LO 6

9. If a child is rewarded for appropriate behavior every 15 minutes, what type of schedule is being used?
   a. fixed ratio
   b. variable ratio
   c. fixed interval
   d. variable interval
      (p. 215) LO 7

10. Salespeople who are paid exclusively by commission are reinforced on which type of schedule?
    a. fixed ratio
    b. fixed interval
    c. variable ratio
    d. variable interval
       (p. 215) LO 7

11. If you wanted to teach a chicken to "play" the piano, you should
    a. wait for a musically inclined chicken to show up
    b. extinguish piano-playing behavior
    c. use shaping
    d. use negative reinforcement
       (p. 217) LO 8

12. Behavior that is reinforced because it causes a negative event to stop is called
    a. shaping
    b. punishment
    c. escape conditioning
    d. avoidance conditioning
       (p. 218) LO 9

13. Both escape conditioning and avoidance conditioning are forms of
    a. superstitious behavior
    b. positive reinforcement
    c. negative reinforcement
    d. secondary reinforcement
       (p. 218) LO 9

14. Which of the following is suggested as a guideline for the use of punishment?
    a. Use the least painful punishment available.
    b. Do not give punishment mixed with rewards.
    c. Make it clear to the individual which behavior is being punished.
    d. all of the above
       (p. 219) LO 10

15. If the consequence of a behavior is negative and the frequency of that behavior decreases, the behavior has been
    a. positively reinforced
    b. negatively reinforced
    c. disinhibited
    d. punished
       (p. 219) LO 10

16. Which of the following is correct?
    a. Classical conditioning usually involves reflexive behavior, while operant conditioning usually involves more complicated, spontaneous behavior.
    b. Classical conditioning usually involves more complicated, spontaneous behavior, while operant conditioning involves reflexive behavior.
    c. In classical conditioning, the reinforcement is contingent on the behavior of the learner.
    d. In operant conditioning the UCS and CS occur independently of the learner's behavior.
       (p. 221) LO 11

17. John loves to receive mail. Over the years, he has learned to tell the difference between the sound of the mail truck and the other cars and trucks that pass his house. What process is at work here?
    a. stimulus discrimination
    b. stimulus generalization
    c. extinction
    d. negative reinforcement
       (p. 222) LO 12

18. After Little Albert was conditioned to fear a white rat, he also displayed fear responses to a white rabbit and a white coat. This is an example of
    a. stimulus generalization
    b. stimulus discrimination
    c. variable interval reinforcement
    d. superstitious behavior
       (p. 223) LO 12

19. When Sandy's disruptive classroom behavior stops because the teacher and other students no longer pay attention to the behavior, the process is called
    a. stimulus discrimination
    b. extinction
    c. stimulus generalization
    d. punishment
       (p. 225) LO 13

20. Behaviors that have been reinforced on a variable schedule are more difficult to extinguish than those that have been continuously reinforced. This is known as
    a. the partial reinforcement effect
    b. an extinction schedule
    c. shaping
    d. avoidance conditioning
       (p. 226) LO 13

21. The most difficult responses of all to extinguish are those learned through
    a. positive reinforcement
    b. variable schedules
    c. escape conditioning
    d. avoidance conditioning
       (p. 226) LO 13

22. Behaviors that appear to be extinguished may return when some dramatic, but unrelated, stimulus event occurs. This is called
    a. spontaneous recovery
    b. stimulus generalization
    c. stimulus discrimination
    d. external disinhibition
       (p. 227) LO 14

23. The neural-connection view of learning is supported by which of the following?
    a. place learning
    b. latent learning
    c. insight learning
    d. none of the above
       (p. 227) LO 15

24. Köhler's research with Sultan supports which theoretical view of learning?
    a. insight learning
    b. latent learning
    c. place learning
    d. modeling
       (p. 232) LO 16

25. Learning to learn insightfully is a characteristic of
    a. latent learning
    b. place learning
    c. learning sets
    d. modeling
       (p. 232) LO 16

26. Those who are concerned about the effects that televised aggression has on children are likely to focus on
    a. insight learning
    b. latent learning
    c. place learning
    d. modeling
       (p. 236) LO 17

27. Learned taste aversion is a form of
    a. operant conditioning
    b. classical conditioning
    c. insight learning
    d. none of the above
       (p. 236) LO 18

28. The fact that fish cannot fly and owls cannot learn to swim is an indication of
    a. lack of adequate reinforcement
    b. their lack of experience
    c. the laziness of these creatures
    d. the effects of biological limits
       (p. 237) LO 18

29. Occasionally, behavior is reinforced when the reinforcing stimulus accidentally follows the response. This is referred to as
    a. classical conditioning
    b. a primary reinforcer
    c. extinction
    d. superstitious behavior
       (p. 239) LO 19

30. According to psychologist Martin Seligman, learned helplessness is a primary cause of
    a. frustration
    b. neurosis
    c. psychosis
    d. depression
       (p. 241) LO 19

Multiple-Choice Answers

1. The answer is *D*. Note that the definition of learning is restricted to *relatively* permanent, as opposed to temporary, changes in behavior.
2. The answer is *B*. The dogs had learned to associate the attendants with the food—the stimulus of the attendant came to elicit the response of salivation.
3. The answer is *C*. In the first phase of classical conditioning, the unconditioned stimulus produces an unconditioned response.
4. The answer is *A*. Since the meat powder is a stimulus that brought about a response (salivation) without any prior conditioning, it is called an unconditioned stimulus.
5. The answer is *D*. Assuming you answered this question correctly (you *did*, didn't you?), before you proceed, be sure that you understand *how* these various responses are classically conditioned.
6. The answer is *B*. The term *operant* is derived from the word *operate*. That is, when our behavior operates on the world, it produces consequences for us. These consequences determine whether or not we will continue the behavior.
7. The answer is *A*. Other important issues in the use of positive reinforcement include the need to be consistent in the delivery of the positive reinforcement and being certain that the positive reinforcer is actually reinforcing.
8. The answer is *A*. Secondary reinforcers, on the other hand, are learned. They take on their reinforcing value through classical conditioning. As an example, consider the process by which money became a powerful reinforcer for you.
9. The answer is *C*. If the reward is based on the passage of a fixed amount of time, it is a fixed interval schedule.
10. The answer is *C*. Variable versus fixed refers to the predictability of the reinforcer. That is, variable reinforcers reward on an unpredictable schedule. Ratio refers to number of behaviors, while interval refers to the amount of time. Thus, a variable ratio implies that the rewards are unpredictable and based on the number of behaviors. A fixed interval schedule, on the other hand, produces a predictable reinforcer after a set amount of time.
11. The answer is *C*. Shaping is a technique that can produce complex behavior by reinforcing behaviors that are successively more similar to the desired behavior. Shaping is also called the method of successive approximations.
12. The answer is *C*. Both escape conditioning and avoidance conditioning are examples of negative reinforcement. Avoidance conditioning is reinforcing because it prevents something negative from happening.
13. The answer is *C*. Negative reinforcement occurs when the reinforcing consequence removes or avoids a negative event.
14. The answer is *D*. In addition to the guidelines mentioned in the question, the text discusses dangers in the use of punishment. These include the fact that the punishment is often reinforcing to the punisher, the generalized inhibiting effect on the individual receiving the punishment, and the criticism trap.
15. The answer is *D*. Punishment and negative reinforcement are often confused. Be sure that you understand the differences between them.
16. The answer is *A*. This is an important question, since it requires you to understand the fundamentals of both classical and operant conditioning. If the answer made sense to you, congratulations! If you struggled with the question, you might wish to review the sections on classical and operant conditioning. Many students find that they need to spend some extra time with this material.
17. The answer is *A*. While stimulus discrimination elicits different responses to different stimuli (at a traffic signal we "go" on green and "stop" on red), stimulus generalization elicits the same response to similar stimuli (we "go" on all green lights regardless of where they are located).
18. The answer is *A*. Little Albert's fear response had generalized to other similar objects. Had he *not* reacted fearfully to these stimuli, he would have demonstrated discrimination.

19. The answer is *B*. Extinction refers to the process of unlearning a learned response due to the removal of the original source of learning. In this instance, Sandy's behavior was conditioned and maintained by the teacher and the other members of the class. When they began to ignore the behavior, they effectively removed the original source of learning.
20. The answer is *A*. Think of examples of specific behaviors that have been partially reinforced and that are difficult to extinguish.
21. The answer is *D*. The person making the response never knows whether or not the stimulus has been removed so the individual persists in making the response.
22. The answer is *D*. In contrast to external disinhibition, spontaneous recovery is likely to occur during extinction and doesn't require the occurrence of a dramatic event. When you suddenly spot your former "significant other" in the mall (the one you thought you were "over") and experience a conditioned emotional response, you have just experienced spontaneous recovery.
23. The answer is *D*. Place learning, latent learning, and insight learning are all examples of the cognitive approach to learning.
24. The answer is *A*. Köhler's research suggested that Sultan learned because of a cognitive change—new insight into the problems he was presented.
25. The answer is *C*. Learning sets suggest that new problems can be solved more quickly when the learner is allowed to practice similar problems.
26. The answer is *D*. Modeling refers to learning based on the observation of another's behavior. In this case, the actors on television may be modeling extremely aggressive behavior.
27. The answer is *B*. Learned taste aversion occurs when we develop a negative reaction to a particular taste because it has been associated with nausea or illness.
28. The answer is *D*. Biological limits also constrain human learning.
29. The answer is *D*. Superstitious behavior is often described as being "resistant to extinction." Can you explain why this is so?
30. The answer is *D*. Learned helplessness is a pattern marked by a lack of effort in avoiding negative events. According to Seligman, it is learned as a consequence of being exposed to unavoidable negative events and is a primary cause of depression.

Learning Objectives

1. Explain the Atkinson and Shiffrin stage theory of memory.
2. Describe the characteristics of the sensory register.
3. Explain the capabilities and functions of short-term memory.
4. Explain how chunking helps to expand the capacity of short-term memory.
5. Explain how the features of long-term memory differ from those of short-term memory.
6. Describe the three kinds of long-term memory: procedural, episodic, and semantic.
7. Discuss the organization of information in long-term memory.
8. Identify different ways of measuring the retrieval of information from long-term memory; explain serial learning and the tip-of-the-tongue phenomenon.
9. Distinguish between deep and shallow processing and explain the role of elaboration.
10. Describe the decay theory of forgetting.
11. Compare and contrast proactive interference and retroactive interference.
12. Explain Bartlett's reconstruction theory and discuss experimental support for the theory.
13. Explain the concept of repression and motivated forgetting.
14. Define and provide examples of flashbulb memories.
15. Describe synaptic theories of memory.
16. Distinguish between anterograde amnesia and retrograde amnesia.
17. Describe Korsakoff's syndrome.
18. (From the "Application" section) Describe the results of research relating eyewitness testimony and memory.

Chapter Overview

The stage theory of memory states that human memory consists of three stages: (1) the sensory register, which holds an exact image of each sensory experience for a very brief interval until it can be fully processed; (2) short-term memory, which holds information for approximately 30 seconds (Information will fade from short-term memory unless the material is rehearsed; the capacity of short-term memory is 7 ± 2 items, but this can be increased by organizing the material into larger chunks.); and (3) long-term memory, which indexes information and stores it primarily in terms of its meaning. Three kinds of long-term memory are procedural, episodic, and semantic. Procedural memory is memory for skills and other procedures. Episodic memory refers to memory for specific experiences that can be defined in terms of time and space, while semantic memory refers to memory for meaning.

The organization of memory in LTM has been characterized as an associative network. One network model is called the spreading activation model.

Three ways that psychologists measure memory retrieval are the recall method, the recognition method, and the relearning method.

An alternative to the stage model is the levels of processing model, which views the differences between short-term and long-term memory in terms of degree rather than separate stages.

Psychologists have identified four ways in which forgetting occurs: (1) decay theory, which states that forgetting occurs simply because time passes; (2) interference theory, which states that forgetting occurs because other memories interfere with retrieval (Interference may occur from memories that were formed by prior learning, called proactive interference, or from memories that were formed by later learning, called retroactive interference.); (3) reconstruction theory, which holds that changes in the structure of a memory make it inaccurate when it is retrieved; and (4) repression, the process by which memories that are upsetting or threatening may be forgotten.

The biological basis of memory is called the memory trace or engram. A theory that has been proposed to explain the biological nature of memory is the synaptic theory, which views learning as a change in the synapses.

Amnesia is a major memory disorder. Anterograde amnesia, caused by damage in the hippocampus, is an inability to store and/or retrieve new information. Retrograde amnesia is the inability to retrieve old, long-term memories.

Research suggests that eyewitness testimony and recall may be inaccurate because of biased questioning or the characteristics of the eyewitnesses. A controversial use of hypnosis to recall past memories is called hypnotic age regression.

Key Terms Exercise

For each of the following exercises, match the key terms on the left with the correct definitions on the right. Page references to the text follow the terms so that you may refer to the text for any items you answer incorrectly or do not understand completely. You may check your responses immediately by referring to the answers that follow each exercise.

Memory (I)

_____ 1. encode (p. 248)
_____ 2. stage theory of memory (p. 248)
_____ 3. sensory register (p. 249)
_____ 4. short-term memory (STM) (p. 249)
_____ 5. rehearsal (p. 249)
_____ 6. acoustic codes (p. 250)
_____ 7. working memory (p. 250)

a. the first stage of memory that briefly holds exact images until they can be processed
b. the second stage of memory that can store five to nine bits of information
c. mental repetition in order to retain information in short-term memory
d. the use of STM to temporarily hold memories from long-term memory
e. The sounds into which information is transformed in STM
f. a theory of memory based on the idea that we store information in three separate but linked memories
g. to represent information in some form in the memory system

ANSWERS

1. g	5. c
2. f	6. d
3. a	7. e
4. b	

Memory (II)

_____ 1. long-term memory (p. 252)
_____ 2. semantic codes (p. 252)
_____ 3. procedural memory (p. 254)
_____ 4. semantic memory (p. 254)
_____ 5. episodic memory (p. 254)
_____ 6. declarative memory (p. 254)
_____ 7. associative network (p. 256)
_____ 8. spreading activation model (p. 256)

a. memory for experiences that can be defined in terms of space and time
b. memory or meaning without reference to time and place of learning
c. memory for skills and other procedures
d. the third stage of memory, which stores information for long periods of time
e. memories that are easily described in words; both semantic and episodic memory
f. Collins and Loftus' model, in which memories spread out along previously formed links to other representations.
g. the general idea that memories are linked together through experience
h. memories that are stored in long-term memory according to their meaning

ANSWERS

1. d	5. a
2. h	6. e
3. c	7. g
4. b	8. f

Memory (III)

_____ 1. recall (p. 256)
_____ 2. recognition (p. 257)
_____ 3. relearning (p. 258)
_____ 4. serial position effect (p. 258)
_____ 5. tip-of-the-tongue (p. 259)
_____ 6. levels of processing model (p. 260)
_____ 7. elaboration (p. 260)

a. the ability to retrieve information from long-term memory without cues
b. the ability to select correct information from among the options provided
c. immediate recall of a list of items is better for items at the beginning and end of the list
d. a measure of memory based on the time it takes to relearn forgotten material
e. trying to recall information we can almost remember
f. creating associations between a new memory and existing memories
g. suggests that the difference between STM and LTM is a matter of degree rather than different stages

ANSWERS

1. a	5. e
2. b	6. g
3. d	7. f
4. c	

Forgetting

_____ 1. decay theory (p. 262)
_____ 2. interference theory (p. 262)
_____ 3. proactive interference (p. 263)
_____ 4. retroactive interference (p. 263)
_____ 5. reconstruction theory (p. 264)
_____ 6. motivated forgetting (p. 266)

a. interference created by prior learning
b. the theory that forgetting occurs when similar memories interfere with storing and retrieving information
c. interference created by later learning
d. the theory that forgetting is based on the threatening nature of the information
e. the theory that forgetting occurs as the memory trace fades over time
f. the theory that forgetting is due to changes in the structure of memory that make it inaccurate when retrieved

ANSWERS

1. e	4. c
2. b	5. f
3. a	6. d

Biological Basis of Memory

_____ 1. engram (p. 268)
_____ 2. anterograde amnesia (p. 269)
_____ 3. retrograde amnesia (p. 271)
_____ 4. Korsakoff's syndrome (p. 271)
_____ 5. Alzheimer's disease (p. 271)
_____ 6. acetylcholine (p. 272)

a. a disorder caused by chronic thiamine deficiency
b. a neurotransmitter assumed to play an important role in memory
c. a severe memory disorder of unknown cause
d. a memory trace that is the biological basis of memory
e. memory disorder characterized by an inability to retrieve old, long-term memories
f. a memory disorder characterized by the inability to store new information in memory

ANSWERS

1. d	4. a
2. f	5. c
3. e	6. b

Guided Review

Three Stages of Memory: An Information-Processing View

Most recent theories of memory borrow a concept used in computer design called _____ _____. In one IP model, information enters the memory system through sensory receptors in _____ form. This raw sensory information

information processing (p. 248)

unprocessed (p. 248)

is represented, or _____, in some form in the memory system. Control mechanisms transfer the information. As information is needed, it is _____ from memory, although some is lost or becomes irretrievable.

The stage theory assumes that we have a _____-_____ memory. The first of these stages is the _____ _____, which holds images until they can be processed. Visual information is retained for about ____ _____, while auditory information can be retained for as long as ____ _____.

The second stage of memory, called ____-_____ _____, stores information for less than ____ _____ unless it is renewed by mental repetition, also called _____. Although information in short-term memory can be stored in many forms, humans seem to prefer transforming information into _____. The capacity of short-term memory, as described by George Miller, is _____ bits of information. Short-term memory also serves as our _____ memory. Research suggests that it takes us about ____ of a second to examine each item in our short-term memory. Miller calls the units of memory _____. The capacity of short-term memory can be expanded by using techniques called _____ _____.

Information is stored for long periods of time in _____-_____ memory. Long-term memory differs from short-term memory in several important ways. Unlike short-term memory, where information can be scanned, the vast amount of information in long-term memory is organized by being _____, and information is retrieved by using _____. In contrast to short-term memory, which stores information in terms of physical qualities, information in long-term memory is primarily stored in terms of its _____. Many psychologists believe that information in long-term memory is not just durable, but it is actually _____. Finally, while STM

encoded (p. 248)

retrieved (p. 248)

three-
stage (p. 248)
sensory register (p. 249)

1/4
second (p. 249)
4 seconds (p. 249)
short-term
memory (p. 249)
30 seconds (p. 249)
rehearsal (p. 249)

sounds (p. 250)

7 ± 2 (p. 250)
working (p. 250)
.04 (p. 251)

chunks (p. 250)
chunking
strategies (p. 251)

long-term (p. 252)

indexed (p. 252)
cues (p. 252)

meaning (p. 252)

permanent (p. 253)

is primarily stored in the _____ lobes of the cerebral frontal (p. 253)

cortex, information in LTM is first held in the _____ hippocampus (p. 253)

and then permanently stored in the language and perception areas

of the _____ _____. cerebral cortex (p. 253)

There appear to be different types of long-term memory.
Memory for skills, such as how to ride a bicycle, is called

_____ memory. Memory associated with meaning is procedural (p. 254)

called _____ memory. Information about specific semantic (p. 254)

experiences is stored in _____ memory. Some episodic (p. 254)

psychologists include semantic memory and episodic memory

under the heading _____ memory. declarative (p. 254)

Organization in LTM helps facilitate the retrieval of
information from the vast amount stored in the LTM. The
organization of memory has been characterized as an

_____ network. An influential network model is called associative (p. 256)

the _____ _____ model. spreading activation (p. 256)

Psychologists have identified three ways of measuring memory

retrieval. In the _____ method, subjects are asked to recall (p. 256)

recall information with few or no cues. In the _____ recognition (p. 257)

method, subjects must recognize the correct information from

among alternatives. The _____ method measures the relearning (p. 258)

relearning of previously memorized information. The superior
recall for items at the beginning and end of a serial list is called

the _____ _____ effect. The tip-of-the-tongue serial position (p. 258)

phenomenon is consistent with the permanence of long-term

memory and suggests that retrieval is not an "_____-_____- all-or-

_____" process. none (p. 259)

An alternative approach to the stage model, called the

_____ _____ _____ model, suggests that levels of processing (p. 260)

there is only one memory store beyond the sensory register. This
model suggests that information will be kept only briefly if it is

processed at a _____ level, but will be kept longer if shallow (p. 260)

processed at a _____ level. Information can be deeply deeper (p. 260)

processed by creating more associations between the new memory

and existing memories, a technique called _____. elaboration (p. 260)

Why Forgetting Occurs

Forgetting occurs because memories that are not used fade over
time, according to the _____ theory. Although it   decay (p. 262)
appears that the passage of time is a cause of forgetting in the
sensory register and _____-_____ memory,   short-term (p. 262)
the decay theory does not appear to explain forgetting in
_____-_____ memory.   long-term (p. 262)

Forgetting in long-term memory occurs because other
memories interfere with the retrieval of information, according to
the _____ theory. Interference is most likely to occur   interference (p. 262)
when memories are _____. Interference due to prior   similar (p. 262)
learning is _____ interference, while interference   proactive (p. 263)
created by later learning is _____ interference.   retroactive (p. 263)

A third theory of forgetting states that memory traces do not
fade but become so distorted that they are unrecognizable; this
approach is called _____ theory. In this view, memories reconstruction (p. 264)
change with time and become less _____, more   complex (p. 264)
consistent, and more congruent with what the person knows and
believes. Recent evidence indicates that reconstructive forgetting
occurs during the process of _____.   retrieval (p. 265)

Sigmund Freud's explanation for forgetting, that the conscious
mind pushes unpleasant information into unconsciousness, is called
_____. Research conducted with _____   repression (p. 266)/flashbulb (p. 267)
memories suggests that even intense emotional experiences are
subject to the normal processes of forgetting.

Biological Basis of Memory: The Search for the Engram

A classical conditioning study conducted on sea snails has provided
support for a theory proposed by Donald Hebb. His theory
suggests that learning is due to a physical change at the
_____. In humans, long-term _____ appears   synapse (p. 269)/potentiation (p. 269)
to lead to synaptic _____.   facilitation (p. 269)

Amnesia: Disorders of Memory

An inability to consciously retrieve new information from long-term memory is found in the memory disorder called

_____ _____. Researchers believe that this   anterograde amnesia (p. 269)

condition is caused by damage in the forebrain structure called the

_____. Individuals who are unable to retrieve old, long-   hippocampus (p. 271)

term memories are experiencing _____   regtrograde

_____. Both retrograde and anterograde amnesia are   amnesia (p. 271)

experienced by individuals with _____ _____.   Korsakoff's syndrome (p. 271)

This disorder is caused by the prolonged loss of the vitamin

_____ from the diet of chronic alcoholics. Individuals   thiamine (p. 271)

with Korsakoff's syndrome engage in _____.   confabulation (p. 271)

Memory enhancement drugs are still controversial and should be viewed with concern.

Research suggests that eyewitness testimony and recall may be

inaccurate due to _____ _____ or due to   biased questioning (p. 273)

characteristics of the eyewitnesses. Research also suggests that the accuracy of eyewitness identification in lineups can be improved by

first presenting a "_____ _____" or by   blank lineup (p. 275)

presenting the persons in the lineup one at a time. With regard to repressed memories of sexual and physical abuse in childhood, a number of studies indicated that some of these memories may be

_____.   erroneous (p. 275)

The use of hypnosis to recall memories of some past event is

called _____ ____ _____. One study found   hypnotic age regression (p. 276)

that memories dredged up during hypnotic age regression are more erroneous than factual. Similar controversy surrounds the use

of hypnosis to aid the recall of eyewitnesses to _____.   crimes (p. 276)

CONCEPT CHECK

Fill in the missing components of the following concept box. The answers are shown below the box.

Theories of Forgetting

I. Theory of forgetting	II. Explanation
a. Decay theory	a. Memories that are not used fade over time.
b. Interference theory	b.
c.	c. Memories get distorted over time.
d. Motivated forgetting	d.

Answers

IIb.   Other memories interfere with recall; proactive interference is created by prior learning, and retroactive interference is created by later learning.

Ic.   Reconstruction theory

IId.   Painful memories are pushed into the unconscious.

Multiple-Choice Questions

1. Which of the following is *not* a stage in the information-processing model of memory?
    a. short-term memory
    b. long-term memory
    c. episodic memory
    d. sensory register
    (p. 248) LO 1

2. The sensory register has all of the following characteristics *except*
    a. Visual information lasts about a quarter of a second.
    b. It holds an exact image of each sensory experience.
    c. Auditory information lasts about 4 seconds.
    d. The capacity is 7 ± 2 bits of information.
    (p. 249) LO 2

3. Suppose that you call the information operator to find a friend's phone number. When you dial your friend's number, you get a busy signal. Later, when you start to dial the number again, you realize you have forgotten it. This experience probably occurred because the phone number was only temporarily stored in your
   a. short-term memory
   b. long-term memory
   c. sensory register
   d. none of the above
   (p. 249) LO 3

4. One technique to help overcome the limited capacity of STM is called
   a. chunking
   b. rehearsal
   c. working memory
   d. semantic codes
   (p. 250) LO 3

5. Working memory is a special function of
   a. the sensory register
   b. short-term memory
   c. long-term memory
   d. any of the above
   (p. 250) LO 4

6. The phone number discussed in question 3 probably could have been remembered for a longer period if you had practiced
   a. chunking
   b. repression
   c. rehearsal
   d. a and c
   (p. 251) LO 4

7. Each of the following is true regarding differences between STM and LTM *except*
   a. information in LTM is indexed
   b. information in STM is stored in terms of physical qualities
   c. information in LTM may be permanent
   d. information in LTM s primarily stored in the frontal lobes of the cortex
   (p. 253) LO 5

8. Although short-term memory stores information in terms of physical qualities, long-term memory stores information in terms of
   a. acoustic codes
   b. sematic codes
   c. attitudes
   d. all of the above
   (p. 254) LO 5

9. You remember some specific football plays from the first half of last week's game; this is
   a. episodic memory
   b. procedural memory
   c. semantic memory
   d. all of the above
   (p. 255) LO 6

10. Which characteristic of long-term memory facilitates the retrieval of information?
    a. unlimited capacity
    b. the organization of material
    c. the chunking of information
    d. the ability of long-term memory to store procedural information
    (p. 255) LO 7

11. Which concept states that memories are linked together through experience?
    a. semantic memory
    b. reconstructive memory
    c. associative network
    d. serial forgetting
    (p. 256) LO 7

12. According to the serial position effect, recall of items in a serial list is better
    a. at the beginning of the list
    b. in the middle of the list
    c. at the end of the list
    d. a and c
    (p. 258) LO 8

13. The "tip-of-the-tongue" phenomenon appears to be caused by a problem in
    a. retrieval
    b. engrams
    c. reconstruction
    d. repression
    (p. 259) LO 8

14. The type of remembering necessary to correctly answer this multiple-choice question is
    a. recall
    b. recognition
    c. relearning
    d. rehearsal
    (p. 257) LO 8

15. Which of the following is a way of testing retrieval of long-term memories?
    a. recall
    b. recognition
    c. relearning
    d. all of the above
    (p. 258) LO 8

16. The process of reading material and relating it to previous learning or to your own life is called
    a. rehearsal
    b. consolidation
    c. elaboration
    d. chunking
    (p. 260) LO 9

17. The levels of processing model states that deep processing involves greater
    _____ than shallow processing.
    a. rehearsal
    b. engrams
    c. consolidation
    d. elaboration
    (p. 260) LO 9

18. Which theory suggests that forgetting is caused by a fading memory trace?
    a. reconstruction theory
    b. repression
    c. decay theory
    d. interference theory
    (p. 262) LO 10

19. The expression "You can't teach an old dog new tricks" would support which theory of forgetting"?
    a. repression
    b. retroactive interference
    c. proactive interference
    d. pass interference
    (p. 263) LO 11

20. After having the same phone number for years, you move into an apartment and get a different, but similar, phone number. Retroactive interference would be demonstrated by your difficulty in remembering
    a. the new phone number
    b. the old phone number
    c. either phone number
    d. your new address
    (p. 263) LO 11

21. Research on reconstructive memories indicates that this process occurs during
    a. the formation of memories
    b. the process of retrieval
    c. proactive inhibition
    d. repression
    (p. 264) LO 12

22. Joe likes to fish. His friends have noticed that every time he tells the story about the "big one" he caught a few years ago, he seems to remember the fish as larger and larger. Joe's behavior is consistent with which theory of forgetting?
    a. decay
    b. interference
    c. reconstruction
    d. repression
    (p. 264) LO 12

23. The theory of forgetting that suggests that the conscious mind pushes information into the unconscious is called
    a. decay
    b. reconstruction
    c. interference
    d. repression
       (p. 266) LO 13

24. The vivid recall of a negative emotional experience is called a
    a. flashbulb memory
    b. flashback
    c. reconstructive flash
    d. none of the above
       (p. 267) LO 14

25. Synaptic facilitation occurs when short bursts of electricity are delivered to the
    a. amygdala
    b. hippocampus
    c. hypothalamus
    d. frontal lobe of the cortex
       (p. 269) LO 15

26. Research into the biological basis of memory has focused on
    a. molecular theories
    b. synaptic theories
    c. the role of the medulla
    d. a and b above
       (p. 269) LO 15

27. An inability to store and/or retrieve new information in long-term memory is characteristic of
    a. RNA
    b. anterograde amnesia
    c. retrograde amnesia
    d. retroactive amnesia
       (p. 269) LO 16

28. A key biological structure that is often damaged in patients with anterograde amnesia is the
    a. hippocampus
    b. cerebral cortex
    c. hypothalamus
    d. amygdala
       (p. 271) LO 16

29. Korsakoff's syndrome
    a. is caused by prolonged thiamine deficiency
    b. is characterized by anterograde and retrograde amnesia
    c. is characterized by confabulation
    d. all of the above
       (p. 271) LO 17

30. According to the work of Loftus and others in the area of eyewitness testimony,
    a. eyewitnesses are likely to repress traumatic information
    b. eyewitnesses are strongly influenced by decay theory
    c. eyewitnesses are not easily misled
    d. eyewitnesses can be misled when they are asked misleading questions.
       (p. 276) LO 18

Multiple-Choice Answers

1. The answer is *C*. According to the Atkinson-Shriffin stage theory of memory, the three stages of memory are each separate, but linked. Episodic memory refers to memory about specific experiences in life.
2. The answer is *D*. The capacity mentioned in *D* refers to the capacity for short-term memory.
3. The answer is *A*. Presumably, since the information was not rehearsed, the phone number faded after a short period of time.

4. The answer is *A*. Chunking is the process of putting more than one bit of information into a unit, thereby expanding the capacity of STM.

5. The answer is *B*. This function further limits the already small capacity of short-term memory.

6. The correct answer is *D*. Chunking is a method of putting bits of information together. For example, you might chunk the first three numbers of the phone number. People frequently do this with their social security numbers. Instead of remembering it as nine individual numbers, we tend to remember it as a chunk of three numbers followed by a chunk of two numbers followed by a chunk of four numbers. A second approach for remembering the phone number is to mentally rehearse it. A third technique, not mentioned in the question, is to use a phone with an "automatic redial."

7. The answer is *D*. Information in LTM is first held in the hippocampus and then permanently stored in the language and perception areas of the cortex.

8. The correct answer is *B*. Although short-term memory is usually stored in terms of the sights, sounds, and touch of experiences, long-term memory primarily stores information in terms of meaning.

9. The answer is *A*. Episodic memory stores information about specific experiences. Procedural memory is memory for skills, such as riding a bicycle. Semantic memory is memory about the meaning of words.

10. The answer is *B*. While LTM appears to have unlimited capacity, this characteristic does not facilitate the retrieval of information. The chunking of information is a process carried about by the short-term memory. Finally, the ability of LTM to store procedural information does not facilitate the retrieval of information.

11. The answer is *C*. According to this view, memories form links that we use to think about information we have stored in memory.

12. The answer is *D*. The serial position effect has important implications for everything from the manner in which evidence is presented in a trial to how you can most effectively prepare for an exam.

13. The correct answer is *A*. The tip-of-the-tongue phenomenon suggests that the information is stored, but for some reason we're not pressing the right mental "buttons" to retrieve it.

14. The answer is *B*. Multiple-choice questions provide more cues for retrieving information than do fill-in questions. The question not only provides the problem; it also provides the correct answer. That's why they are so easy for students. Sure.

15. The answer is *D*. Each method measures a different aspect of long-term memory.

16. The answer is *C*. Elaboration is the process of creating more associations between the new memory and existing memories.

17. The answer is *D*. Elaboration refers to the creation of more associations between a new memory and existing memories. When you tie in the concepts you are reading about in your psychology text to events in your own life, you are elaborating.

18. The answer is *C*. Decay theory suggests that the change in the brain that occurs after something is learned gradually fades unless the material is rehearsed.

19. The answer is *C*. The expression implies that any attempt to teach a dog would be interfered with by the dog's prior learning; proactive interference suggests that prior learning interferes with later learning. Retroactive interference suggests that something learned later interferes with something previously learned.

20. The answer is *B*. Retroactive interference refers to interference created by later learning.

21. The answer is *B*. Reconstruction most likely occurs when we try to remember things, that is, during the process of retrieval.

22. The answer is *C*. Reconstruction theory, unlike decay theory, suggests that, over time, the structures of memories get distorted. Thus, reconstructed memories are inaccurate when they are retrieved.

23. The answer is *D*. Repression is Freud's theory. It is often used synonymously with the term *motivated forgetting.*

24. The answer is *A*. Although flashbulb memories can be recalled in vivid detail, they are nonetheless subject to the normal processes of forgetting.

25. The answer is *B*. This process, also called long-term potentiation, causes the hippocampal neurons to be more responsive to additional stimulation for several weeks.

26. The answer is *D*. While molecular theories have focused on the roles played by proteins and RNA, synaptic theories have explored the physical changes that occur at the synapses.
27. The answer is *B*. Retrograde amnesia is the disorder characterized by an inability to retrieve old, long-term memories. Interestingly, in both anterograde and retrograde amnesia, there is little or no disruption to STM.
28. The answer is *A*. Isn't it interesting that the hippocampus keeps turning up as a key brain structure throughout this chapter?
29. The answer is *D*. Confabulation may be thought of as an exaggerated version of reconstructive distortion.
30. The answer is *D*. Loftus and others have shown that misleading questions presented to eyewitnesses can actually cue the recall of items that were not present.

Learning Objectives

1. List and explain three major components of the definition of cognition.
2. Distinguish between conjunctive concepts and disjunctive concepts.
3. Describe the process of concept formation.
4. Describe the basic and prototypical features of natural concepts.
5. List and explain the three types of cognitive operations involved in problem solving.
6. Distinguish among the following problem-solving strategies: trial-and-error, algorithmic operations, and heuristic operations.
7. Explain the relationship between artificial intelligence and the cognitive process.
8. Distinguish between convergent thinking and divergent thinking.
9. Describe the results of research into the creative process.
10. Distinguish between the surface structure and deep structure of language.
11. Distinguish among phonemes, morphemes, and syntax.
12. Explain Benjamin Whorf's linguistic relativity hypothesis.
13. Discuss the results of research regarding the language capabilities of animals.
14. Compare the position of psychologists who view intelligence as a general ability with those who view it as several specific abilities.
15. List and explain the components of Robert Sternberg's triarchic theory of intelligence.
16. Explain the concept of intelligence quotient; distinguish between the ratio IQ and the deviation IQ.
17. List the characteristics of good intelligence tests.
18. Discuss the predictive abilities of intelligence tests and explain the concept of "everyday intelligence."
19. Discuss the evidence that supports the role of heredity in determining intelligence; discuss the evidence that supports the role of the environment in determining intelligence.
20. Describe the controversy concerning ethnic differences in intelligence scores.
21. Describe the extremes in intelligence: mental retardation and giftedness. Then discuss the results of studies by Terman and others on those with high intelligence.
22. (From the "Application" section) Identify techniques to help improve everyday problem solving.

Chapter Overview

Cognition refers to the process by which information is obtained through the senses, transformed through the processes of perception and thinking, stored and retrieved through the processes of memory, and used in the processes of problem solving and language.

The basic units of thinking are called concepts. Concepts are categories of things, events, or qualities linked together by some common feature or features. Some concepts are based on a single common feature, while others are more complex. Conjunctive concepts are defined by the simultaneous presence of two or more common characteristics, while disjunctive concepts are defined by the presence of one of two common characteristics, or both of them. Concept formation is a type of learning in which hypotheses about the characteristics of a concept are tested by examining positive and negative instances of the concept. All concepts are not equally easy to learn; some are more natural than others. Natural concepts are both basic and prototypical.

Problem solving is the use of information to reach a goal that is blocked. Problem solving uses cognitive operations, which include formulating the problem, understanding the elements of the problem, and generating and evaluating alternative solutions. The term *artificial intelligence* describes computers that are programmed to think like humans. Algorithmic and heuristic operations are two types of cognitive strategies used to solve problems. Creative problem solving requires the ability to think in flexible and unusual ways, called divergent thinking; problem solving that is more logical and conventional is called convergent thinking.

Language is a symbolic code used in human communication. The meaning that is communicated is called the semantic content of language. Human language is highly efficient and generative; an infinite set of utterances can be made using a finite set of elements and rules. These rules are referred to as syntax. Phonemes are the smallest units of sound, while morphemes are the smallest units of meaning in a language.

Psychologists have long been interested in the relationship between language and thought. The Whorfian or linguistic relativity hypothesis states that the structure of language influences thinking.

Intelligence refers to the cognitive abilities of an individual to learn from experience, to reason well, and to cope effectively with the demands of daily living. Some psychologists believe that intelligence is a single factor, while others view intelligence as many different kinds of intellectual abilities. Intelligence tests measure a small sample of the cognitive abilities that constitute intelligence. The intelligence quotient (IQ) is obtained by dividing an individual's mental age by his or her chronological age. This approach to calculating intellectual ability has been replaced by the deviation IQ, which compares individual scores to a normal distribution. Useful IQ tests must be standardized, objective, reliable, valid, and evaluated against proper norms. Some psychologists feel that intelligence tests do not measure "everyday intelligence." In response, tests of everyday intelligence measuring such skills as sales and decision-making have been developed. An individual's level of intelligence is determined both by inherited and environmental factors.

Mental retardation varies in degree, from mild to profound. Retardation can result from a variety of causes, including genetic factors, birth trauma, maternal drug use, or early deprivation.

Key Terms Exercise

For each of the following exercises, match the key terms on the left with the correct definitions on the right. Page references to the text follow the terms so that you may refer to the text for any items you answer incorrectly or do not understand completely. You may check your responses immediately by referring to the answers that follow each exercise.

Concepts

_____ 1. cognition (p. 284)
_____ 2. concept (p. 284)
_____ 3. conjunctive concepts (p. 285)
_____ 4. disjunctive concepts (p. 285)
_____ 5. prototypes (p. 288)

a. concepts defined by the simultaneous presence of two or more common characteristics
b. concepts defined by the presence of one of two common characteristics, or both characteristics
c. a characteristic of natural concepts; they are good examples
d. a category of objects or events that are linked together by some common feature or features
e. intellectual process through which information is obtained, transformed, stored, and used

ANSWERS

1. e	4. b
2. d	5. c
3. a	

Problem Solving

_____ 1. mental set (p. 291)
_____ 2. algorithm (p. 292)
_____ 3. heuristic (p. 292)
_____ 4. artificial intelligence (p. 293)
_____ 5. expert systems (p. 293)
_____ 6. convergent thinking (p. 294)
_____ 7. divergent thinking (p. 294)
_____ 8. incubation (p. 294)
_____ 9. illumination (p. 295)

a.   in creative problem solving, a period of rest or setting aside of problem
b.   computer programs designed to think like humans
c.   a pattern of reasoning that maximizes the probability of finding the correct solution
d.   loosely organized, unconventional thinking
e.   sudden insight into a problem's solution
f.   logical, conventional thinking
g.   a pattern of reasoning that guarantees finding a correct solution
h.   a habitual way of viewing a problem
i.   problem-solving computer programs that operate in a narrow area

ANSWERS

1. h	6. f
2. g	7. d
3. c	8. a
4. b	9. e
5. i	

Language

_____ 1. language (p. 297)
_____ 2. semantic content (p. 297)
_____ 3. surface structure (p. 297)
_____ 4. deep structure (p. 297)
_____ 5. phoneme (p. 297)
_____ 6. morpheme (p. 298)
_____ 7. syntax (p. 298)
_____ 8. prescriptive rules (p. 298)
_____ 9. linguistic relativity hypothesis (p. 299)

a.   the underlying structure that contains a statement's meaning
b.   the meaning in symbols such as language
c.   the smallest unit of meaning in a language
d.   a symbolic code used in communication
e.   the formal rules of a language, typically taught by parents and teachers
f.   the smallest unit of sound in a language
g.   the grammatical rules of a language
h.   the superficial structure of a statement
i.   the idea that the structure of a language influences thinking

ANSWERS

1. d	6. c
2. b	7. g
3. h	8. e
4. a	9. i
5. f	

Intelligence

_____ 1. intelligence (p. 304)
_____ 2. triarchic theory of intelligence (p. 306)
_____ 3. intelligence quotient (p. 309)
_____ 4. normal distribution (p. 309)
_____ 5. standardization (p. 310)
_____ 6. norm (p. 310)
_____ 7. objectivity (p. 311)
_____ 8. reliability (p. 311)
_____ 9. validity (p. 311)
_____ 10. neural pruning (p. 314)

a. a numerical value of intelligence derived from an intelligence test
b. methods for administering tests in the same way to all individuals
c. the cognitive ability of an individual to learn from experience, to reason well, and to cope with the demands of daily living
d. the destruction of excess neural circuits
e. a standard used as the basis of comparison for test scores
f. a symmetrical pattern of scores in which most scores are clustered near the center
g. similarity in test scores even if the test is administered at different times or by different examiners
h. a test's ability to measure what it's supposed to measure
i. scoring a test question so that the same score is produced regardless of who does the scoring
j. theory of intelligence that distinguishes learning new information, solving specific problems, and solving problems in general

ANSWERS

1. c	6. e
2. j	7. i
3. a	8. g
4. f	9. h
5. b	10. d

Who Am I?

Match the psychologists on the left with their contributions to the field of psychology on the right. Page references to the text follow the names of the psychologists so that you may refer to the text for further review of these psychologists and their contributions. You may check your responses immediately by referring to the answers that follow each exercise.

_____ 1. Benjamin Whorf (p. 299)
_____ 2. Sir Francis Galton (p. 304)
_____ 3. Alfred Binet (p. 309)
_____ 4. David Wechsler (p. 307)
_____ 5. Robert Sternberg (p. 306)
_____ 6. Howard Gardner (p. 304)

a. I developed intelligence scales for children and adults.
b. I developed the first useful intelligence test (in France).
c. I believe there are seven independent types of intelligence, including artistic and athletic.
d. It's my belief that language influences thinking.
e. I proposed the triarchic theory of intelligence.
f. My writings in the late 1800s helped popularize the concept of intelligence.

ANSWERS

1. d	4. a
2. f	5. e
3. b	6. c

Guided Review

Definition of Cognition

The intellectual processes through which information is obtained,

transformed, stored, retrieved, and used is _____.   cognition (p. 284)

Cognition processes _____; it is active and it is   information (p. 284)

_____.   useful (p. 284)

Concepts: The Basic Units of Thinking

Categories of objects and events linked together by common

features are called _____. These basic units of thought   concepts (p. 284)

may involve one common feature, or they may be more complex.

When two or more common characteristics are simultaneously

present, this is a _____ concept. Concepts that have one   conjunctive (p. 285)

or another characteristic, or both of them, are _____   disjunctive (p. 285)

concepts.

    A special kind of thinking that tests hypotheses about the

characteristics of a concept is called _____   concept

_____. Some concepts are easier to learn than others;   formation (p. 286)

these are _____ concepts. Natural concepts have two   natural (p. 286)

primary characteristics: they are _____ and   basic (p. 286)

_____. Basic concepts have a medium degree of   prototypical (p. 286)

_____. In contrast, a high degree of inclusiveness is   inclusiveness (p. 286)

found in _____ concepts, and a low degree of   superordinate (p. 286)

inclusiveness is found in _____ concepts. Among the   subordinate (p. 287)

important characteristics of basic concepts are (1) they share many

common _____; (2) they share similar _____;   attributes (p. 287)/shapes (p. 288)

(3) they often share motor _____; and (4) they are   movements (p. 288)

easily _____.   named (p. 288)

Problem Solving: Using Information to Reach Goals

The type of thinking that uses information to reach a goal that is blocked is called _____ _____. There are three major steps in problem solving: (1) _____ the problem, (2) understanding and _____ the elements of the problem, and (3) _____ and evaluating alternative solutions.

    A habitual way of viewing a problem is called a _____ _____. Three types of cognitive strategies are used in problem solving: (1) trial-and-error, (2) a type in which every possible solution is examined and which guarantees a solution, called an _____, and (3) a shortcut strategy that maximizes the probability of finding a correct solution, known as _____. Two examples of heuristics that humans commonly use in problem solving are representativeness and _____.

    The term *artificial intelligence* describes _____ that are programmed to think like humans. Problem-solving computer programs, such as MYCIN, that operate in a very narrow area, are called _____ _____. Generally, computers are best at solving problems when the problem area is _____-_____.

    The ability to produce novel and socially valued products or ideas is _____. Thinking that is logical and conventional is called _____ thinking, while thinking that is loosely organized, only partially directed, and unconventional is called _____ thinking. Most formal education emphasizes _____ thinking. Divergent thinking produces answers that must be evaluated _____. One explanation of the creative process suggests that it proceeds in four steps: preparation, _____, illumination, and _____. According to Hayes, three ways of increasing the likelihood of creative thinking are a good knowledge base, the right atmosphere, and the use of _____.

problem solving (p. 290)

formulating (p. 290)

organizing (p. 290)

generating (p. 290)

mental set (p. 291)

algorithm (p. 292)

heuristics (p. 292)

availability (p. 293)

computers (p. 293)

expert systems (p. 293)

well-defined (p. 294)

creativity (p. 294)

convergent (p. 294)

divergent (p. 294)

convergent (p. 294)

subjectively (p. 294)

incubation (p. 294)/verification (p. 295)

analogies (p. 295)

Language: Symbolic Communication

Language is a symbolic code used in communication. The meaning that is communicated is referred to as _____ _____. Noam Chomsky has distinguished between the superficial structure of a statement, called _____ _____, and the underlying structure that contains the statement's meaning, called _____ _____. Language gives us the ability to create an infinite number of utterances from a fixed set of elements and rules; this is called the _____ property of language. The smallest unit of sound in a language is a _____, while the smallest unit of meaning in a language is a _____. The rules of a language are called _____. The hypothesis that the structure of a language influences thinking, proposed by Benjamin Whorf, is called the _____ _____ _____.

    The experiences of Washoe and Koko suggest that chimps are able to learn to use _____. Terrace, however, questions whether chimps can use language spontaneously and whether they can exhibit an understanding of _____.

semantic

content (p. 297)

surface

structure (p. 297)

deep structure (p. 297)

generative (p. 297)

phoneme (p. 297)

morpheme (p. 298)

syntax (p. 298)

linguistic relativity

hypothesis (p. 299)

language (p. 301)

syntax (p. 302)

Intelligence: The Sum Total of Cognition

The ability of an individual to learn from experience, to reason well, and to cope well with daily life is _____. Sir Francis Galton popularized the notion of intelligence in the late 1800s. He believed intelligence is inherited and is composed of a single _____ factor. Charles Spearman uses the term _____ to refer to this general factor, but other psychologists believe intelligence is a collection of many separate abilities. Louis Thurstone, for example, devised a test to measure _____ different abilities, while J. P. Guilford believes intelligence is made up of _____ different abilities. According to Howard Gardner, there are _____ independent types of intelligence. Robert Sternberg has proposed a theory that specifies the _____ _____ of intelligence. Sternberg

intelligence (p. 304)

general (p. 304)

g (p. 304)

7 (p. 304)

150 (p. 304)

seven (p. 304)

cognitive components (p. 305)

suggests that there are three components; he refers to his view as the _____ theory of intelligence.

    Around 1900, Alfred _____ became the first person to develop a useful measure of intelligence. Binet's test was refined by Lewis _____ of Stanford University. A similar intelligence test was also developed by David _____. Intelligence tests are designed to be a _____ of some of the cognitive abilities that constitute intelligence. They are useful in predicting the performance of individuals in situations that require _____.

    To calculate an IQ score, it is necessary to know both the child's _____ age and _____ age. IQ scores are calculated by dividing a subject's _____ age by this _____ age and multiplying the result by ____. For example, a child with a mental age of 12 and a chronological age of 10 would have an IQ score of ____, while a child with a mental age of 6 and a chronological age of 8 would have an IQ score of ____. Binet's approach, which calculates the ratio IQ, is no longer used in contemporary intelligence tests.

    A newer approach to measuring intellectual ability, termed the _____ IQ, assumes that the scores of large numbers of individuals who take an intelligence test will fall in a normal distribution. Most scores will be clustered around the _____, and as scores deviate from the average they become progressively less common. Using this approach, the average intelligence score is set at ____.

    Good intelligence tests, as well as other psychological tests, are characterized by (1) _____, so that tests are given the same way to all who take the test; (2) _____, in which the test is given to a large representative sample of the population; (3) _____, so that there is little or no ambiguity as to what constitutes a correct answer; (4) _____, so that the scores obtained would be the same if administered on two different occasions or by two different examiners; and (5) _____, so that a test measures what it is supposed to measure.

triarchic (p. 306)

Binet (p. 307)

Terman (p. 307)

Wechsler (p. 307)

sample (p. 307)

intelligence (p. 307)

mental (p. 309)/chronological (p. 309)

mental (p. 309)

chronological (p. 309)/100 (p. 309)

120 (p. 309)

75 (p. 309)

deviation (p. 309)

average (p. 309)

100 (p. 309)

standardization (p. 310)

norms (p. 310)

objectivity (p. 311)

reliability (p. 311)

validity (p. 311)

While intelligence tests are useful in predicting "school intelligence," they have been criticized for not accurately measuring _____ intelligence. One researcher suggests that everyday intelligence tests primarily assess _____ knowledge and skills in getting things done.

everyday (p. 312)

practical (p. 312)

Although the evidence from both twin studies and adoption studies suggests that intelligence is partly determined by heredity, research by Skeels underscores the importance of _____ influences. Research by Haier suggests that higher intelligence may result from success in a normal maturational process called _____ _____.

environmental (p. 313)

neural pruning (p. 313)

The differences between the IQ scores of African Americans and whites have been attributed to the facts that the tests are based on items common to white culture and that African Americans face _____ environments. Group IQ differences appear to be dwindling as prejudice and _____ barriers are weakening.

prejudiced (p. 315)

economic (p. 315)

Degrees of retardation range from mild to _____. Retardation can result from genetic disorders, _____ trauma, maternal infections, use of alcohol or psychoactive _____, or early sensory or maternal _____. Approximately 90 percent of the population with retardation is _____ retarded; thus, the vast majority of retarded people can lead productive and satisfying lives.

profound (p. 315)

birth (p. 315)

drugs (p. 315)/deprivation (p. 315)

mildly (p. 315)

Although "gifted" is usually defined in terms of IQ scores, attention is also paid to _____. Gifted programs are founded on two assumptions: (1) that the nation needs to enrich the education of its brightest future leaders, and (2) that bright children occasionally need help to avoid having _____ problems. The results of the Terman study and others on highly intelligent people indicates that they function very well in every evaluated area of life. IQ scores don't become stable until age ____ to ____.

creativity (p. 316)

psychological (p. 316)

7 (p. 316)/10 (p. 316)

Application of Psychology: Improving Everyday Problem Solving

One of the most common barriers to effective problem solving is

_____ _____. One type of mental set, in   mental set (p. 318)

which we have difficulty in seeing new uses for objects, is called

_____ _____. A common problem in   functional fixedness (p. 318)

reasoning about probabilities is called the _____   conjunction

_____. A general strategy for effective problem solving   fallacy (p. 320)

involves the following steps: (1) identify the problem;

(2) _____ all possible solutions; (3) eliminate any poor   generate (p. 321)

choices; (4) examine the likely consequences of each possible

solution and select the best solution; (5) _____ all   generate (p. 321)

possible ways to implement the solution; (6) implement the

_____.   solution (p. 321)

CONCEPT CHECK

Fill in the missing components of the following concept box. The answers are shown below the box.

Differing Views of Intelligence

I. Theorist	II. Concept
a. Galton, Spearman, and Wechsler	a. Intelligence is a single general factor.
b.	b. There are seven independent types of intelligence including linguistic, logical-mathematical, musical, spatial, kinesthetic, intrapersonal, and interpersonal.
c. Sternberg	c.

Answers

Ib. Howard Gardner

IIc. Sternberg's triarchic theory of intelligence distinguishes three components of intelligence: knowledge-acquisition components, performance components, and metacomponents.

Multiple-Choice Questions

1. Which of the following is an important characteristic of cognition?
   a. Cognition processes information.
   b. Cognition is active.
   c. Cognition is functional.
   d. all of the above
   (p. 284) LO 1

2. If a concept has two or more common characteristics present at the same time, it is a
   a. disjunctive concept
   b. conjunctive concept
   c. natural concept
   d. novel concept
   (p. 285) LO 2

3. Which of the following is part of the process of concept formation?
   a. Hypotheses about the defining characteristics of the concept are tested.
   b. Positive instances are examined.
   c. Negative instances are examined.
   d. all of the above
   (p. 285) LO 3

4. According to Eleanor Rosch, basic concepts
   a. are very inclusive
   b. are difficult to name
   c. share many common attributes
   d. rarely share similar shapes
   (p. 287) LO 4

5. Which of the following represents the proper sequence of cognitive operations involved in problem solving?
   a. generate and evaluate solutions, formulate the problem, understand the elements
   b. understand the elements, generate and evaluate solutions, formulate the problem
   c. formulate the problem, generate and evaluate solutions, understand the elements
   d. formulate the problem, understand the elements, generate and evaluate solutions
   (p. 290) LO 5

6. According to the text, which type of problem-solving strategy is more likely to be used?
   a. heuristics
   b. algorithms
   c. expert systems
   d. none of the above
   (p. 292) LO 6

7. Amy is trying to solve a problem by using a strategy that guarantees a correct solution. The technique she is using is
   a. algorithms
   b. representativeness
   c. heuristics
   d. availability
   (p. 292) LO 6

8. The MYCIN program
   a. is an example of an expert system
   b. has replaced the need for physicians to diagnose and treat some diseases
   c. agreed with medical experts in almost every case
   d. all of the above
   (p. 293) LO 7

9. People who are creative tend to use
   a. convergent thinking
   b. divergent thinking
   c. subordinate thinking
   d. little or no thinking
   (p. 294) LO 8

10. Each of the following is a step in the creative process *except*
    a. illumination
    b. creation
    c. elimination
    d. verification
    (p. 295) LO 9

11. According to Hayes, which of the following is a technique that makes the creative process more likely?
    a. firm knowledge base
    b. the right atmosphere
    c. the use of analogies
    d. all of the above
    (p. 295) LO 9

12. Which of the following contains the underlying meaning in a statement?
    a. deep structure
    b. surface structure
    c. phonemes
    d. syntax
       (p. 297) LO 10

13. Which of the following is the correct sequence used by children in language development?
    a. morphemes, phonemes, and then syntax
    b. syntax, phonemes, and then morphemes
    c. phonemes, morphemes, and then syntax
    d. syntax, morphemes, and then phonemes
       (p. 298) LO 11

14. Which of the following statements is *not* true?
    a. Morphemes are the smallest units of meaning.
    b. Phonemes are the smallest units of sound.
    c. The English language contains more phonemes than morphemes.
    d. The rules governing phonemes and morphemes are called syntax.
       (p. 297) LO 11

15. The belief that language influences thinking is
    a. peripheralism
    b. the linguini hypothesis
    c. the linguistic relativity hypothesis
    d. none of the above
       (p. 299) LO 12

16. The Whorfian hypothesis
    a. was strongly supported by Rosch's research with the Dani tribe
    b. was not supported by Rosch's research
    c. was not supported by research regarding labels for personality types and their influence on how we think about people
    d. is just the opposite of the linguistic relativity hypothesis
       (p. 299) LO 12

17. Although apes have been taught American Sign Language (ASL), according to Terrace,
    a. they generally do not use language spontaneously
    b. they rarely express their emotions
    c. they show little evidence of understanding syntax
    d. a and c above
       (p. 302) LO 13

18. All of the following psychologists have believed in a single general factor of intelligence *except*
    a. Galton
    b. Binet
    c. Wechsler
    d. Guilford
       (p. 304) LO 14

19. Each of the following is a component of Sternberg's triarchic theory of intelligence *except*
    a. knowledge-acquisition components
    b. performance components
    c. intellectual components
    d. metacomponents
       (p. 306) LO 15

20. According to Gardner, which of the following is a type of intelligence?
    a. linguistic
    b. spatial
    c. kinesthetic
    d. all of the above
       (p. 304) LO 15

21. According to Sternberg's triarchic theory of intelligence, which component refers to knowledge about general strategies for problem solving?
    a. knowledge-acquisition
    b. performance
    c. metacomponents
    d. none of the above
       (p. 306) LO 15

22. Joe has a mental age of 10 and a chronological age of 8. his IQ score is
    a. 80
    b. 100
    c. 120
    d. 125
    (p. 309) LO 16

23. When a test measures what it claims to measure it is
    a. valid
    b. reliable
    c. standardized
    d. objective
    (p. 311) LO 17

24. Intelligence tests can predict success in
    a. school achievement
    b. practical knowledge
    c. personal organization
    d. a and b above
    (p. 312) LO 18

25. Research done with twins as well as with adopted children has tended to support the influence of which factor on intelligence?
    a. environment
    b. learning
    c. heredity
    d. none of the above
    (p. 312) LO 19

26. Neural pruning refers to
    a. the destruction of excess neural connections
    b. a maturational process that occurs between the ages of 5 and the early teens
    c. a process that leads to greater neural efficiency
    d. all of the above
    (p. 314) LO 19

27. The results of a 1975 study of German children—half with African-American fathers and white mothers and half with two white parents—showed that the IQ scores of the children with African-American fathers
    a. surpassed those of the children with two white parents
    b. were lower than those of the children with two white parents
    c. were similar to those of the children with two white parents
    d. depended on the IQ scores of the white parents
    (p. 315) LO 20

28. The longitudinal study of highly intelligent people initiated by Louis Terman has revealed
    a. that the intellectually gifted have a greater likelihood of experiencing mental disorders
    b. no significant differences in achievement when compared with a group of normal IQ individuals
    c. that the gifted group was shorter than average
    d. higher achievements and lower death rates for the intellectually gifted
    (p. 316) LO 21

29. An effective strategy for dealing with functional fixedness is to
    a. break out of the set and see new uses for objects
    b. ignore the problem and just focus on the end result
    c. stay with the problem and eventually a solution will "pop" into your head
    d. all of the above
    (p. 318) LO 22

30. According to the text, such reasoning skills as the conjunction fallacy support the notion that human reasoning is frequently
    a. logical
    b. illogical
    c. rational
    d. nonexistent
    (p. 320) LO 22

1. The answer is *D*. While cognition is involved in virtually every aspect of psychology, it is an integral part of thinking, language, and intelligence.
2. The answer is *B*. Disjunctive concepts, in contrast to conjunctive concepts, are defined by the presence of one common characteristic, *or* a second characteristic, or *both* characteristics.
3. The answer is *D*. Concept formation results from the interaction of the three events described in the question.
4. The answer is *C*. Natural concepts are both basic and prototypical. Basic concepts have a medium degree of inclusiveness, share many common attributes, share similar shapes, often share motor movements, and *are easily named*. The second quality of natural concepts is that they are good prototypes; that is, they are good examples. Generally, natural concepts are easily learned.
5. The answer is *D*. Following this strategy may help you to improve your own problem-solving abilities.
6. The answer is *A*. We tend to use heuristics more often than algorithms because algorithms require too much cognitive capacity, and most of life's problems don't readily lend themselves to algorithmic thinking.
7. The answer is *A*. The use of algorithms is a time-consuming strategy, which makes them ideal for computer use.
8. The answer is *A*. While MYCIN is an example of an expert system, it agreed with medical experts 72 percent of the time and is *not* considered a replacement for physicians.
9. The answer is *B*. While convergent thinking is logical, conventional, and focused, divergent thinking is unconventional and loosely organized.
10. The answer is *B*. The missing second step in the creative process is called incubation, in which the problem is set aside for a while after the initial preparation period.
11. The answer is *D*. Each of these techniques has been suggested by Hayes as a way to increase the likelihood of creative thinking.
12. The answer is *A*. According to Chomsky, the superficial spoken or written structure of a statement is the surface structure, while the underlying meaning of the statement is held by the deep structure.
13. The answer is *C*. Children first babble in the sounds of their language (phonemes), then progress to morphemes, and finally acquire syntactic rules.
14. The answer is *C*. In fact, the English language contains more morphemes than phonemes.
15. The answer is *C*. Although the concept might make common sense, the hypothesis has not always been supported by research results.
16. The answer is *B*. The Whorfian hypothesis (also called the linguistic relativity hypothesis) was supported by research regarding labels and their impact on how we think about people, but was NOT supported by Rosch's study on the Dani tribe.
17. The answer is *D*. According to Terrace, who has taught chimps ASL, the chimps fail to use language spontaneously and do not understand syntax. This contradicts the findings of Patterson, who has taught Koko over 600 signs.
18. The answer is *D*. Guilford suggested that 150 different abilities are part of intelligence. The debate over intelligence as a general ability or as multiple specific abilities continues at the present time.
19. The answers is *C*. Sternberg's theory distinguishes between learning new information (knowledge-acquisition components), solving specific problems (performance components), and a general understanding of how to solve problems (metacomponents).
20. The answer is *D*. Gardner suggests there are seven independent types of intelligence; in addition to those listed in the question, the others are logical-mathematical, musical, interpersonal, and intrapersonal.
21. The answer is *C*. According to Sternberg, the most important differences between more intelligent and less intelligent people involve the use of metacomponents.
22. The answer is *D*. Using the IQ formula (IQ = MA/CA × 100), $10/8 \times 100 = 1.25 \times 100 = 125$.

23. The answer is *A*. Reliability implies that the scores would be the same if the test was repeated. A test that is standardized is administered the same way to all who take the test. An objective test has agreed-upon right and wrong answers.
24. The answer is *A*. The inability of intelligence tests to measure "everyday intelligence" has led to the development of a variety of tests measuring abilities in such areas as sales, business management, decision-making, and medical diagnosis.
25. The answer is *C*. While the environment is also widely recognized as an important factor in intelligence, the question asked about the research conducted specifically with twins and adopted children.
26. The answer is *D*. According to some researchers, more pruning of the neural circuits may lead to greater neural efficiency and higher intelligence.
27. The answer is *C*. One implication of this study is that environmental factors may be responsible for the measured racial differences in IQ.
28. The answer is *D*. Terman's study has exploded some myths about intellectually gifted people. According to the research, they were considered more honest and trustworthy, enjoyed higher incomes, and had lower rates of alcoholism and criminal convictions when compared with their peers of average IQ.
29. The answer is *A*. While some of the other strategies may occasionally be effective, overcoming functional fixedness means breaking out of the set.
30. The answer is *B*. Human problem solvers typically have difficulty being logical when evaluating probabilities.

Chapter **8** **Development Psychology**

Learning Objectives

1. Describe the nature-nurture issue; discuss the role of maturation in development.
2. Discuss the phenomenon of imprinting; explain the importance of the critical period.
3. Describe the Harlows' research with monkeys on early social deprivation.
4. Explain the notion of individual variation in development.
5. Describe Kohlberg's three levels of moral reasoning: premoral, conventional, and principled.
6. Describe Gilligan's three levels of moral reasoning: individual survival, self-sacrifice, and equality.
7. List and describe Erikson's stages of personality and summarize the major features of his theory.
8. Describe development during the neonatal period.
9. Explain cognitive development during the sensorimotor period; include the role of object permanence and early language acquisition.
10. Describe the results of research using the visual cliff; explain the concepts of attachment and separation anxiety.
11. Discuss the kinds of thinking errors that characterize the preoperational stage.
12. Describe changes in play patterns that occur in early childhood.
13. Describe the thinking abilities of children in the concrete operational stage; include the concepts of reversibility, conservation, and decentering.
14. Describe physical development during puberty, including primary and secondary sex characteristics, menarche, and the adolescent growth spurt.
15. Discuss the characteristics of formal operational thinking.
16. Explain adolescent egocentrism and distinguish among pseudostupidity, the imaginary audience, and the personal fable.
17. Contrast the popular view and the results of research regarding adolescent emotions.
18. Describe physical and cognitive development in adulthood.
19. Discuss emotional and social development in adulthood.
20. Contrast Erikson's and Levinson's views of adult personality development.
21. Discuss the biological and psychological changes that are involved in aging; describe the factors that are associated with "happy aging."
22. Discuss the controversies raised by stage theories.
23. Describe the stages of dying identified by Elisabeth Kübler-Ross.
24. (From the "Application" section) Identify the following: secure and insecure attachment, Baumrind's discipline styles, and the "two-way street" of parenting.
25. (From the "Application" section) Describe the effects of day care and divorce on parenting.

Chapter Overview

Psychologists differ on the issue of how much our development is biologically determined (nature) or is shaped by the learning environment (nurture). Today, most psychologists believe that nature and nurture combine to influence our actions, thoughts, and feelings.

Research on imprinting in some animals shows that experiences during critical periods of early development can have long-lasting effects on behavior. Research conducted by the Harlows on the effects of early deprivation in monkeys showed the lasting effects of early social deprivation. Opinions are divided regarding the effects of abnormal early experiences in humans.

Stage theorists believe that all children pass through the same qualitatively different stages in the same order. For example, Piaget identified four stages of cognitive development from infancy to adulthood. According to Piaget, the process of assimilation adds new information to existing concepts, or schemas, that results in quantitative changes in a child's cognitions. The process of changing schemas in qualitative ways to incorporate new experiences is called accommodation. Piaget's four stages include (1) the sensorimotor stage (birth to 2 years), during which an infant conceptualizes the world in terms of schemas that incorporate sensory information and motor activities; (2) the preoperational stage (2 to 7 years), during which children can think in mental images, but exhibit egocentric thinking; (3) the concrete operational stage (7 to 11 years), during which children increase their ability to reason logically; and (4) the formal operational stage (11 years on), during which an individual uses full adult logic and can understand abstract concepts.

Kohlberg's theory of moral development is concerned with the logical process of arriving at answers to moral dilemmas. Kohlberg's theory proposes the following levels of moral development: (1) the premoral level, when the child has no sense of morality as adults understand the term; (2) the conventional level, when a child's moral view is based on what others will think of him or her; and (3) the principled level, when individuals judge right and wrong according to ethical principles rather than by the consequences of the actions.

Gilligan suggests that females progress through three stages of moral development: (1) morality as individual survival, (2) morality as self-sacrifice, and (3) morality as equality.

Erikson's theory of personality development suggests that individuals experience eight stages or crises, the outcomes of which will partly determine the future course of personality development. The development of the child proceeds through the following periods: (1) the neonatal period, the first two weeks of life marking the transition from the womb to independent life; (2) infancy, a time of rapid change in physical, perceptual, cognitive, linguistic, social, and emotional development; (3) early childhood, a period of great improvements in the coordination of small and large muscle groups; and (4) middle childhood, during which physical growth is slowed, but important cognitive changes occur, such as the ability to conserve and decenter.

Adolescence is the development period from the onset of puberty until the beginning of adulthood. The production of sex hormones in puberty triggers biological changes known as the primary sex characteristics. Menarche, the fist menstrual period, occurs in American females at about 12 years and 6 months, while males produce sperm about two years later. Within each sex, there is wide variation in the age at which puberty begins. Secondary sex characteristics appear in both sexes during puberty. The adolescent growth spurt lasts for slightly more than a year in early adolescence. In late adolescence weight gain is common due to a decline in the basal metabolism rate. For both sexes different parts of the body grow at different rates, weight and physique change in irregular ways, and many adolescents experience skin problems. According to Piaget, the formal operational stage, which is characterized by the ability to use abstract concepts, occurs in some individuals by about age 11. Adolescence can be a stormy, emotional period for some, but most adolescents experience emotional difficulties only some of the time. Peers replace the family as the most important influence on the adolescent; however, most adolescents remain relatively close to their parents in terms of values and attitudes.

Adulthood is not a single phase of life. Challenges involving love, work, and play continue throughout adulthood. Psychologists disagree about whether the changes in adulthood are the result of programmed stages of biological development or are reactions to significant events, such as marriage and the birth of children.

Intelligence appears stable throughout adulthood in healthy adults. Some relatively positive personality changes that occur for many people during adulthood include becoming more insightful, dependable, and candid. Also, whereas women become less traditional shortly after marriage, men gradually become less traditional the longer they are married.

Erikson's developmental theory refers to early adulthood as the stage of intimacy vs. isolation. It is a time during which many individuals enter committed loving relationships. Erikson calls middle adulthood the stage of generativity vs. stagnation, the goal of which is to find meaning in work and family lives.

The period from the late 60s and beyond is referred to by Erikson as the stage of integrity vs. despair. According to Erikson, older adults who see meaning in their lives continue to live a satisfying existence.

Psychological variables associated with happy aging are whether one stays engaged in life's activities and whether one believes the myths about old age. Older adults tend to be less frightened by death than younger adults. Studies by Elisabeth Kübler-Ross suggest that people who learn of their impending death tend to pass through five distinct stages: denial, anger, bargaining, depression, and acceptance.

Human infants who are securely attached enjoy physical contact with parents and move out quickly to explore; insecurely attached infants, however, cling excessively and are extremely upset by separation from parents. According to Baumrind, the three types of parental discipline styles are authoritarian, permissive, and authoritative. Children and parents are affected by each other's behavior. Research suggests that day-care children do not differ from those raised by others in their own homes in terms of physical health, emotional or intellectual development, or attachment.

Key Terms Exercise

For each of the following exercises, match the key terms on the left with the correct definitions on the right. Page references to the text follow the terms so that you may refer to the text for any items you answer incorrectly or do not understand completely. You may check your responses immediately by referring to the answers that follow each exercise.

Nature, Nurture, and Maturation

_____ 1. development (p. 329)
_____ 2. maturation (p. 330)
_____ 3. imprinting (p. 331)
_____ 4. critical period (p. 331)
_____ 5. early experiences (p. 332)
_____ 6. stage (p. 336)

a. a time period in development that is qualitatively different from the periods that come before and after
b. the more-or-less predictable changes in behavior associated with increasing age
c. a biologically determined period during which certain forms of learning can take place most easily
d. a form of early learning that takes place in some animals
e. systematic physical growth of the body
f. experience occurring early in development, believed by some to have lasting effects

ANSWERS

1. b	4. c
2. e	5. f
3. d	6. a

Development in Infancy and Childhood (I)

_____ 1. neonatal period (p. 343)
_____ 2. sensorimotor stage (p. 344)
_____ 3. object permanence (p. 345)
_____ 4. attachment (p. 345)
_____ 5. separation anxiety (p. 346)

a. the first 2 weeks of life following birth
b. the psychological bond between infants and caregivers
c. the period of cognitive development from birth to 2 years
d. the distress expressed by infants when they are separated from their caregivers
e. the understanding that objects continue to exist even after they are removed from view

ANSWERS
1. a 4. b
2. c 5. d
3. e

Development in Infancy and Childhood (II)

_____ 1. preoperational stage (p. 346)
_____ 2. egocentrism (p. 346)
_____ 3. animism (p. 346)
_____ 4. transductive reasoning (p. 347)
_____ 5. concrete operational stage (p. 349)
_____ 6. conservation (p. 349)

a. the period of cognitive development from ages 2 to 7
b. the belief that inanimate objects are alive
c. the period of cognitive development from ages 7 to 11
d. the concept that quantity does not change just because superficial features have changed
e. self-centered thinking, characteristic of preoperational children
f. errors in inferring cause and effect relationships

ANSWERS
1. a 4. f
2. e 5. c
3. b 6. d

Adolescence

_____ 1. adolescence (p. 351)
_____ 2. puberty (p. 351)
_____ 3. formal operational stage (p. 352)
_____ 4. adolescent egocentrism (p. 353)

a. characterized by the ability to use abstract concepts
b. imaginary audience, the personal fable, hypocrisy, and pseudostupidity
c. the point at which the individual is physically capable of sexual reproduction
d. the period from the onset of puberty until the beginning of adulthood

ANSWERS
1. d 3. a
2. c 4. b

Who Am I?

Match psychologists on the left with their contributions to the field of psychology on the right. Page references to the text follow the names of the psychologists so that you may refer to the text for further review of these psychologists and their contributions. You may check your responses immediately by referring to the answers that follow each exercise.

_____ 1. Konrad Lorenz (p. 331)
_____ 2. Harry and Margaret Harlow (p. 332)
_____ 3. Jean Piaget (p. 337)
_____ 4. Lawrence Kohlberg (p. 337)
_____ 5. Carol Gilligan (p. 337)
_____ 6. Erik Erikson (p. 340)
_____ 7. Elisabeth Kübler-Ross (p. 365)

a. While studying geese, I observed imprinting.
b. My stage theory focuses on the development of moral reasoning, especially in boys.
c. My theory focuses on personality development and assumes that people pass through eight important stages.
d. Our studies of early social deprivation led to some surprising results.
e. I developed a theory explaining the stages that occur leading to the acceptance of death.
f. I studied children extensively and proposed an important theory of cognitive development.
g. My research showed that the moral development of girls is different from that of boys.

ANSWERS

1. a	5. g
2. d	6. c
3. f	7. e
4. b	

Guided Review

Preview: Development

The more-or-less predictable changes in behavior throughout our

lives are described as the process of _____.   development (329)

Nature, Nurture, and Maturation: Molding or Unfolding?

Most contemporary psychologists believe that behavior and

developmental changes are controlled both by biological factors,

called _____, and the psychological environment, called   nature (p. 330)

_____.   nurture (p. 330)

   The most important biological factor in development is the

systematic physical growth of the body, including the nervous

system; this process is called _____. Research done with   maturation (p. 330) infants on toilet training supports the importance of

_____.   maturation (p. 330)

Early Experience and Critical Periods

Konrad Lorenz has observed that goslings will follow any moving

object that they are exposed to after hatching. He called this

behavior _____. Imprinting can occur only during a   imprinting (p. 331)

brief period of a bird's life, called the _____   critical

_____.   period (p. 331)

     Harry and Margaret Harlow's research with monkeys focused

on the effects of early _____ deprivation. Infant   social (p. 332)

monkeys were raised in complete _____ for the first few   isolation (p. 332)

months of life and never lived with a _____. When the   mother (p. 332)

monkeys reached adulthood and were placed in cages with normal

monkeys, the Harlows noticed that their behavior was distinctly

_____. When the mother-deprived monkeys became   abnormal (p. 332)

mothers themselves, they _____ their own infants.   rejected (p. 333)

Opinions among psychologists are divided regarding the effects of

abnormal early experiences among _____.   humans (p. 333)

     Normal development is highly variable in two respects: (1) the

differences _____ children in their development and   between (p. 335)

(2) the differences _____ individual children in the rates within (p. 335)

at which they move from one developmental period to the next.

Stage Theories of Development

Psychologists who believe that behavior goes through a series of

abrupt changes are called _____ theorists. They believe   stage (p. 336)

that the changes occurring from one stage to the next are

_____ different, while changes that occur within each   qualitatively (p. 336)

stage are _____ different. Stages are believed to be   quantitatively (p. 336)

_____ programmed, and all children pass through the   biologically (p. 336)

same stages in the same order. A well-known stage theory is

Piaget's theory of _____ development.   cognitive (p. 337)

     The stage theories of Kohlberg and Gilligan focus on the

development of _____ reasoning. According to   moral (p. 337)

Kohlberg, we pass through three major levels in the development of moral reasoning. The first level, in which children make moral judgment to obtain rewards and avoid punishment, is called the

_____ level. At the second level, moral decisions are   premoral (p. 338)
based on what others, particularly parents, will think of them; this
level is referred to as the _____ level. At the third level,   conventional (p. 338)
called the _____ level, decisions are based on ethical   principled (p. 338)
principles rather than the consequences. According to Kohlberg,

_____ people ever reach a stage in which they reason   few (p. 338)
mostly in principled ways. Gilligan has claimed that Kohlberg's
theory does not always accurately describe the moral development
in _____. According to Gilligan, female moral   girls (p. 338)
development centers on the needs of people rather than on

_____. Gilligan's theory suggests that moral   abstractions (p. 339)
development progresses from morality as individual

_____, to morality as ____-_____, and   survival (p. 339)/self-sacrifice (p. 339)
finally to morality as _____.   equality (p. 339)

Erik Erikson's theory, which focuses on developing
relationships with people, describes major turning points or

_____ that all people experience. According to Erikson,   crises (p. 340)
the outcome of these crises will help determine future

_____ development.   personality (p. 340)

Development in Infancy and Childhood

The first two weeks of life are termed the _____ period.   neonatal (p. 343)
When stimulated on the cheek, the neonate engages in the

_____ reflex. Apparently, neonates cannot see beyond   rooting (p. 343)
about _____ inches from their eyes. Neonates can show memory   12 (p. 343)
for a _____ form; the emotions of the neonate are   visual (p. 344)

_____.   diffuse (p. 344)

At 2 weeks of age, the baby is called an _____.   infant (p. 344)
Infancy is characterized by rapid _____ development   physical (p. 344)
and rapid change in all _____. According to Piaget, the   senses (p. 344)
infant is in the _____ stage. According to Piaget, later   sensorimotor (p. 344)
in the sensorimotor stage, the child understands that objects exist

even when they are out of sight; this is called _____ _____ .

object permanence (p. 345)

By 9 months, infants begin to understand some nouns. By age 2, the infant can communicate in word combinations called _____ speech.

telegraphic (p. 345)

At 2 months of age, the infant engages in true social behavior—_____ in response to a human face. Fear of strangers, of separation from parents, and of heights begins at _____ to _____ months of age. The 2-year old displays a strong bond toward his or her caregiver, referred to as an _____ . When infants are separated from their caregivers, they experience distress referred to as _____ _____ .

smiling (p. 345)

6 (p. 345)/9 (p. 345)

attachment (p. 345)

separation
anxiety (p. 346)

In early childhood, from ages 2 to 7, the child's physical growth is less explosive. According to Piaget, the child has entered the _____ stage. At the age of 2, most children can think in _____ images. The preoperational child's thought is self-centered, or _____ , and the young child believes that inanimate objects are alive, a trait called _____ . The preoperational child also makes errors in understanding cause-and-effect relationships, called _____ reasoning. The preoperational stage is also characterized by dramatic growth in _____ .

preoperational (p. 346)

mental (p. 346)

egocentric (p. 346)

animism (p. 346)

transductive (p. 347)

language (p. 347)

The sequence of development in a child's play activities is: (1) playing alone, called _____ play; (2) playing near other children, called _____ play; and (3) playing with others, or _____ play. By the age of 2, most boys and girls have begun to act in _____ - _____ ways.

solitary (p. 348)

parallel (p. 348)

cooperative (p. 348)

sex-typed (p. 348)

The elementary school years occur while the child is in Piaget's _____ _____ stage. Children in this stage are able to use most adult concepts, with the exception of _____ concepts. They can order objects according to size and weight, called _____ , and they understand that logical propositions can be reversed, called _____ . Children in this stage also understand that the quantity of objects

concrete operational (p. 349)

abstract (p. 349)

seriation (p. 349)

reversibility (p. 349)

does not change if the shape or other superficial features have changed; this concept is called _____.   conservation (p. 349)

Piaget has stated that conservation is possible when a child can think of more than one thing at a time, referred to as the ability to

_____. Although ties to parents remain important, after   decenter (p. 349)

age 7 friendships with _____ become more important to   peers (p. 349)

children. Friendship groups, called _____, also emerge   cliques (p. 350)

during this stage.

Adolescence begins with the onset of _____. The   puberty (p. 351)

hormones produced at puberty trigger a series of changes that lead

to _____ and menstruation in females and to the   ovulation (p. 351)

production of _____ _____ in males; these   sperm cells (p. 351)

are called the _____ ____ _____. The first   primary sex characteristics (p. 351)

menstrual period, called _____, begins at about 12 years   menarche (p. 352)

and 6 months in females. Sperm cell production in males begins

about ____ years later. For males and females, the more obvious   two (p. 352)

physical changes occurring during puberty, such as lowering of the

voice in males and development of the breasts in females, are

called _____ ____ _____. Around the onset   secondary sex characteristics (p. 352)

of puberty, adolescents experience a rapid increase in height and

weight that is referred to as the _____ _____   adolescent growth

_____.   spurt (p. 352)

At about age 11, some adolescents demonstrate an ability to

use abstract concepts, which Piaget calls the _____   formal

_____ stage. Adolescents often possess a self-centered   operational (p. 352)

type of thinking which Elkind has termed _____   adolescent

_____. The primary characteristic of this type of   egocentrism (p. 353)

thinking is that the adolescent feels that he or she is the focus of

everyone's attention; this is termed the _____   imaginary (p. 353)

_____. Adolescents may also feel that their problems   audience (p. 353)

are unique, which Elkind calls the _____   personal

_____. Another characteristic of adolescent egocentrism   fable (p. 354)

involves criticizing others for actions and traits that they find

acceptable in themselves, called _____. A final   hypocrisy (p. 354) characteristic, involving oversimplified logic, is called

_____.

pseudostupidity (p. 354)

Although about _____ to _____ percent of adolescents experience a difficult, tumultuous time, adolescents are no more likely than other age groups to experience severe emotional turmoil. Typically, however, the topics over which adolescents and parents have conflict are upsetting to both sides, and about

15 (p. 355)/20 (p. 355)

_____ of all teenagers break the law at least once. Also, adolescence marks a period of dramatic increase in

half (p. 356)

_____, anorexia nervosa, anxiety, and _____.

schizophrenia (p. 356)/suicide (p. 356)

Adulthood

Throughout adulthood, from the twenties to the seventies, small but steady increases occur in the knowledge of _____

facts (p. 357)

and word _____. Research suggests that older adults do

meanings (p. 357)

not remember less, but need cues to assist their _____

retrieval (p. 358)

of information. Some facets of personality change more across the adult life span than others. For example, enjoyment of others and enjoyment of excitement are fairly stable throughout adulthood, while the desire for _____ and _____ are

power (p. 358)/achievement (p. 358)

more subject to change.

Some psychologists believe that adulthood consists of a series of _____ of development. Stage theories of adulthood

stages (p. 358)

have been proposed by _____ and Levinson. These

Erikson (p. 358)

stages differ from the stages of child development in that (1) not every adult is believed to go through every stage, (2) the order of the stages can _____ for some individuals, and (3) the

vary (p. 358)

timing of the stages is not controlled by _____

biological (p. 358)

maturation.

Erikson refers to early adulthood as the stage of

_____ vs. _____. According to Levinson,

intimacy (p. 359)/isolation (p. 359)

early adulthood consists of three briefer stages: (1) creating an adult manner of working and living independently characterize the

_____ to early adulthood; (2) reevaluating one's start

entry (p. 359)

into adult life occurs in the _____ _____ _____; and

age 30 transition (p. 359)

(3) working hard toward one's goals characterizes the

_____ _____ _____ _____.

    Erikson believes that the challenges of middle adulthood are
to find meaning in our lives and to continue to be

_____. He calls this stage _____ _____

_____. Levinson describes four brief stages of middle
adulthood. The first of these stages reaches a peak in the early
forties and is sometimes a period of anguish; it is called the

_____ _____. A period of calm and stability
follows, called _____ _____

_____. Another period of reassessment occurs for most
individuals in the _____ _____ _____, followed by
another stable period from about age 55 to 65, called the

_____ _____ _____ _____.

    The _____, which begins around age 45, is marked
by a loss of the capacity to reproduce in women and by a decline
in the reproductive capacity of men. In women, the end of
menstruation is called _____. About 50 percent of
women experience some discomfort during menopause and 10
percent experience _____ distress. Research suggests
that the difficulties of menopause experienced by some women
may be influenced by their _____. According to
Erikson, individuals in their late 60s and beyond are in the stage
called _____ vs. _____.

    Aging is partly a biological process, but it involves many

_____ aspects as well. Two keys to happy aging are
(1) staying _____ in life's activities and (2) ignoring
_____ about old age.

    Not all psychologists believe that adulthood can be thought of
as a series of stages. Some theorists cite studies suggesting that
predictable changes do not take place at the times indicated by the
_____ theorists.

culmination of early adulthood (p. 360)

productive (p. 360)/generativity vs.
stagnation (p. 360)

midlife transition (p. 361)
entering middle
adulthood (p. 361)
age 50 transition (p. 361)

culmination of middle adulthood (p. 361)
climacteric (p. 361)

menopause (p. 361)

severe (p. 361)

expectations (p. 362)

integrity (p. 362)/despair (p. 362)

psychological (p. 363)
engaged (p. 363)
myths (p. 364)

stage (p. 364)

Death and Dying: The Final "Stage"

Elisabeth Kübler-Ross has developed a theory stating that people who learn of their impending death (and sometimes of the impending death of loved ones) pass through five distinct stages. In the first stage, the individual strongly resists the idea of death; this is called _____. In stage two, the reaction is _____. In stage three, the individual tries to prolong his or her life by _____. In stage four, the terminally ill person experiences a loss of hope called _____. Finally, the depression is lifted and there is an _____ of death.

denial (p. 365)

anger (p. 365)

bargaining (p. 365)

depression (p. 365)

acceptance (p. 365)

Application of Psychology: Parenting

At 6 to 9 months, infants typically become closely attached to their caretakers and develop _____ _____. By 18 to 24 months, toddlers prefer to be near their caregiver, but, if _____ _____, the toddler is able to explore the world and play. Children who are _____ attached cling excessively to the caretaker and become upset when separated. Secure attachment is a result both of a child's inborn _____ and parental _____.

stranger anxiety (p. 367)

securely attached (p. 367)

insecurely (p. 367)

temperament (p. 367)/behaviors (p. 367)

According to Baumrind, parental discipline styles are of three types: (1) the _____ parent provides strict rules with little discussion of the reasons for the rules; (2) the _____ parent gives the child few rules and rarely punishes misbehavior; and (3) the _____ parent is an authority figure to the child, but explains and discusses rules. According to Baumrind, middle class white children of _____ parents are happier and better behaved. However, that style may not be best in all American cultures.

authoritarian (p. 368)

permissive (p. 368)

authoritative (p. 368)

authoritative (p. 368)

According to Richard Bell and others, children affect their _____ behavior as much as parents affect their _____ behavior.

parents' (p. 368)

children's (p. 368)

Research suggests that there are generally no differences between children in _____ _____ and children being raised by parents in their own home in terms of

day care (p. 370)

their physical health, emotional or intellectual development, or attachment. Furthermore, children whose parents divorce may experience _____ _____, but usually the disruptions are for a relatively brief period of time.

emotional turmoil (p. 370)

CONCEPT CHECK

Fill in the missing components of the following concept box. The answers are shown below the box.

Developmental Theorists

I. Theorist	II. Developmental Areas	III. Proposed Stages
a. Piaget	a. Cognitive	a. Sensorimotor, preoperational, concrete operational, and formal operational.
b. Kohlberg	b.	b. Premoral, conventional, and principled reasoning.
c. Gilligan	c. Moral	c.
d.	d. Social	d. Eight stages or crises the outcome of which will determine future personality development.
e. Kübler-Ross	e.	e. Denial, anger, bargaining, depression, and acceptance.

Answers

IIb. Moral
IIIc. Morality as individual survival, morality as self-sacrifice, and morality as equality.
Id. Erik Erikson
IIe. Death and dying

Multiple-Choice Questions

1. The debate among psychologists regarding the relative contributions of environment and heredity to the developmental process is called
   a. the critical period
   b. the nature-nurture controversy
   c. the stage controversy
   d. behaviorism
   (p. 330) LO 1

2. Research on toilet training conducted with identical twins illustrates the importance of which developmental factor?
   a. maturation
   b. imprinting
   c. nurture
   d. genetics
   (p. 330) LO 1

3. Lorenz observed that after hatching, baby goslings will follow any moving object to which they are exposed. He called this behavior
   a. maturation
   b. exprinting
   c. imprinting
   d. follow-the-leader
   (p. 331) LO 2

4. Research conducted by the Harlows underscores the profound importance of
   a. imprinting
   b. maturation
   c. early experience
   d. all of the above
   (p. 332) LO 3

5. With regard to variation in development, the text asserts that
   a. different children develop at different rates
   b. children vary in their *own* rate of development from one period to the next
   c. little variation exists between children beyond the age of seven
   d. a and b above
   (p. 335) LO 4

6. According to Kohlberg, at what level of moral development would a child most likely be concerned about pleasing his parents and teachers?
   a. the preconventional level
   b. the premoral level
   c. the conventional level,
   d. the principled level
   (p. 338) LO 5

7. According to Gilligan, a woman in the most advanced stage of moral development experiences morality as
   a. individual survival
   b. self-sacrifice
   c. inequality
   d. equality
   (p. 339) LO 6

8. The stage during which Erikson believes a child learns to meet the demands imposed by society is
   a. basic trust vs. mistrust
   b. autonomy vs. shame and doubt
   c. industry vs. inferiority
   d. identity vs. role confusion
   (p. 340) LO 7

9. The neonatal period refers to the first
   a. 2 hours of life
   b. 2 days of life
   c. 2 weeks of life
   d. 2 months of life
   (p. 343) LO 8

10. Which of the following is *not* developed during the infancy period?
    a. object permanence
    b. telegraphic speech
    c. separation anxiety
    d. transductive reasoning
    (p. 345) LO 9

11. The visual cliff has been used with infants to study
    a. depth perception
    b. separation anxiety
    c. fear of heights
    d. a and c above
       (p. 345) LO 10

12. Which of the following is characteristic of the preoperational child?
    a. The child is egocentric.
    b. The child uses transductive reasoning.
    c. The child is capable of abstract thought.
    d. a and b above
       (p. 346) LO 11

13. Which of the following describes the correct developmental sequence of play?
    a. parallel play, solitary play, cooperative play
    b. solitary play, cooperative play, parallel play
    c. solitary play, parallel play, cooperative play
    d. cooperative play, solitary play, parallel play
       (p. 348) LO 12

14. The recognition that the volume of water remains the same whether it is in a short, wide beaker, or a long, narrow beaker is called
    a. reversibility
    b. conservation
    c. decentering
    d. formal operations
       (p. 349) LO 13

15. Which of the following is *not* a primary sex characteristic?
    a. ovulation in females
    b. lowering of the voice in males
    c. menstruation in females
    d. production of sperm in males
       (p. 351) LO 14

16. The concept of liberty and justice can be understood by an adolescent who
    a. has achieved the concrete operational stage
    b. has achieved the formal operational stage
    c. does not exhibit pseudostupidity
    d. does not exhibit hypocrisy
       (p. 352) LO 15

17. Debbie, an adolescent, feels that she is the only person in the world who has ever had a crush on the boy who sits next to her, argued with her parents, and had complexion problems. Which component of adolescent egocentrism is she experiencing?
    a. imaginary audience
    b. personal fable
    c. hypocrisy
    d. pseudostupidity
       (p. 353) LO 16

18. According to Erikson, the challenge of adolescence is to establish
    a. enduring friendships
    b. career goals
    c. a deeper relationship with parents
    d. a sense of identity
       (p. 358) LO 17

19. Which of the following cognitive abilities improves throughout adulthood?
    a. reasoning about everyday problems
    b. knowledge of facts and word meanings
    c. abstract problem solving and divergent thinking
    d. general recall
       (p. 358) LO 18

20. Adult personalities are likely to change in each of the following areas *except*
    a. enjoyment of being with other people
    b. becoming more dependable
    c. becoming more candid
    d. becoming more accepting of life's hardships
       (p. 358) LO 19

21. Jerry, age 67, and Al, age 65, are acquaintances. Jerry feels his life is meaningful and enjoys his existence, but he has noticed that Al has lately withdrawn and sees his life as a "bunch of unmet goals." These individuals illustrate which of Erikson's stages?
    a. basic trust vs. mistrust
    b. intimacy vs. isolation
    c. generativity vs. stagnation
    d. integrity vs. despair
       (p. 359) LO 20

22. Hank, age 47, has recently changed careers and has joined a health club. His behavior falls into which of Levinson's stages?
    a. entering middle adulthood
    b. midlife transition
    c. age 50 transition
    d. settling down
       (p. 361) LO 20

23. Which of the following appears to affect the aging process?
    a. diet
    b. stress
    c. heredity
    d. all of the above
       (p. 361) LO 21

24. One common myth about menopause is that
    a. the body will rapidly age after menopause
    b. menopause is associated with an increase in illness
    c. sexual interest decreases after menopause
    d. all of the above
       (p. 361) LO 21

25. Which of the following is *not* a belief of stage theorists?
    a. Changes between stages are qualitatively different.
    b. Changes during each stage are quantitatively different.
    c. All children pass through the same stages in the same order.
    d. Some children seem to skip some stages.
       (p. 336) LO 22

26. The final stage of Elisabeth Kübler-Ross's theory is labeled
    a. denial
    b. bargaining
    c. acceptance
    d. none of the above
       (p. 365) LO 23

27. According to Baumrind, the best behaved and happiest children have parents who use what style of parenting?
    a. authoritarian
    b. permissive
    c. authoritative
    d. disciplinarian
       (p. 368) LO 24

28. The "two-way street" concept in childrearing suggests that
    a. both mothers *and* fathers need to accept responsibility for childrearing
    b. parents need to be consistent in their childrearing approaches with *all* their children
    c. children act as important influences on their siblings
    d. children's behavior affects their parents' behavior just as parents' behavior affects their children's behavior.
       (p. 368) LO 24

29. According to research comparing children in day-care centers versus children raised by mothers in their own homes, the biggest differences were found in the children's
    a. physical health
    b. intellectual development
    c. attachment
    d. none of the above
       (p. 368) LO 25

30. The children who are affected the longest by the divorce of their parents
    a. have parents who quietly and subtly argued with each other before and after the divorce
    b. have parents who were openly conflictual before and after the divorce
    c. have parents with serious psychological difficulties
    d. b and c above
       (p. 370) LO 25

1. The answer is *B*. "Nature" refers to biological factors and "nurture" refers to environmental factors.
2. The answer is *A*. Maturational factors refer to the systematic physical growth of the body, including the nervous system. The experience of the twins suggests that, with potty training, a child isn't ready until he's ready.
3. The answer is *C*. According to Lorenz, imprinting is a special form of learning because it is highly constrained by biological factors. Goslings will imprint on the first noisy, moving object they see, and this generally occurs only during a brief "window" of time, called the critical period.
4. The answer is *C*. The Harlows conducted research with monkeys who were raised in isolation for the first few months of their lives. Later in the monkey's lives, they exhibited gross abnormalities in their behavior.
5. The answer is *D*. Although many psychologists are engaged in trying to describe and understand the normal developmental changes that take place in childhood, it is important to realize that development is highly variable.
6. The answer is *C*. According to Kohlberg, children at the conventional level are concerned with making moral decisions on the basis of what others, especially parents, will think of them. At the next level, called the principled level, actions come to be based on the ethical principles involved.
7. The answer is *D*. According to Gilligan, in this most advanced stage of morality, the woman views her own needs as equal to those of others.
8. The answer is *C*. According to Erikson, each stage presents a crisis or turning point, the outcome of which will determine future personality development. The challenge of the stage of industry vs. inferiority, which occurs between the ages of 5 and 11, is to meet the demands imposed by school and home; if these demands are not met, the child will come to feel inferior to others.
9. The answer is *C*. During this period of time, the infant engages in a variety of reflexes, displays well-developed sensory abilities, and exhibits the following emotional states: surprise, happiness, discomfort, distress, and interest (and, or course, sleep!).
10. The answer is *D*. Transductive reasoning refers to errors in cause-and-effect reasoning that are commonly made by preoperational children. Before proceeding, be sure you can describe object permanence, telegraphic speech, and separation anxiety.
11. The answer is *D*. One interesting result of the visual cliff research has been that infants apparently perceive the visual cliff several months before they show any fear of it. The development of the fear response coincides with the development of the ability to crawl.
12. The answer is *D*. According to Piaget, another characteristic of the preoperational stage is animism (the belief that inanimate objects are alive). The child is not ready for abstract thought, according to Piaget, until the formal operational stage.
13. The answer is *C*. This sequence seems to parallel cognitive development. That is, children whose thinking is still highly egocentric might be expected to engage in solitary play. As egocentric thinking declines, cooperative play becomes possible.
14. The answer is *B*. Reversibility is the concrete operational concept that logical operations can be reversed. Decentering allows the concrete operational child to consider more than one feature of an object at a time. Formal operations is the last stage of Piaget's theory.
15. The answer is *B*. Primary sex characteristics indicate that the adolescent has the ability to reproduce; thus, ovulation and menstruation in females and the production of mature sperm cells in males are considered primary sex characteristics. The more obvious changes, such as development of the breasts and hips in females and the lowering of the voice in males, are considered secondary sex characteristics.
16. The answer is *B*. The formal operational stage is characterized by an ability to use abstract concepts, such as liberty and justice. Pseudostupidity and hypocrisy are characteristics of adolescent egocentrism, discussed in the next question.

17. The answer is *B*. The imaginary audience is characterized by the belief that others are watching the adolescent's every move; hence, any blunder will be noticed by everyone! Adolescent egocentrism is also characterized by excessive hypocrisy and by pseudostupidity, the use of oversimplified logic.

18. The answer is *D*. Until adolescents establish an adult identity, they often experience a great deal of anguish.

19. The answer is *B*. Reasoning about everyday problems does not decline before age 75. Slight declines occur in abstract problem solving, perceptual integration, and divergent thinking. The ability to recall words without using cues seems to decline, but when cues are added, no declines are seen.

20. The answer is *A*. Some traits, such as enjoyment of being with other people, enjoyment of excitement, and the general level of activity are stable throughout adulthood.

21. The answer is *D*. According to Erikson, the older adult who sees meaning in his or her life continues to live a satisfying existence, while the person who sees life as a series of unmet goals may come to experience despair.

22. The answer is *A*. According to Levinson, the entry into middle adulthood generally takes place from ages 45 to 50 and is occasionally marked by career and other dramatic changes such as divorce or geographical moves. For most, however, it is a period of calm and stability.

23. The answer is *D*. Aging is a psychological as well as a biological process. Two important variables associated with happy aging are (1) the extent to which one stays engaged in life's activities and (2) the extent to which one believes myths about aging.

24. The answer is *C*. Menopause refers to the cessation of menstruation and the capacity to reproduce. About 50 percent of women experience some discomfort, and about 10 percent of women experience severe distress. According to Masters and Johnson, many women actually experience an increase in sexual interest after menopause.

25. The answer is *D*. While stage theories have been popular in developmental psychology, some critics argue that the transition from one stage to the next is often gradual and/or variable.

26. The answer is *C*. The sequence described by Kübler-Ross is denial, anger, bargaining, depression, and acceptance.

27. The answer is *C*. At first glance the words *authoritarian* and *authoritative* might seem similar, but there are important differences. According to Baumrind, authoritarian parents dole out strict rules and little discussion. Authoritative parents, however, act as authority figures for their children, but encourage their children to voice their opinions as well. Permissive parents provide few rules and rarely punish misbehavior.

28. The answer is *D*. The concept is actually quite logical: The child's behavior influences the style of discipline used by the parents and vice versa.

29. The answer is *D*. Research has not found any differences between day care children and children raised by parents at home.

30. The answer is *D*. Although divorce is stressful to all parties involved, children are capable of adapting well to divorce if parents can cease arguing in front of the children and come to agreement regarding the sharing of parental responsibilities.

Learning Objectives

1. Distinguish between motivation and emotion.
2. Discuss the relationship between primary motives and homeostatic mechanisms.
3. Describe the biological and psychological regulation of hunger.
4. Discuss the biological and psychological regulation of thirst.
5. Describe the following three psychological motives: the need for novel stimulation, the need for affiliation, and the need for achievement.
6. Explain the optimal arousal theory and the Yerkes-Dodson Law.
7. Compare research findings regarding the fear of failure and the fear of success.
8. Explain Richard Solomon's opponent-process theory of motivation.
9. Distinguish between intrinsic and extrinsic motivation.
10. Identify the components of Maslow's hierarchy of motives.
11. Distinguish among the James-Lange theory, the Cannon-Bard theory, and the cognitive theory of emotion.
12. Discuss the effectiveness of lie-detector tests.
13. Describe the role of learning and culture in emotions.
14. Distinguish among the following theories of aggression: Freud's instinct theory, the frustration-aggression theory, and the social learning theory.
15. Discuss the effects of culture on aggressive behavior.
16. (From the "Applications" section) Describe the current American obsession with being thin.

Chapter Overview

Motivation refers to an internal state that activates behavior and gives direction to our thoughts. Emotions are positive or negative feelings usually accompanied by behavior and physiological arousal that generally occur in response to stimulus situations.

Primary motives are motives for things that are necessary for survival, such as food, water, and warmth. Homeostatic mechanisms in the body help to regulate biological imbalances and stimulate actions to restore the proper balance.

Hunger is a primary motive that is biologically regulated by two systems that involve separate parts of the hypothalamus; one is referred to as the feeding system; the other is called the satiety system. Among humans, the cues that help regulate hunger on a daily basis are stomach contractions and blood sugar levels; blood fat appears to be involved in the long-term regulation of hunger. Psychological factors, such as learning, emotions, and incentives, are also involved in the regulation of food intake.

Thirst is also regulated by the hypothalamus. The cues that help regulate drinking include mouth dryness, loss of water by cells, and reductions in blood volume. Psychological factors such as learning and incentives also help to regulate thirst.

Psychological motives are motives that are related to the individual's happiness and well-being, but not to survival. Among the important psychological motives are (1) seeking novel stimulation; (2) seeking an optimal level of arousal (the Yerkes-Dodson law states that if arousal is too low, performance will be inadequate, but if arousal is too high, it may disrupt performance); (3) the motive for affiliation, the preference to be with others; and (4) achievement motivation (*n Ach*), the psychological need for success.

Richard Solomon has proposed the opponent-process theory to explain how we learn new motives. Motivation can also be characterized as either intrinsic, which refers to motives stimulated by the inherent nature of the activity, or extrinsic, those stimulated by external rewards. According to Maslow, motives are organized in a hierarchy, arranged from the most basic to the most personal and advanced.

Emotions are the experiences that give color, meaning, and intensity to our lives. Theories that attempt to explain emotions include the James-Lange theory, the Cannon-Bard theory, and cognitive theories. According to Schachter and Singer, the cognitive process involves interpreting stimuli from both the environment and the body. Most psychologists believe that many basic emotions are primarily inborn but that learning plays an important role in emotions.

Aggression is a complex phenomenon, and its origins are the subject of continuing controversy. Freud suggested that all people are born with potent aggressive instincts released through the process of catharsis, while other psychologists believe that aggression is a reaction to the blocking of important motives (the frustration-aggression hypothesis). A third view, held by social learning theorists, explains aggression as learned behavior.

Key Terms Exercise

For each of the following exercises, match the key term on the left with the correct definitions on the right. Page references to the text follow the terms so that you may refer back to the text for any items that you answer incorrectly or do not understand completely. You may check your responses immediately by referring to the answers that follow each exercise.

Primary Motives

_____ 1. motivation (p. 380)
_____ 2. emotion (p. 380)
_____ 3. primary motives (p. 381)
_____ 4. homeostatic mechanism (p. 381)
_____ 5. hypothalamus (p. 381)
_____ 6. incentive (p. 383)

a. motives for things that are necessary for survival
b. an internal mechanism that regulates bodily functions
c. an external cue that activates motivation
d. an internal state that activates behavior and gives it direction
e. positive and negative feelings that are accompanied by physiological arousal
f. the area of the forebrain involved with motives, emotions, and the autonomic nervous system

ANSWERS

1. d   4. b
2. e   5. f
3. a   6. c

Psychological Motives (I)

_____ 1. psychological motives (p. 386)
_____ 2. novel stimulation (p. 386)
_____ 3. optimal level of arousal (p. 388)
_____ 4. Yerkes-Dodson law (p. 388)
_____ 5. motive for affiliation (p. 389)

a. new or changed experience
b. effective performance is more likely if the level of arousal is suitable for the activity
c. individuals are motivated to achieve an optimal level of arousal by increasing or decreasing their stimulation
d. motives related to happiness and well-being, but not to survival
e. the general preference to be with other people

ANSWERS

1. d	4. b
2. a	5. e
3. c	

Psychological Motives (II)

_____ 1. achievement motivation (p. 390)
_____ 2. opponent-process theory of motivation (p. 393)
_____ 3. intrinsic motivation (p. 394)
_____ 4. extrinsic motivation (p. 394)
_____ 5. Maslow's hierarchy of motives (p. 394)
_____ 6. self-actualization (p. 395)

a. the inner drive of humans to use their potential to the fullest
b. motives stimulated by external rewards
c. The psychological need for success in competitive situations
d. a theory that states we learn new motives when feelings contrast and when they lose intensity
e. motives stimulated by the inherent nature of the activity
f. the view that human motives are organized from the most basic (biological) to the most advanced (self-actualization)

ANSWERS

1. c	4. b
2. d	5. f
3. e	6. a

Theories of Emotion and Aggression

_____ 1. James-Lange theory (p. 398)
_____ 2. Cannon-Bard theory (p. 399)
_____ 3. cognitive theory of emotion (p. 400)
_____ 4. Freud's instinct theory (p. 406)
_____ 5. frustration-aggression theory (p. 406)

a. states that emotional experience and physical arousal are simultaneous and mostly independent events
b. the view that humans have inborn aggressive instincts that must be released in some way
c. the theory that aggression is a natural reaction to the frustration of important motives
d. states that sensations from bodily reactions to stimuli produce the emotions we feel
e. views the cognitive interpretation of emotional stimuli as the key event in emotions

ANSWERS

1. d   4. b
2. a   5. c
3. e

Guided Review

Definitions of Motivation and Emotion

Motivation refers to an _____ state that activates and gives direction to our thoughts. The positive or negative feelings in response to stimulus situations are called _____.

internal (p. 380)

emotions (p. 380)

Emotions are accompanied by _____ arousal.

physiological (p. 380)

Motivation and emotion are closely linked in the following ways: (1) both motivation and emotion _____ behavior;

activate (p. 380)

(2) motives are often accompanied by emotions; and (3) emotions often have motivational properties of their own. Human motives for things that are necessary for survival are called

_____ motives. The essential life elements in the body are regulated by an internal mechanism called the

primary (p. 381)

_____ mechanism.

homeostatic (p. 381)

The biological control center for hunger is a network of body organs whose key structure appears to be the _____.

hypothalamus (p. 381)

Hunger is regulated by two systems: the one that initiates eating when food is needed is called the _____

feeding

_____; the second, which signals the body to stop eating, is called the _____ _____. Destruction

system (p. 381)

satiety system (p. 381)

of the part of the hypothalamus associated with the satiety system leads to a condition called _____. The hypothalamus uses two cues to regulate hunger on a daily basis: _____ _____ and _____ _____ levels. The islets of Langerhans secrete two hormones that help regulate hunger. A feeling of hunger is produced when _____ is secreted into the bloodstream; conversely, a person no longer feels hungry when _____ is injected into the bloodstream. Long-term maintenance of body weight is apparently regulated by the hypothalamus as it monitors _____ _____ levels.

hyperphagia (p. 382)

stomach

contractions (p. 382) /blood sugar (p. 383)

insulin (p. 383)

glucagon (p. 383)

blood fat (p. 383)

Psychological factors, such as learning and _____, also regulate food intake. People trying to limit their food intake may have trouble with external cues (such as the sight of a dessert) that activate motivation; these are referred to as _____.

emotions (p. 383)

incentives (p. 383)

The hypothalamus also contains two centers that control drinking, the _____ system and the _____ _____ system. The hypothalamus uses three main cues in regulating drinking: mouth _____, _____ _____ levels, and total _____ _____.

drink (p. 384)/stop

drinking (p. 384)

dryness (p. 384)/cell

fluid (p. 384)/blood

volume (p. 384)

Psychological Motives

Motives that are not directly related to biological survival are called _____ motives.

psychological (p. 386)

Most people are easily bored if there is little stimulation; we have an apparently inborn motive to seek _____ _____. Too much stimulation or too little stimulation makes us feel uncomfortable; individuals strive for an _____ _____ ____ _____. In the brain, arousal is linked to the activity of the _____ _____. To achieve an effective performance, the level of arousal must be suitable for the activity, according to the _____-_____ _____.

novel

stimulation (p. 386)

optimal level of arousal (p. 388)

reticular

formation (p. 388)

Yerkes-Dodson law (p. 388)

Another psychological motive is the preference to be with other people, called the motive for _____. Some psychologists believe that this motivation is an _____ need, while others believe it is a _____ motive. Researchers have found that _____ increases our need for affiliation.

affiliation (p. 389)

inborn (p. 389)

learned (p. 389)

anxiety (p. 389)

The psychological motive to succeed in competitive situations is called _____ _____, or ____ _____. Researchers believe that achievement motivation is probably _____.

achievement motivation (p. 390)

n Ach (p. 390)

learned (p. 391)

Many people low in *n Ach* fear failure, but Horner's research showed that many people fear _____. Richard Solomon's theory, which explains how people learn new motives, is called the _____-_____ _____ ____ _____. Two concepts that are important to Solomon's theory are: (1) every state of positive feeling is followed by a _____ negative feeling, and (2) any feeling that is experienced many times in succession loses some of its _____.

success (p. 391)

opponent-process theory of motivation (p. 393)

contrasting (p. 393)

intensity (p. 393)

When people are motivated by the inherent nature of the activity or its natural consequences, the situation is referred to as _____ motivation. Motivation which is external to an activity is called _____ motivation. Although low frequency behaviors can be increased with extrinsic motivation, adding incentives to an activity that is already intrinsically motivated may _____ from the intrinsic motivation.

intrinsic (p. 394)

extrinsic (p. 394)

detract (p. 394)

Abraham Maslow's theory states that motives are arranged in a _____. If lower needs are not met, then higher motives will generally not operate. According to Maslow, individuals are motivated to realize their full potential, a process he called ____-_____.

hierarchy (p. 394)

self-actualization (p. 394)

Emotions: Feelings, Physiology, and Behavior

Most definitions of emotion include the following four elements: (1) a _____ _____ that provokes the

stimulus situation (p. 396)

reaction; (2) a positively or negatively toned conscious experience—the _____; (3) a bodily state of _____ _____; and (4) related _____ that accompanies emotions. Psychologists are not in agreement about how many emotions exist or how the elements of emotion relate to each other.

emotion (p. 396)
physiological arousal (p. 396)
behavior (p. 396)

William James believed that emotional stimuli first produce _____ reactions; the sensations from these reactions then produce the emotions we feel. This theory today is called the _____-_____ theory of emotion.

bodily (p. 398)

James-Lange (p. 398)

Conscious emotional experience and physiological arousal are two simultaneous events according to the _____-_____ _____ _____.

Cannon-
Bard theory of emotion (p. 399)

A third theory of emotion emphasizes the _____ interpretation of events. Cognitive theorists hold that cognitive interpretation of emotions involves interpreting stimuli from both the _____ and the _____.

cognitive (p. 400)

environment (p. 400)/body (p. 400)

According to Schachter and Singer's model of emotion, the autonomic arousal that accompanies all emotions is similar; our _____ _____ of the arousal is important.

cognitive interpretation (p. 400)

A device used in a lie-detector test that measures sympathetic arousal in response to questions is called a _____. The procedure used in a lie-detector examination is called the _____ knowledge test. Among the problems with lie-detector tests are (1) that emotions other than guilt may be falsely interpreted as guilt and that (2) some hardened criminals feel little or no guilt about their crimes, so they do not appear _____ in the examination.

polygraph (p. 402)

guilty (p. 402)

guilty (p. 402)

_____ _____ influences the expression of emotions. Learning also has a great deal to do with the stimuli that produce emotional reactions.

Cultural learning (p. 404)

According to Nisbett, some groups in this country have higher rates of violence than others because they have passed along attitudes favorable to violence from generation to generation through _____ _____.

social learning (p. 407)

Aggression: Emotional and Motivational Aspects

Sigmund Freud believed that aggression is the result of potent
aggressive _____. Freud believed that aggressive energy   instincts (p. 406)
must be released in some way. This process is called

_____.   catharsis (p. 406)

The belief that aggression is a natural reaction to the
frustration (blocking) of important motives is called the

_____-_____ _____. By contrast,   frustration-aggression hypothesis (p. 406)
social learning theorists believe that people act aggressively in
reaction to frustration only if they have _____ to do so.   learned (p. 407)

Application of Psychology: Should You Lose Weight? If So, How?

Our society generally values thinness. _____ and past   Heredity (p. 409)
history of _____ and _____ determine, to a   eating (p. 409)/exercise (p. 409)
great extent, how thin we can be. Two dangerous eating disorders
particularly for women, are _____ _____ and   anorexia nervosa (p. 410)
_____. When dieters establish a pattern of gaining and   bulimia (p. 410)
then losing weight, this is referred to as ____-____ dieting. In the   yo-yo (p. 410)
Framingham health study, repeated yo-yo dieting was associated
with increased _____ _____. Among the   heart disease (p. 410)
suggestions from the text are: don't "diet"—eat _____,   differently (p. 410)
emphasize _____, and don't let yourself lapse.   exercise (p. 411)

CONCEPT CHECK

Fill in the missing components of the following concept box. The answers are shown below the box.

Models of Motivation and Emotion

I. Proposed by	II. Basic Elements of Theory
a. Solomon	a. In the opponent-process theory every state of positive feeling is followed by a negative feeling. Any feeling experienced many times in succession loses some of its intensity.
b. Maslow	b.
c.	c. Emotional stimuli first produce bodily reactions. These reactions then produce the emotions we feel.
d. Cannon-Bard	d.
e.	e. We interpret stimuli from the environment and we interpret our autonomic arousal.

Answers

IIb. Our motives are arranged in a hierarchy from the most basic to the most personal and advanced. When lower motives have been met, self-actualizing needs become important.

Ic. James-Lange

IId. Conscious emotional experience and physiological arousal occur simultaneously.

Ie. Schachter and Singer

Multiple-Choice Questions

1. An internal state or condition that activates and gives direction to our thoughts is called
   a. motivation
   b. emotion
   c. aggression
   d. all of the above
      (p. 380) LO 1

2. Homeostatic mechanisms are involved in
   a. drinking
   b. eating
   c. maintaining body temperature
   d. all of the above
      (p. 381) LO 2

3. Each of the following is a primary motive *except*
   a. hunger
   b. thirst
   c. avoidance of pain
   d. desire to be competent
   (p. 381) LO 2

4. Hyperphagic rats are the result of
   a. surgically destroyed satiety centers in the hypothalamus
   b. surgically destroyed feeding centers in the hypothalamus
   c. artificially raised blood sugar levels
   d. blood fat levels that have been lowered
   (p. 382) LO 3

5. Each of the following is a cue that helps the hypothalamus regulate eating *except*
   a. stomach contractions
   b. blood sugar levels
   c. red blood cell levels
   d. blood fat levels
   (p. 382) LO 3

6. According to the text, which of the following is a psychological factor in hunger?
   a. incentives
   b. learning
   c. anxiety
   d. all of the above
   (p. 383) LO 3

7. Each of the following is a cue in regulating drinking *except*
   a. mouth dryness
   b. cell fluid levels
   c. blood sugar levels
   d. total blood volume
   (p. 384) LO 4

8. What happens when cell fluid levels in the body decrease?
   a. sodium salts draw water out of cells
   b. the hypothalamus signals the pituitary gland to secrete ADH
   c. the hypothalamus signals the cerebral cortex to initiate a search for liquids
   d. all of the above
   (p. 384) LO 4

9. The general preference among humans to be with others is called the
   a. affiliation motive
   b. need for achievement
   c. need for self-actualization
   d. group motive
   (p. 389) LO 5

10. Which of the following might characterize individuals who are low in achievement motivation?
    a. a lack of interest in achieving status or material success
    b. anxiety in competitive situations and the fear of failure
    c. a sense of accomplishment and enjoyment of the fruits of one's labor
    d. a and b above
    (p. 391) LO 5

11. According to Schachter, when subjects are anxious, their need to affiliate with others
    a. increases
    b. decreases
    c. virtually disappears
    d. is not changed
    (p. 390) LO 5

12. An effective performance is more likely if the level of arousal is suitable for the activity, according to the
    a. optimal level of arousal
    b. performance-arousal model
    c. Yerkes-Dodson law
    d. James-Lange theory of motivation
    (p. 388) LO 6

13. Arousal is linked to what brain structures?
    a. the amygdala
    b. the reticular formation
    c. the sympathetic nervous system
    d. b and c above
    (p. 388) LO 6

14. According to Solomon's opponent-process theory of motivation
    a. every positive feeling is followed by a negative feeling
    b. every negative feeling is followed by a positive feeling
    c. any feeling that is experienced many times in succession loses some of is intensity
    d. all of the above
       (p. 393) LO 8

15. People who donate anonymously to charity are probably motivated by
    a. intrinsic motivation
    b. extrinsic motivation
    c. biological motivation
    d. affective habituation
       (p. 394) LO 9

16. If an individual is already intrinsically motivated to perform an activity, adding an extrinsic reward will probably
    a. sharply increase the intrinsic motivation
    b. increase both the intrinsic and extrinsic motivation
    c. decrease the intrinsic motivation
    d. none of the above
       (p. 394) LO 9

17. According to Maslow, the highest motive people can experience is
    a. biological
    b. intellectual
    c. self-esteem
    d. self-actualization
       (p. 395) LO 10

18. Which of the following is *not* an element commonly used by psychologists to describe "emotion"?
    a. a stimulus situation
    b. the emotion we feel
    c. an aggressive response
    d. physiological arousal
       (p. 396) LO 11

19. According to which theory of emotion does the thalamus simultaneously relay information to the cortex and the hypothalamus?
    a. the James-Lange theory of emotion
    b. the Cannon-Bard theory of emotion
    c. the cognitive theory of emotion
    d. none of the above
       (p. 399) LO 11

20. "We feel sorry because we cry" is an explanation of emotion associated with
    a. the James-Lange theory of emotion
    b. the Cannon-Bard theory of emotion
    c. the cognitive theory of emotion
    d. all of the above
       (p. 398) LO 11

21. Which of the following theories emphasizes the interpretation both of incoming stimuli and bodily stimuli in explaining emotions?
    a. cognitive theory of emotion
    b. Cannon-Bard theory of emotion
    c. James-Lange theory of emotion
    d. a and b above
       (p. 400) LO 11

22. According to the text, lie-detector tests
    a. are an accurate measure of one's guilt or innocence
    b. use physiological measures from the parasympathetic division of the autonomic nervous system
    c. have strict licensing requirements for polygraph operators
    d. are increasingly used by large companies to screen potential employees
       (p. 403) LO 12

23. Which of the following processes may influence the role of learning in our emotions?
    a. modeling
    b. reinforcement
    c. classical conditioning
    d. all of the above
       (p. 404) LO 13

24. Which of the following is true regarding the roles of learning and culture on emotions?
    a. Learning and culture play minimal roles, since all emotions are genetic.
    b. Cultural learning influences the expression of emotions.
    c. Learning affects our emotional reactions to various stimuli.
    d. b and c above
       (p. 404) LO 13

25. Which explanation of aggression involves the process of catharsis?
    a. Freud's instinct theory
    b. the frustration-aggression hypothesis
    c. social learning theory
    d. none of the above
       (p. 406) LO 14

26. According to the frustration-aggression hypothesis, aggression is a natural reaction to
    a. frustration
    b. pain
    c. heat
    d. all of the above
       (p. 407) LO 14

27. Which of the following correctly summarizes the positions taken on televised violence?
    a. Both the social learning and Freudian positions favor televised aggression as an outlet for people.
    b. Neither the social learning nor the Freudian positions view televised aggression favorably.
    c. The social learning theorists opposed televised aggression, while the Freudians view it as catharsis.
    d. The social learning theorists favor televised aggression while the Freudians oppose it.
       (p. 407) LO 14

28. Nisbett's research on violence supports what type of explanation?
    a. Freudian
    b. genetic
    c. social learning
    d. all of the above
       (p. 407) LO 15

29. According to the text, yo-yo dieting is
    a. a reasonable way to lose a lot of weight quickly
    b. effective because it moves the body's metabolism up and down
    c. self-defeating and leads to a slowed metabolism
    d. linked to anorexia nervosa
       (p. 410) LO 16

30. According to the text, regular exercise is advantageous when dieting because it
    a. can burn calories
    b. helps the metabolism to fall while you are dieting
    c. helps keep the metabolism from falling
    d. a and c above
       (p. 411) LO 16

Multiple-Choice Answers

1. The answer is *A*. Emotions are positive or negative feelings in reaction to stimuli. Motivation and emotion are closely linked concepts; motives are often accompanied by emotions, and emotions typically have motivational properties of their own.

2. The answer is *D*. Homeostatic mechanisms refer to internal mechanisms that help to regulate many bodily functions. Among the functions that are regulated are eating, drinking, and maintaining body temperature.

3. The answer is *D*. Primary motives refer to biological needs; these needs must be met or else the organism will die. The desire to be competent is an important psychological need, but not a primary motive.

4. The answer is *A*. Although the rats don't eat more often daily, they eat much longer—the signal to stop eating apparently has been destroyed.

5. The answer is *C*. Stomach contractions and blood sugar levels help to regulate hunger on a daily basis; blood fat levels help to regulate hunger on a long-term basis.

6. The answer is *D*. Incentives are external cues that activate motivation. In the case of hunger, the smell or sight of a favorite food can start those neurons firing in your hypothalamus. Learning and emotions are other psychological factors that impact on hunger.

7. The answer is *C*. In the same manner that the hypothalamus regulates eating with a feeding system and a satiety system, it likewise regulates drinking with "drink" and "stop drinking" systems.

8. The answers is *D*. A complex process, initiated largely by the cells of the hypothalamus, is set into motion when cell fluid levels decrease.

9. The answer is *A*. Explanations of the motive for affiliation once again raise the nature-nurture issue. Some psychologists believe that the need for affiliation is inborn, while others suggest that motive is learned.

10. The answer is *D*. Although some people who are low in *n Ach* (need to achieve) seem uninterested in achieving status and in acquiring material possessions, others avoid competitive situations because of their fear of failure.

11. The answer is *A*. In Schachter's research, subjects who were frightened about their well-being preferred to wait in a room with others.

12. The answer is *C*. The Yerkes-Dodson law suggests that if arousal is too low (to use the vernacular, if you're not "psyched up" enough), performance will be inadequate, but if arousal is too high, performance may become disrupted.

13. The answer is *D*. Although biological factors are involved in arousal, there is no biological need for a moderate or optimal level of arousal.

14. The answer is *D*. Solomon's theory helps to explain our learning of new and seemingly unusual motives, such as seeking out dangerous experiences or hanging around with people we no longer particularly enjoy.

15. The answer is *A*. Presumably, people who donate anonymously to a charity are motivated by the desire to do a "good thing," but do not seek the recognition or attention that often comes with such donations. Therefore, their behavior seems to be an example of intrinsic motivation.

16. The answer is *C*. The basic idea is that if somebody already enjoys something (intrinsic motivation), don't risk diminishing that motivation with extrinsic rewards.

17. The answer is *D*. According to Maslow's theory, our motives are organized in a hierarchy. The "higher" human motives, however, cannot operate until the more basic, lower needs, such as hunger, thirst, and safety, have been met. At the highest level, according to Maslow, we are "dreaming our impossible dream" and realizing our full potential.

18. The answer is *C*. The missing element in the description of emotion is the related behavior that usually accompanies emotions, such as trembling, running, and punching, for example.

19. The answer is *B*. The James-Lange theory suggests that the hypothalamus first produces a bodily reaction, which is then interpreted as the emotion we experience. By contrast, the Cannon-Bard theory suggests that information is first processed in the thalamus, from which it is simultaneously sent both to the cortex and the hypothalamus. Thus, the emotional experience and the physiological arousal are two simultaneous and independent events.

20. The answer is *A*. According to the James-Lange theory, the bodily reaction occurs first and is then processed by the cortex to produce the conscious experience of emotion.

21. The answer is *A*. The cognitive theory emphasizes the cognitive interpretation of stimuli as the major influence in emotions.

22. The answer is *D*. In fact, polygraph tests are estimated to be wrong at least 5 percent of the time, measure sympathetic arousal, and are often conducted by operators who have historically not been well regulated.

23. The answer is *D*. Although most psychologists who study emotions would agree that basic human emotions are inborn, the study of individuals in different cultures, in different families, and under different circumstances also underscores the importance of learning in many of our emotions.

24. The answer is *D*. Although basic emotions are inborn, culture and learning affect the expression of emotions and our reactions to various stimuli.

25. The answer is *A*. According to Freud, aggression is instinctual, and aggressive energy must be released. Catharsis refers to the process of releasing instinctual energy. Freud believed that societies should find nonviolent ways for its members to release this energy.

26. The answer is *D*. Whereas Freud viewed aggression as an inborn part of human nature, frustration-aggression advocates view aggression as a natural reaction to the blocking of important motives.

27. The answer is *C*. The position of the social learning theorists is that people will behave aggressively only if they have learned to do so. Televised aggression, therefore, will increase violence. The Freudian position, on the other hand, suggests that watching televised aggression and experiencing violence vicariously lead to a good cathartic release.

28. The answer is *C*. Nisbett believes that some groups have higher rates of violence because of attitudes toward violence that have been passed down from generation to generation.

29. The answer is *C*. Yo-yo dieting is not only self-defeating; it was found to be associated with increased heart disease.

30. The answer is *D*. The body tends to try to compensate for dieting by lowering the metabolic rate. Exercise, however, helps to keep the metabolic rate from falling while dieting.

Learning Objectives

1. Distinguish between gender identity and gender role.
2. Discuss the results of research regarding gender similarities and gender differences.
3. Compare and contrast the psychoanalytic and social learning theories of gender identity.
4. Discuss the results of research regarding the origins of homosexuality.
5. Describe the controversies regarding the admission of openly homosexual men and women into the military.
6. Discuss the efforts of those who pioneered the scientific study of sexual behavior.
7. Identify and describe the major structures of the sexual anatomy of females and males.
8. Trace the course of sexual differentiation in males and females.
9. Identify and explain the stages in the human sexual response cycle.
10. Compare sexual motivation with other primary motives.
11. Discuss the relationship between hormones and sexual behavior.
12. Distinguish between transvestism and transsexualism.
13. Identify the following abnormal sexual behaviors: fetishism, sexual sadism, sexual masochism, voyeurism, exhibitionism, and forced sexual behavior.
14. Identify and discuss sexual harassment.
15. identify and describe common sexual dysfunctions.
16. Describe the following health problems: cancers of sexual anatomy, sexually transmitted diseases, and AIDS.
17. (From the "Application" section) Discuss the problem of date rape.

Chapter Overview

Although a person's sex is defined by their male and female genitals, a person's gender is the psychological experience of one's sex. The subjective experience of being a male or female is referred to as gender identity. Gender identity develops early in childhood.

Although small cognitive differences exist between men and women in some areas, there are far more gender similarities than differences. Although women on the average receive higher grades in math courses at all levels, they still lag behind men in success in careers that require math. Explanations for this phenomenon include both prejudice and a lack of confidence on the part of women.

A person's sexual orientation is likely developed through the interaction of biological and sociocultural factors. Controversy swirls around President Clinton's proposal to ban discrimination against homosexual men and women in the military.

The study of human sexuality, often mired in controversy, was advanced by Kinsey's surveys of sexuality, Money's studies of sexual development and gender roles, and Masters and Johnson's research on the human sexual response cycle.

The sexual anatomy of men and women is discussed, as well as the process of sexual differentiation.

The human sexual response cycle is characterized by four stages: the excitement phase, the plateau phase, the orgasmic phase, and the resolution phase. The sexual motive is similar to other primary motives in that it is subject to hypothalamic control, and it is affected by external stimuli, learning, and emotions. The sexual motive differs from other primary motives in that sex is not necessary for survival. Other differences relate to our motivation to both increase and decrease our sexual arousal, the role of deprivation, and the fact that, unlike other motives, sexual behavior decreases energy.

Atypical sexual behavior discussed in the chapter includes transvestism, transsexualism, fetishism, sexual sadism, voyeurism, and exhibitionism. The traumas of rape and child rape are discussed, as well as the difficulties raised by sexual harassment.

Most sexual dysfunctions are caused by psychological factors. Dysfunctions are categorized as dysfunctions of desire, arousal, and orgasm.

Among health problems related to sexual anatomy are cancers of sexual anatomy, and sexually transmitted diseases, such as syphilis, gonorrhea, chlamydia, and a fatal STD, AIDS.

Date rape is a common occurrence on college campuses. In many cases, date rape begins with a miscommunication. Differing beliefs and attitudes about sexuality and the use of alcohol and other drugs are important factors in understanding and preventing date rape.

Key Terms Exercise

For each of the following exercises, match the key terms on the left with the correct definitions on the right. Page references to the text follow the terms so that you may refer to the text for any items you answer incorrectly or do not understand completely. You may check your response immediately by referring to the answers that follow each exercise.

Definitions of Sex, Gender, Sexuality and Sexual Orientation

_____ 1. gender (p. 418)
_____ 2. gender identity (p. 418)
_____ 3. gender role (p. 418)
_____ 4. sexual orientation (p. 418)
_____ 5. androgynous (p. 418)
_____ 6. heterosexual (p. 422)
_____ 7. homosexual (p. 422)

a. a person who has both masculine and feminine characteristics
b. the subjective experience of being a female or male
c. persons who are sexually attracted to members of the same sex
d. persons who are sexually attracted to members of the other sex
e. the overall psychological way in which a person experiences his or her sex
f. the behaviors that communicate the degree of our masculinity or femininity
g. the preference for romantic and sexual partners of the same or different sex

ANSWERS
1. e   5. a
2. b   6. d
3. f   7. c
4. g

Biological and Psychological Aspects of Sexuality

_____ 1. uterus (p. 428)
_____ 2. ovaries (p. 428)
_____ 3. fallopian tubes (p. 428)
_____ 4. testes (p. 428)
_____ 5. vas deferens (p. 428)
_____ 6. prostate gland (p. 428)
_____ 7. penis (p. 428)
_____ 8. excitement phase (p. 432)
_____ 9. plateau phase (p. 432)
_____ 10. orgasm (p. 432)

a. a pair of structures in the female reproductive system that produce estrogen, other hormones and ova

b. a structure in the male reproductive system that produces hormones and sperm cells

c. responsible for the production of semen, which carries sperm cells

d. a muscle structure that carries the fetus during pregnancy

e. the tube that carries sperm from the epididymis towards the outside of the body

f. part of the male reproductive system, its three tubes fill with blood during sexual arousal

g. part of the female reproductive system, they help transport the ova from the ovaries to the uterus.

h. part of the sexual response cycle, characterized by high levels of arousal

i. part of the sexual response cycle, characterized by an initial increase in physiological arousal

j. part of the sexual response cycle, characterized by a reflexive peak of physiological pleasure and arousal

ANSWERS

1. d	6. c
2. a	7. f
3. g	8. i
4. b	9. h
5. e	10. j

Atypical and Abnormal Sexual Behavior/Sexual Dysfunction and Sexual Health

_____ 1. atypical sexual behavior (p. 438)
_____ 2. transvestism (p. 438)
_____ 3. transsexualism (p. 438)
_____ 4. rape trauma syndrome (p. 439)
_____ 5. pedophilia (p. 441)
_____ 6. sexual harassment (p. 441)
_____ 7. sexual dysfunction (p. 443)
_____ 8. sexually transmitted diseases (p. 445)

a. obtaining sexual pleasure by dressing in the clothes of the other sex

b. diseases caused by microorganisms that are spread through sexual contact

c. physical and/or psychological disturbances in any phase of the sexual response cycle

d. unwanted sexual advances or touching, sexually suggestive comments, and any form of coercive sexual behavior

e. unusual sexual behavior

f. characterized by feelings of anxiety and fear, and disturbances in sleep, relationships, and daily functioning

g. adults who experience sexual pleasure primarily through sexual contact with children

h. a condition in which an individual feels trapped in the body of the wrong sex

ANSWERS

1. e	5. g
2. a	6. d
3. h	7. c
4. f	8. b

Guided Review

Gender and Sexuality

Although a person's sex is defined by their male or female genitals, a person's _____ is the psychological experience of one's sex. The subjective experience of being a male or female is _____ _____. The behaviors that communicate the degree to which we are feminine or masculine refer to a person's _____ _____. The behaviors in which we engage for sexual pleasure, as well as the related feelings and beliefs, are referred to as _____. The tendency to prefer romantic and sexual partners of the same or different sex is _____ _____.

gender (p. 418)

gender identity (p. 418)

gender role (p. 418)

sexuality (p. 418)

sexual orientation (p. 418)

Gender _____ develops early in childhood. Recent views of gender roles have conceived them as being on a _____, with people displaying varying degrees of both masculinity and femininity. A person who has both female and male characteristics is referred to as _____. _____ people are more likely to adapt well to a variety of situations.

identity (p. 418)

continuum (p. 418)

androgynous (p. 418)

Androgynous (p. 418)

Although small cognitive differences exist between men and women in some areas, there are far more gender _____ than differences. Research suggests the possibility that _____ factors that influence one's gender _____ may be more important in the development of mental abilities than one's sex. Although women, on the average, receive higher grades in math courses at all levels, they still lag behind men in success in careers that involve _____. Explanations for the differences in achievement range from _____ barriers against women to a lack of _____ in these fields. From about two years of age on, boys are more _____ aggressive; from an early age, girls are more likely to express their _____ and to be helpful to others. It is likely that both biological differences and _____ factors work together to shape human behavior.

similarities (p. 419)

sociocultural (p. 420)

identity (p. 420)

math (p. 420)

prejudicial (p. 420)

confidence (p. 421)

physically (p. 421)

emotions (p. 421)

sociocultural (p. 421)

According to Freud, young children take on the manners and ways of the same-sexed parent through a process called

_____. According to social learning theorists, children   identification (p. 422)

learn gender appropriate behavior through _____ and   reinforcement (p. 422)

_____.   punishment (p. 422)

People who are attracted to members of the other sex are

termed _____, while those who are attracted to the   heterosexual (p. 422)

same sex are _____. Approximately ____ to ____   homosexual (p. 422)/1 to 2 (p. 422)

percent of the population has an exclusively homosexual

orientation. People who are attracted both to members of the

same sex and to members of the other sex are called

_____.   bisexual (p. 422)

A person's sexual orientation is likely to be developed through

the interaction of _____ and _____ factors.   biological (p. 423)/sociocultural (p. 423)

Some researchers believe that genetic and _____ factors   hormonal (p. 423)

may predispose a person toward homosexuality or heterosexuality.

Persecution and discrimination against gays and lesbians is

widespread and often reaches extreme forms of _____.   violence (p. 424)

President Clinton sparked controversy shortly after his

inauguration by seeking to ban discrimination against homosexual

men and women in the _____ _____. A   armed forces (p. 424)

review of research has found no convincing evidence that gays and

lesbians are poor _____ risks or are unfit for military   security (p. 425)

service. According to Herek, it would be useful to conduct active

campaigns against _____ and to protect gays and   prejudice (p. 425)

lesbians in the military against retaliation.

Biological and Psychological Aspects of Sexuality

A Viennese neurologist, Richard von Krafft-Ebing, extensively

studied variations and _____ in human sexual behavior.   deviations (p. 427)

Krafft-Ebing incorrectly concluded that _____ was the   masturbation (p. 427)

cause of sexual deviation. An English physician, Henry Havelock

Ellis, studied the role of _____ and _____   social (p. 427)/cultural (p. 427)

influences in shaping human sexual behavior. Alfred Kinsey

conducted large _____ that allowed him to describe the   surveys (p. 427) range of human sexual behavior. John Money studied sexual development and _____ _____. Albert Ellis applied _____ psychology to sexual problems. Masters and Johnson conducted groundbreaking research on the human

_____ _____ _____.

The pear-shaped structure that carries the fetus during pregnancy is the _____. The structures that produce estrogen and other hormones, as well as the ova, are called _____. The ova are transported to the uterus through the _____ _____. At the bottom of the uterus, connected to the vagina, is the _____. The female external genitals, collectively called the _____, consist of (1) a fleshy mound called the _____, (2) the outer lips of the vagina called _____ _____, (3) the inner lips of the vagina, called _____ _____, and (4) the structure at the upper part of the vagina highly responsive to sexual stimulation, called the _____.

In the male, hormones and sperm are produced by the _____. After mature sperm have been produced, they are held in the _____. The tube that carries sperm from the epididymis to the outside of the body is called the _____ _____. The sperm cells are carried in a fluid called _____; semen is produced by the _____ gland and held in the seminal vesicle. The external genitals of the male consist of a tubular structure called a penis and a loose skin structure that supports the testes, called the _____.

The prenatal development of the sexual organs is called _____ _____. This process is controlled by a pair of chromosomes called the X and Y chromosomes. Females have two ____ chromosomes and males have one X and one Y chromosome. The sex of the embryo is determined by the combination of the mother's X and the father's ____ or ____ chromosome. All _____ have internal and external

gender roles (p. 428)

cognitive (p. 428)

sexual response cycle (p. 428)

uterus (p. 428)

ovaries (p. 428)

fallopian tubes (p. 428)

cervix (p. 428)

vulva (p. 428)

mons (p. 428)

labia majora (p. 428)

labia minora (p. 428)

clitoris (p. 428)

testes (p. 428)

epididymis (p. 428)

vas deferens (p. 428)

semen (p. 428)

prostate (p. 428)

scrotum (p. 428)

sexual differentiation (p. 431)

X (p. 431)

X (p. 430)/Y (p. 431)

embryos (p. 431)

structures that could develop into either male or female sex organs. Externally, in females the genital tubercle will develop into the _____, the genital groove will form the opening of the vagina and the labioscrotal swelling will develop into the labia majora. In males, the genital tubercle will develop into the _____, the labioscrotal swelling will develop into the scrotum, and the genital groove will close. The second wave of major changes in sexual development takes place during _____.

clitoris (p. 431)

penis (p. 431)

puberty (p. 431)

The sexual response cycle consists of four stages: (1) an initial increase of physiological arousal occurs in the _____ phase; (2) high levels of arousal take place in the _____ phase; (3) a peak of physical arousal and pleasure is reached in the _____ stage; and (4) the body's level of physical arousal rapidly declines in the _____ phase. The resolution phase is accompanied by a time during which the male is unresponsive to additional stimulation; this is called the _____ period. The sexual motive contains important similarities to and differences from other primary motives. As with other motives (1) the _____ plays a key regulatory role; (2) sexual motivation is sensitive to _____ stimuli; (3) our motives are powerfully shaped by _____; and (4) sexual motivation is greatly influenced by our _____. Unlike the other primary motives (1) the sexual motive is not necessary for _____ survival; (2) while we seek to decrease the arousal created by hunger, thirst, etc., we are motivated to both _____ and _____ our sexual arousal; (3) sexual motivation is less related to _____ than the other primary motives; and (4) while other primary motives help to increase our energy, sexual behavior _____ our energy. Although hormones secreted from the endocrine system play a major role in regulating the sexual behavior of animals, the sexual behavior of humans is much less influenced by _____ factors.

excitement (p. 432)

plateau (p. 432)

orgasmic (p..432)

resolution (p. 433)

refractory (p. 433)

hypothalamus (p. 434)

external (p. 434)

learning (p. 434)

emotions (p. 435)

individual (p. 435)

increase (p. 435)/decrease (p. 435)

deprivation (p. 435)

decreases (p. 435)

hormonal (p. 435)

Atypical and Abnormal Sexual Behavior

Sexual practices that are unusual are called _____ sexual behavior.

    Individuals who obtain sexual pleasure by dressing in the clothes of the opposite sex are _____. Transvestites are almost always males. When an individual feels trapped in a body of the wrong sex, the condition is referred to as _____. In some cases, the person will undergo _____ injections and _____ surgery.

    Some individuals are primarily or exclusively aroused by specific objects; this practice is called _____. Receiving sexual pleasure by inflicting pain on others is called

_____ _____. A condition in which receiving pain is sexually exciting is called _____

_____.

    The practice of obtaining sexual pleasure by watching members of the opposite sex undress or engage in sexual activities is called _____. Voyeurs are generally not considered _____. Individuals who obtain sexual pleasure from exposing their genitals to others are _____.

    When an individual forces another person to engage in a sexual act, it is called _____. Many rape victims experience feelings of _____ and fear, as well as disturbances in _____, relationships, and daily functioning; these behaviors are labeled _____

_____ _____. Theories of rape suggest that male rapists are driven by aggressive impulses or by the need to feel _____ and _____. Many communities provide assistance and support to rape victims through

_____ _____ centers.

    Sexual contact with a child perpetuated by a family member is called _____. When there is force or the threat of force, the assault is called _____ _____. When non-forceful means are used, the abuse of children is called child

_____. Many of the effects of child sexual abuse are

atypical (p. 438)

transvestites (p. 438)

transsexualism (p. 438)

hormone (p. 438)

plastic (p. 438)

fetishism (p. 438)

sexual sadism (p. 439)

sexual

masochism (p. 439)

voyeurism (p. 439)

dangerous (p. 439)

exhibitionists (p. 439)

rape (p. 439)

anxiety (p. 439)

sleep (p. 439)

rape

trauma syndrome (p. 439)

powerful (p. 440)/dominating (p. 440)

rape crisis (p. 440)

incest (p. 440)

child rape (p. 440)

molestation (p. 441)

believed to be long-term. Adults who experience sexual pleasure through contact with children are called _____. In the vast majority of cases, the molester or rapist is known and _____ by the child victim.

pedophiles (p. 441)

trusted (p. 441)

Unwanted sexual advances, touching, sexually suggestive comments, and any form of coercive behavior all constitute _____ harassment. Sexual harassment occurs between persons with different amounts of _____, often in schools or in the workplace. In some cases, sexual harassment can provoke serious levels of anxiety and _____.

sexual (p. 441)

power (p. 441)

depression (p. 441)

Disturbances that occur in any phase of the sexual response cycle are called sexual _____. Most sexual dysfunctions are caused by psychological factors. Dysfunctions of sexual desire include (1) infrequent or nonexistent sexual desire, called _____ sexual desire and (2) fearful avoidance of sexual contact, called sexual _____ _____. Dysfunctions of sexual arousal include, for females, female sexual _____ disorder, characterized by a lack of vaginal lubrication and minimal sexual excitement, involuntary contractions of the vagina, called _____, and pain during intercourse, called _____. Male sexual arousal disorders include _____ dysfunction. Orgasm dysfunctions include, for women, inhibited female orgasm, and for men, _____ ejaculation or retarded ejaculation. People who experience sexual dysfunctions often are _____ to discuss the problem, may believe they are the only ones with such problems and may believe there is nowhere to turn for help.

dysfunctions (p. 443)

inhibited (p. 443)

aversion disorder (p. 443)

arousal (p. 444)

vaginismus (p. 444)

dyspareunia (p. 444)

erectile (p. 444)

premature (p. 445)

embarrassed (p. 445)

Among health problems related to sexual anatomy are _____ of sexual anatomy, including, for women, the cervix, _____, ovaries, and breasts. A low-dose X ray that is accurate at detecting cancers is called a _____. For men, cancers of the _____ and testicles are potential health problems.

cancers (p. 445)

uterus (p. 445)

mammogram (p. 446)

prostate (p. 446)

Diseases that are caused by micro-organisms spread through sexual contact are called _____ _____

sexually transmitted

_____. Caused by a spiral-shaped bacteria called a
spirochete, _____ has been increasing in incidence in
the United States. Primary syphilis is characterized by
_____ sores. _____ syphilis is characterized
by rashes, fever, headache, and nausea. During these first two
stages, syphilis can be treated with _____. If untreated,
syphilis develops into the _____ stage, which is
characterized by numerous serious health problems. A second STD
spread by bacterial infection is called _____. The most
common STD is _____. An STD commonly referred to
as "crabs" is _____ _____. An STD caused
by the herpes simplex virus, genital herpes is treatable but not
_____. Another viral infection, usually not painful, is
genital _____. A fatal STD caused by the human
immunodeficiency virus (HIV) is _____. HIV is
transmitted through blood, semen, and _____ fluids.
HIV destroys _____ cells, which aid the body's immune
response. A variety of misconceptions exists about AIDS. The
following facts about AIDS are important: (1) a person with HIV
looks _____ for a long time; (2) no evidence exists that
AIDS can be spread through _____ _____;
(3) although no cure exists, there are treatments that can help
people with HIV to stay _____; (4) a person cannot get
the AIDs virus by sharing kitchens and bathrooms with someone
with AIDS or if someone who is infected sneezes near you or by
donating blood or by _____ someone with AIDS; (5) a
person can get the AIDS virus after having sex _____
time with someone who has the virus; (6) men and women can
transmit the AIDS virus to each other; (7) a person who got the
AIDS virus through _____ drug use can transmit the
virus to someone by having sex. The use of _____ helps
protect against pregnancy as well as most STDs.

diseases (p. 446)

syphilis (p. 446)

chancre (p. 446)/Secondary (p. 446)

antibiotics (p. 446)

tertiary (p. 446)

gonorrhea (p. 467)

chlamydia (p. 447)

pubic lice (p. 448)

curable (p. 448)

warts (p. 448)

AIDS (p. 448)

vaginal (p. 449)

T-Helper (p. 449)

healthy (p. 449)

casual contact (p. 449)

healthy (p. 449)

touching (p. 450)

one (p. 450)

intravenous (p. 450)

condoms (p. 450)

Application of Psychology: Date Rape

Date rape is a common occurrence on _____   college

_____. One estimate is that 33 percent of women have   campuses (p. 452)

experienced date rape. In many cases, date rape begins with a

_____ between the persons. One reason for the   miscommunication (p. 452)

miscommunication is a difference in beliefs and _____   attitudes (p. 452)

about sexuality. Another factor that is related to date rape is the

use of _____. Guidelines for men include the following;   alcohol (p. 452)

(1) It is always rape when she says "____"; (2) if it is not clear   no (p. 453)

that she has consented to sex, then she has ____   not

_____; and (3) if she is drunk or high, she cannot   consented (p. 453)

_____ to sex. Guidelines for women include: consent (p. 453)

(1) communicate your wishes about sex _____ and   clearly (p. 453)

_____; (2) _____ and _____   early (p. 453)/alcohol (p. 453)/sexual (p. 453)

situations are a dangerous combination; and (3) even

"_____" guys can commit rape. Many _____   nice (p. 453)/resources (p. 453)

exist, both on campus and off-campus, to assist victims of date

rape.

CONCEPT CHECK

Fill in the missing components of the following concept box. The answers are shown below the box.

Sexually Transmitted Diseases

I. Disease	II. Symptoms/Cures
a. Syphilis	a.
b. Gonorrhea	b.
c.	c. The most common STD. It has vague symptoms that can be treated with antibiotics. It is difficult to treat and may be recurrent.
d.	d. Commonly called "crabs," this disease causes skin itching and may be treated with medicated shampoo.
e. Genital herpes	e.
f.	f. Caused by a virus, they are not usually painful and not considered dangerous, but they are related to the development of other serious conditions. They may be removed by surgery or by freezing.
g. AIDS	g.

Answers

IIa. Caused by a bacteria called a spirochete; progresses through three stages of infection; one early symptom is a sore called a chancre; secondary symptoms may include fever, nausea, headaches, swollen glands, and so on; primary and secondary syphilis can usually be treated with antibiotics; tertiary stage syphilis can cause serious health problems and can be fatal.

IIb. Caused by a bacteria; symptoms involve discharge from genital area. If left untreated, it can lead to serious health complications. It is usually cured with antibiotics.

Ic. Chlamydia

Id.   Pubic lice

IIe.   Causes small painful lesions in the genital area. The lesions are highly contagious. Herpes is
        treatable, but not curable.

If.   Genital warts

IIg.   Caused by HIV and transmitted through blood, semen, and vaginal fluids. A person may be infected
        with HIV for a long period of time before becoming ill. There is no cure for AIDS.

Multiple-Choice Questions

1. The subjective experience of being either
   male or female is referred to as
   a. gender
   b. gender identity
   c. gender role
   d. sex
      (p. 418) LO 1

2. The expectations that we have for each
   others' behavior that are linked to our sex are
   referred to as
   a. gender
   b. gender identity
   c. gender role
   d. sex
      (p. 418) LO 1

3. Recent studies of gender difference in
   cognitive abilities have shown that
   a. males' scores in mathematical reasoning
      are increasing
   b. males' scores in mathematical reasoning
      are decreasing
   c. females' scores in mathematical reasoning
      are increasing
   d. females' scores in mathematical reasoning
      are decreasing
      (p. 420) LO 2

4. Starting at an early age, researchers have
   found that
   a. boys are more physically active
   b. girls are more likely to express their
      emotions
   c. girls are better able to understand the
      emotions of others
   d. all of the above
      (p. 421) LO 2

5. The process of identification is central to the
   development of gender identity according to
   which theory?
   a. psychoanalytic
   b. social learning
   c. humanistic
   d. sociocultural
      (p. 422) LO 3

6. The process of reinforcing appropriate gender
   roles is central to gender development
   according to which theory?
   a. psychoanalytic
   b. social learning
   c. humanistic
   d. sociocultural
      (p. 422) LO 3

7. According to researcher John Money, sexual
   orientation has its origins
   a. during the first two years of life
   b. during adolescence
   c. during fetal development
   d. in one's social environment
      (p. 422) LO 4

8. Some researchers have identified differences
   in the brains of heterosexual and homosexual
   men in an area called the
   a. amygdala
   b. cerebral cortex
   c. hippocampus
   d. hypothalamus
      (p. 423) LO 4

9. Which of the following best reflects the view of researchers regarding admitting homosexual men and women into the military?
   a. Homosexuals should be admitted, but they should be in separate units.
   b. Homosexuals should not be admitted because the morale of the military would suffer.
   c. Homosexuals should be admitted, and programs should be initiated to reduce prejudice and stereotyping.
   d. The present policy of not directly addressing the issue has worked for centuries and should continue.
   (p. 424) LO 5

10. In the mid-1950s, large-scale sexual surveys were conducted by
    a. Masters and Johnson
    b. Alfred Kinsey
    c. John Money
    d. Albert Ellis
    (p. 427) LO 6

11. Estrogen, ova (eggs), and other hormones are produced by the
    a. uterus
    b. fallopian tubes
    c. cervix
    d. ovaries
    (p. 428) LO 7

12. Sperm cells are produced by the
    a. prostate gland
    b. scrotum
    c. testes
    d. vas deference
    (p. 428) LO 7

13. During the prenatal development of the sexual organs, which of the following is true?
    a. In the female, the genital tubercle develops into the labioscrotal swelling.
    b. In the female, the genital tubercle develops into the clitoris.
    c. In the male, the genital tubercle develops into the genital groove.
    d. In the male, the genital tubercle develops into the scrotum.
    (p. 431) LO

14. Which of the following describe the correct sequence of the human sexual response cycle?
    a. excitement, plateau, resolution, orgasm
    b. plateau, excitement, resolution, orgasm
    c. excitement, plateau, orgasm, resolution
    d. plateau, excitement, orgasm, resolution
    (p. 432) LO 9

15. During the sexual response cycle, the refractory period is experienced by
    a. males in the excitement phase
    b. females in the excitement phase
    c. males in the resolution phase
    d. females in the resolution phase
    (p. 433) LO 9

16. Each of these factors represents a difference between the sexual motive and other primary motives *except*
    a. sexual behavior decreases one's energy
    b. sexual motivation is not necessary for individual survival
    c. sexual motivation is less related to deprivation than are other primary motives
    d. the hypothalamus seems unrelated to the sexual motive
    (p. 435) LO 10

17. How does the hormonal control of human sexual behavior compare with the hormonal control of other animals?
    a. Humans are more influenced by hormonal factors.
    b. Humans are less influenced by hormonal factors.
    c. Humans and animals are equally influenced by hormonal factors.
    d. Hormonal factors play no role in human sexual behavior.
    (p. 436) LO 11

18. The feeling that one is trapped in the body of the wrong sex is called
    a. transvestism
    b. transsexualism
    c. fetishism
    d. exhibitionism
    (p. 438) LO 12

19. Individuals who obtain sexual pleasure by watching members of the opposite sex undress or engage in sexual behaviors are called
    a. exhibitionists
    b. sadists
    c. voyeurs
    d. pedophiles
       (p. 439) LO 12

20. Each of the following is true regarding sexual masochism *except*
    a. masochists derive sexual pleasure by receiving pain
    b. masochists derive sexual pleasure by inflicting pain on others
    c. some masochists prefer to substitute verbal abuse for physical pain
    d. masochism is the preferred method of sexual stimulation for large numbers of individuals
       (p. 439) LO 12

21. Which of the following behaviors or feelings are likely of children who have been sexually victimized?
    a. acting out sexually
    b. feeling stigmatized
    c. feeling personally betrayed
    d. all of the above
       (p. 441) LO 13

22. Pedophiles are people who experience sexual pleasure primarily
    a. through sexual contact with shoes
    b. through sexual contact with children
    c. through sexual contact by exposing themselves to others
    d. by watching others engaging in sexual activities
       (p. 441) LO 13

23. Each of the following is a characteristic of sexual harassment *except*
    a. it consists of unwanted sexual advances
    b. it consists of sexually suggestive comments
    c. it occurs between persons with different amounts of power
    d. all of the above
       (p. 441) LO 14

24. A nearly complete fearful avoidance of sexual contact with others is called
    a. inhibited sexual desire
    b. sexual aversion disorder
    c. dyspareunia
    d. vaginismus
       (p. 443) LO 15

25. Which of the following is a female sexual dysfunction?
    a. dyspareunia
    b. premature ejaculation
    c. erectile dysfunction
    d. all of the above
       (p. 444) LO 15

26. Which of the following is (are) common beliefs about sexual dysfunctions?
    a. They are often embarrassing to discuss.
    b. People experiencing sexual dysfunctions may believe they are psychologically abnormal.
    c. People often believe they have nowhere to turn for help.
    d. all of the above
       (p. 445) LO 15

27. During which stage(s) of syphilis is it usually curable with antibiotics?
    a. primary
    b. secondary
    c. tertiary
    d. a and b above
       (p. 446) LO 16

28. The most common sexually transmitted disease is
    a. gonorrhea
    b. syphilis
    c. genital herpes
    d. chlamydia
       (p. 447) LO 16

29. A person with HIV is diagnosed as having AIDS when he or she
    a. is first infected with HIV
    b. experiences one of several specific infectious diseases
    c. loses a specific number of T-Helper blood cells
    d. b or c above
       (p. 449) LO 16

30. Which of the following demonstrates the relationship between alcohol and date rape?
    a. A person cannot give consent to sex when they are drunk.
    b. Alcohol lowers inhibitions and increases the likelihood of the use of force.
    c. Drinking alcohol allows people to attribute their behavior to the effects of alcohol.
    d. all of the above
       (p. 452) LO 17

Multiple-Choice Answers

1. The answer is *B*. Gender role refers to the behaviors that communicate the degree to which we are feminine or masculine, while one's sex is determined by their male or female genitals.
2. The answer is *C*. Appropriate gender roles are strongly determined by one's culture.
3. The answer is *C*. The changes in scores over the years support the importance of sociocultural factors and gender identity in the development of mental abilities.
4. The answer is *D*. Researchers continue to debate the relative contributions of biological and sociocultural factors to gender differences.
5. The answer is *A*. According to the psychoanalysts, young children usually take on the behavior of the parent of the same sex through the process of identification.
6. The answer is *B*. The social learning approach suggests that gender roles are learned from society.
7. The answer is *C*. According to Money, the fetal interplay of hormones and genetics predispose an individual toward homosexuality or heterosexuality.
8. The answer is *D*. Interestingly, the area of the hypothalamus where researchers found differences is directly related to sexual behavior.
9. The answer is *C*. Researchers suggest that when people with prejudices work together, the prejudice diminishes dramatically.
10. The answer is *B*. Kinsey's surveys demonstrated that such phenomena as masturbation, sexual fantasies, and homosexual contact were widespread.
11. The answer is *D*. The uterus carries the fetus during pregnancy, the fallopian tubes transport the ova to the uterus, and the cervix, located at the bottom of the uterus, connects the uterus to the vagina.
12. The answer is *C*. The prostate gland produces semen, the scrotum supports the testes, and the vas deferens is the tube that carries sperm toward the outside of the body.
13. The answer is *B*. In the male, the genital tubercle develops into the penis.
14. The answer is *C*. If you need an acronym to remember the sequence, how about *Every Person Ought to Relax* (EPOR).
15. The answer is *C*. During the refractory period, males are unresponsive to further sexual stimulation.
16. The answer is *D*. The sexual motive resembles the other primary motives with respect to hypothalamic control, the role of external stimuli, and the roles played by learning and emotions.
17. The answer is *B*. Although humans are far less influenced by hormonal factors than other animals, a strong relationship does exist between hormonal factors and human sexuality.
18. The answer is *B*. Transvestism refers to those who derive sexual pleasure by dressing in the clothes of the opposite sex. Fetishism refers to those who are aroused by specific physical objects, and exhibitionism refers to those who obtain sexual pleasure by exposing themselves to others.

19. The answer is *C*. Exhibitionists obtain sexual pleasure by exposing their genitals to others. Sexual sadists receive pleasure by inflicting pain on others. Pedophiles obtain pleasure from sexual contact with children.

20. The answer is *B*. While masochists enjoy receiving pain, sexual sadists derive sexual pleasure by inflicting pain on others.

21. The answer is *D*. In addition, children who have been sexually victimized are likely to feel powerless and a lack of control.

22. The answer is *B*. Child molesters and rapists are usually known and trusted by their victims.

23. The answer is *D*. Although there are laws that attempt to protect people from sexual harassment, most instances of harassment probably still go unreported.

24. The answer is *B*. Inhibited sexual desire refers to infrequent desire for sexual contact. Dyspareunia refers to painful intercourse for women, and vaginismus refers to involuntary contractions of the vaginal wall that make it too narrow to allow sexual intercourse.

25. The answer is *A*. Premature ejaculation and erectile dysfunction are male sexual dysfunctions.

26. The answer is *D*. Our society is still generally reluctant to discuss sexual matters openly, especially sexual dysfunctions. However, as the text suggests, help for these dysfunctions is widely available.

27. The answer is *D*. The tertiary stage is characterized by numerous serious health complications.

28. The answer is *D*. Recent research suggests that as many as 20 percent of college students may be infected with chlamydia.

29. The answer is *D*. Most people who are infected with HIV go several years before they become ill with AIDS.

30. The answer is *D*. All of these issues argue for the cautious use of alcohol.

Chapter

Learning Objectives

1. Define the term *personality*.
2. Distinguish among Freud's concepts of the conscious mind, the preconscious mind, and the unconscious mind.
3. Describe the following three parts of the mind according to Freud: the id, the ego, and the superego.
4. Distinguish among the following: displacement, sublimation, and identification.
5. List and describe Freud's five psychosexual stages of development.
6. Discuss Carl Jung's theory of the mind; distinguish between extroversion and introversion and between the personal unconscious and the collective unconscious.
7. Describe the roles of inferiority feelings, social interest, and goals in Alfred Adler's personality theory.
8. Discuss the role of anxious insecurity in the personality theory of Karen Horney; describe Horney's criticisms of Freud's view of women.
9. Describe Albert Bandura's social learning theory, including the role of cognition in personality development.
10. Identify the basic concepts of humanistic theory, including inner-directedness and subjectivity.
11. Distinguish between the "self" and the "ideal self" and discuss the importance of congruence and conditions of worth in Carl Rogers' personality theory.
12. Identify the characteristics of a self-actualized person according to Abraham Maslow.
13. Compare and contrast humanistic, psychoanalytic, and social learning theories of personality.
14. Distinguish among Allport's cardinal, central, secondary, and common traits; compare Allport's approach with Cattell's trait theory.
15. List and describe the "big five" personality traits.
16. Discuss the alternative explanations to trait theories called situationism and interactionism.
17. Explain the use of interviews and observational methods to assess personality.
18. Describe the use of projective tests and distinguish between the TAT and the Rorschach inkblot test.
19. Describe the use of objective tests such as the MMPI-2.
20. Discuss the usefulness and accuracy of personality tests.
21. (From the "Application" section) Discuss the role of situational influences in everyday life.

Chapter Overview

Personality is the sum total of the typical ways of acting, thinking, and feeling that make each person unique. One influential theory of personality, psychoanalytic theory, was developed in the late nineteenth century by Sigmund Freud. Freud's theory distinguished three levels of conscious awareness—the conscious mind, the preconscious mind, and the unconscious mind. According to Freud, the mind is composed of the following three parts: (1) the id, which operates on the pleasure principle and seeks to obtain immediate pleasure and to avoid pain; (2) the ego, which operates on the reality principle and seeks safe and realistic ways of satisfying the id; and (3) the superego, which opposes the id by imposing moral restrictions and striving for perfection. Freud suggested that when the ego cannot find ways to satisfy the id, it seeks a substitute. The process of substituting a more acceptable goal is called displacement; the displacement of a socially desirable goal is termed sublimation. Another process that allows individuals to operate in society without friction is called identification; we tend to model our actions after individuals who are successful in gaining satisfactions from life.

Freud's theory also distinguishes five stages in the development of personality: the oral stage, the anal stage, the phallic stage, the latency stage, and the genital stage. According to Freud, events that happen as the individual passes through these stages can be critical in the formation of personality.

Alfred Adler and Carl Jung were two associates of Freud. They both developed influential personality theories of their own. Jung differed with Freud over his emphasis on sexual motivation. Jung believed that the unconscious mind contains positive and even spiritual motives. He also felt that we each possess both a personal unconscious and a collective unconscious. Adler felt that the primary struggle in personality development was the effort to overcome feelings of inferiority in social relationships and to develop feelings of superiority. Karen Horney was another influential revisionist of Freudian psychoanalysis. She felt that anxious insecurity, which stems from inadequate childrearing experiences, is the source of all personality conflicts. Horney is also an important contributor to the psychology of women.

Other personality theorists, the social learning theorists, emphasize classical conditioning, operant conditioning, and modeling in the development of personality. Albert Bandura, a prominent social learning theorist, believes that social learning is determined by the actions of behavior on the environment, and vice versa. Bandura also believes that behavior is self-regulated by our internalized cognitive standards for self-reward and limited by our perception of our own self-efficacy.

Members of a third group of personality theorists, humanistic theorists, believe that humans possess an inner-directedness that pushes them to grow. To the humanist, reality is subjective. The concept of "self" is central to the personality theory of Carl Rogers and other humanists. Our self-concept is our subjective perception of who we are and what we are like. Rogers distinguishes between the self (the person I think I am) and the ideal self (the person I wish I were). Problems result when there are major discrepancies between the self and the ideal self, or when a person's self-concept is not congruent with the way he or she actually acts, thinks, and feels.

Some psychologists believe that personality can be described in terms of traits. Traits are relatively enduring and consistent ways of behaving. Other psychologists believe that situations determine behavior; this is known as situationism. Social learning theorists have suggested a compromise termed interactionism, which says that behavior is influenced by a combination of personality traits and the situation.

Personality assessment is the use of psychological methods to learn about a person's personality. The most widely used method is the interview. Personality is also assessed by observing the person's behavior in a natural or simulated situation. Rating scales are used to help make observational methods more objective. The second most widely used method of personality assessment is the projective test, which psychoanalysts believe reveals the motives and conflicts of the unconscious mind. Objective personality tests, such as the MMPI-2, consist of questions that measure different aspects of personality. Objective personality tests are generally better at assessing personality than projective techniques, but all personality tests are only partly accurate.

Key Terms Exercise

For each of the following exercises, match the key terms on the left with the correct definitions on the right. Page references to the text follow the terms so that you may refer to the text for any items you answer incorrectly or do not understand completely. You may check your responses immediately by referring to the answers that follow each exercise.

Psychoanalytic Theory (I)

_____ 1. personality (p. 460)
_____ 2. psychoanalytic theory (p. 461)
_____ 3. unconscious mind (p. 461)
_____ 4. repression (p. 462)
_____ 5. id (p. 462)
_____ 6. pleasure principle (p. 463)

a. the theory of personality developed by Sigmund Freud
b. the sum total of ways of acting, thinking, and feeling that make each person unique
c. the part of the mind of which we are never directly aware
d. pushing unpleasant information into unconsciousness
e. the attempt of the id to seek immediate pleasure
f. the inborn part of the unconscious mind

ANSWERS

1. b	4. d
2. a	5. f
3. c	6. e

Psychoanalytic Theory (II)

_____ 1. primary process thinking (p. 463)
_____ 2. ego (p. 463)
_____ 3. reality principle (p. 463)
_____ 4. superego (p. 463)
_____ 5. ego ideal (p. 463)
_____ 6. displacement (p. 464)

a. the part of the mind that enforces strict moral restrictions
b. formation by the id of wish-fulfilling mental images
c. substitution of an acceptable goal for an unacceptable goal of the id
d. the ego's attempt to find realistic ways to meet the needs of the id
e. the standard of perfect conduct of the superego
f. the part of the mind that uses the reality principle to satisfy the id

ANSWERS

1. b.	4. a
2. f	5. e
3. d	6. c

Psychoanalytic Theory (III)

_____ 1. sublimation (p. 464)
_____ 2. identification (p. 464)
_____ 3. psychosexual stages (p. 464)
_____ 4. Oedipus complex (p. 466)
_____ 5. Electra complex (p. 466)
_____ 6. feelings of inferiority (p. 466)

a. unconscious childhood wishes of boys
b. unconscious childhood wishes of girls
c. developmental periods in Freud's theory
d. the process of modeling one's actions after others
e. substitution of a socially desirable goal for one that is socially harmful
f. according to Adler, the feelings that result from children being less powerful than adults

ANSWERS

1. e	4. a
2. d	5. b
3. c	6. f

Social Learning Theory

_____ 1. social learning theory (p. 470)
_____ 2. reciprocal determination (p. 471)
_____ 3. self-efficacy (p. 472)
_____ 4. self-regulation (p. 472)

a. the perception of being capable of achieving one's goals
b. the view that the individual and the social learning environment continually influence each other
c. the theory that our personalities are formed through learning from others
d. the process of cognitively reinforcing and punishing ourselves, depending on our personal standards

ANSWERS
1. c   3. a
2. b   4. d

Humanistic Theory

_____ 1. humanistic theory (p. 473)
_____ 2. inner-directedness (p. 473)
_____ 3. subjective reality (p. 474)
_____ 4. self-concept (p. 474)
_____ 5. self-actualization (p. 475)
_____ 6. symbolization (p. 474)
_____ 7. conditions of worth (p. 475)

a. an internal force that leads people to grow and improve
b. the third force in psychology
c. the human drive to use our potential to the fullest
d. our subjective perceptions of who we are
e. representation of experience, thought, or feelings in mental symbols
f. standards that are used by others or ourselves in judging our worth
g. each individual's unique perception of reality

ANSWERS
1. b   5. c
2. a   6. e
3. g   7. f
4. d

Personality Traits and Assessment

_____ 1. traits (p. 478)
_____ 2. situationism (p. 479)
_____ 3. person X situation interactionism (p. 480)
_____ 4. projective test (p. 482)

a. the view that behavior is relatively consistent only if situations remain consistent
b. relatively enduring and consistent ways of behaving
c. a test that uses ambiguous stimuli designed to reveal the client's mind
d. the view that behavior is influenced by the characteristics of both the person and the situation

ANSWERS
1. b   3. d
2. a   4. c

Who Am I?

Match the psychologists on the left with their contributions to the field of psychology on the right. Page references to the text follow the names of the psychologists so that you may refer to the text for further review of these psychologists and their contributions. You may check your responses immediately by referring to the answers that follow each exercise.

_____ 1. Sigmund Freud (p. 461)
_____ 2. Alfred Adler (p. 468)
_____ 3. Carl Jung (p. 467)
_____ 4. Karen Horney (p. 468)
_____ 5. Albert Bandura (p. 471)
_____ 6. Abraham Maslow (p. 475)
_____ 7. Carl Rogers (p. 474)
_____ 8. Gordon Allport (p. 478)
_____ 9. Raymond Cattell (p. 479)

a. The personal unconscious and the collective unconscious are important to my theory.
b. I developed psychoanalytic theory.
c. I am a cognitive behaviorist and a leader in social learning theory.
d. My theory emphasizes overcoming feelings of inferiority, developing social interest, and achieving goals.
e. The concept of "self" is central to my personality theory.
f. I described the process of self-actualization.
g. My personality test measures 16 source traits.
h. I believe that personality traits are either cardinal, central, or secondary.
i. It was my belief that anxious insecurity is the source of all personality conflicts.

ANSWERS

1. b	6. f
2. d	7. e
3. a	8. h
4. i	9. g
5. c	

Guided Review

Definition of Personality

Personality is the sum total of all the ways of acting, thinking, and

feeling that are _____ for a person and make that   typical (p. 460)

person _____ from all others.   different (p. 460)

Psychoanalytic Theory: Sigmund Freud

Freud believed that individuals are not aware of the contents of the

part of the mind called the _____. While working with   unconscious (p. 461)

patients experiencing conversion disorders, Freud became

convinced that all such cases were caused by unexpressed

_____ motives.   sexual (p. 461)

Freud believed that conscious awareness exists on three levels. The portion of the mind of which an individual is presently aware is the _____ mind. Memories that are not presently conscious but that can be easily brought into consciousness are found in the _____ mind. The storehouse for primitive instinctual motives and repressed memories and emotions is the _____ mind.

conscious (p. 461)

preconscious (p. 461)

unconscious (p. 461)

Freud also divided the mind in a different, but related, way. He viewed the mind as being composed of the _____, the _____, and the _____. At birth, the mind has only one part, the _____. The id is composed of two sets of instincts, the _____ instinct and the _____ instinct. The two most important motives of the life instinct are _____ and _____ motives. According to Freud, the id functions entirely at the _____ level. The id operates according to the _____ principle and attempts to satisfy its needs by using wish-fulfilling mental images, a process Freud called _____ _____ _____. As we grow up, we develop a second part of the mind, called the _____. The ego helps us to deal with the world through the _____ principle. The ego can be thought of as the _____ of the personality.

id (p. 462)

ego (p. 462)/superego (p. 462)

id (p. 462)

life (p. 462)

death (p. 462)

sexual (p. 462)/aggressive (p. 462)

unconscious (p. 462)

pleasure (p. 462)

primary process thinking (p. 463)

ego (p. 463)

reality (p. 463)

executive (p. 463)

The only part of the mind containing a sense of morality is the _____. The superego is created mainly by _____. Parental punishment creates the moral inhibitions called _____, while parental rewards establish a standard of conduct called the _____ _____.

superego (p. 463)

parents (p. 463)

conscience (p. 463)

ego

ideal (p. 463)

Sometimes the ego must settle for a substitute for the goals of the id. This process is called _____. A form of displacement in which a socially desirable goal is substituted for a socially harmful goal is called _____. The process of thinking, acting, and feeling like individuals who are successful in gaining satisfactions from life is called _____.

displacement (p. 464)

sublimation (p. 464)

identification (p. 464)

Freud believed that our personalities are formed as we pass through a series of developmental stages from infancy to adulthood. Stressful events experienced during a stage can leave the personality _____ at that stage. Since these stages represent a shifting of sexual energy from one part of the body to another, they are called _____ stages. The first stage, from birth to 1 year, is called the _____ stage. Fixations here may lead to overeating and drinking, and the person is called an _____ _____ personality. If oral pleasures are frustrated, the infant may grow to be an _____ _____ personality.

fixated (p. 464)

psychosexual (p. 464)

oral (p. 465)

oral receptive (p. 465)

oral

aggressive (p. 465)

The second stage of development, from 1 to 3 years, is called the _____ stage. Fixations at this stage may lead to a personality that is either stingy and compulsive, called _____ _____, or cruel and disorderly, called _____ _____.

anal (p. 465)

anal retentive (p. 465)

anal expulsive (p. 465)

From ages 3 to 6, children are in the _____ stage, in which the genitals become the primary source of pleasure. During this stage, boys develop a sexual attraction to their mothers, referred to as the _____ _____. Boys also develop a fear of their fathers, called _____ _____. Girls develop desires for their fathers, called the _____ _____. The desire of young girls to possess a penis is called _____ _____.

phallic (p. 465)

Oedipus complex (p. 466)

castration

anxiety (p. 466)

Electra complex (p. 466)

penis envy (p. 466)

From ages 6 to 11, children enter the _____ stage, during which sexual interest is relatively inactive. From age 11 through adulthood, the individual is in the _____ stage, in which sexual and romantic interest is directed toward one's peers. Most modern revisions of psychoanalysis agree that Freud overemphasized _____ motivation and _____.

latency (p. 466)

genital (p. 466)

sexual (p. 467)/aggression (p. 467)

Carl Jung believed that people have a pair of opposite personality traits—a desire to be open and friendly, called _____, and a desire to be shy and focus attention on ourselves, called _____. He also felt that the unconscious contained two elements: motives that have been

extroversion (p. 467)

introversion (p. 467)

repressed because they are threatening, called the _____   personal (p. 468)

unconscious, and an unconscious mind with which all humans are

born, called the _____ unconscious.   collective (p. 468)

    According to Alfred Adler, the task of personality development

is to overcome feelings of _____ . Later in his career,   inferiority (p. 468)

Adler felt that all humans are born with _____   social

_____ and that people's lives are governed by   interest (p. 468)

_____ .   goals (p. 468)

    Another influential revisionist of Freudian psychoanalysis is

Karen Horney. She believed that anxious _____ , which   insecurity (p. 469)

stems from inadequate _____ experiences, is the source   childrearing (p. 469)

of all personality conflicts. Horney rejected the importance Freud

placed on _____ _____ .   penis envy (p. 469)

Social Learning Theory: Albert Bandura

According to social learning theorists, personality is

_____ from other members of society. Albert Bandura   learned (p. 471)

is a leading social learning theorist. Although he is a behaviorist,

he emphasizes the importance of _____ in personality   cognition (p. 471)

and believes that people play an _____ role in   active (p. 471)

determining their actions. Bandura has observed that the individual

and the social learning environment continually influence each

other; that is, they are _____ _____ .   reciprocally determined (p. 471)

According to Bandura, the perception of being able to achieve

one's goals is called _____-_____ . Bandura   self-efficacy (p. 472)

believes that we cognitively reinforce or punish ourselves,

depending on whether or not our behavior has met our personal

standards; this process is called _____ _____ .   self-regulation (p. 472)

Humanistic Theory: Maslow and Rogers

Humanistic psychology is often referred to as the _____   third

_____ . Humanists believe that all people possess an   force (p. 473)

internal force that leads them to grow and improve. This force is

called _____-_____ . To the humanist, reality   inner-directedness (p. 473)

is _____ .   subjective (p. 474)

Our selective perception of who we are is called our

_____-_____. Carl Rogers distinguishes

between the person one thinks he is, called the _____,

and the person one wishes to be, called the _____

_____. An obscure view of ourselves may arise when

our self-concept is not _____ with the way we actually

are. According to Rogers, when a person denies feelings that are

incongruent with her self-concept, she fails to _____ her

experience. The process of denying awareness to certain feelings

begins when parents _____ some behaviors but

_____ others. This creates standards which Rogers calls

_____ ____ _____. We often deny these

feelings that are _____ with our internalized conditions

of worth.

self-concept (p. 474)

self (p. 474)

ideal

self (p. 474)

congruent (p. 474)

symbolize (p. 474)

praise (p. 475)

punish (p. 475)

conditions of worth (p. 475)

inconsistent (p. 475)

According to Abraham Maslow, the ultimate in completed
growth is self-actualization. Among the characteristics of self-
actualized people are the following: they (1) have reached a high
level of moral development; (2) are usually committed to some
cause or task; (3) experience life in intense, vivid ways; (4) are
open and honest; (5) are not particularly interested in fads and
fashion; (6) enjoy positive and caring friendships but enjoy privacy
and independence; (7) find life challenging and fresh; (8) have an
accurate, positive view of life; (9) are spontaneous and natural.
Although many of us may occasionally have a peak experience,
according to Maslow, these experiences are more common for self-
actualizing individuals.

Humanistic psychology, psychoanalysis, and social learning

theory all differ in their views of the basic _____ of

human beings and society.

nature (P. 476)

Traits and Situations: Describing the Consistencies of Personality
Psychologists refer to relatively enduring and consistent ways of

behaving as _____. Trait theories of personality are

more concerned with _____ traits than with

_____ their origins.

traits (p. 478)

describing (p. 478)

explaining (p. 478)

According to Gordon Allport, the most important traits are those that relate to our _____. Allport called the traits that dominate a person's life _____ traits. He felt that few people possess these traits. Allport labeled those traits which influence much of our behavior _____ traits. The traits that are specific to a situation are _____ traits.

values (p. 478)

cardinal (p. 478)

central (p. 478)

secondary (p. 478)

Raymond B. Cattell has used sophisticated statistical techniques to identify traits. According to Cattell, the relatively unimportant clusters of behavior are called _____ traits, while the important underlying traits are _____ traits. There is considerable agreement among trait theorists that there are _____ basic personality traits.

surface (p. 479)

source (p. 479)

five (p. 479)

Some psychologists believe that behavior is determined by the situations people find themselves in rather than by the traits inside the person; this approach is called _____. A more recent compromise view, called _____ ____ _____ _____, suggests that behavior is influenced both by the characteristics of the person as well as by the situation. Interactionism is complicated by two factors: (1) evidence exists that people select situations that are consistent with their _____ _____; and (2) according to Bem, some people are influenced more than others by _____.

situationism (p. 479)

person ×

situation interactionism (p. 480)

personality characteristics (p. 480)

situations (p. 480)

Personality Assessment: Taking a Measure of the Person

Psychologists use personality assessment techniques to develop a picture of their client's personality in a relatively brief amount of time. The most universally used method of personality assessment is the _____. Although widely used, interviews have limitations; they are inherently _____, and they are _____ situations. An alternative to the interview is to watch the person's behavior in a natural or simulated situation; this is called the _____ method. In an attempt to make observational methods more objective, a variety of _____ _____ have been developed.

interview (p. 482)

subjective (p. 482)

artificial (p. 482)

observational (p. 482)

rating scales (p. 482)

A personality test that uses ambiguous stimuli to reveal the
contents of the client's unconscious mind is the _____
test. The individual is asked to make up a story about ambiguous
pictures in the _____ _____ _____
(TAT); symmetrical inkblots are used in the _____

_____ _____.

An example of an objective personality test is the

_____ _____ _____

_____ (MMPI-2). Recently, MMPI-2 scores have been

interpreted by computers; these have been criticized for being too

_____.

Research with projective tests indicates they are generally not
successful in distinguishing between individuals with and without
psychological problems. Although objective personality tests fare
somewhat better, _____ is recommended in interpreting
the results of personality tests.

projective (p. 482)

Thematic Apperception Test (p. 483)

Rorschach

inkblot test (p. 483)

Minnesota Multiphasic Personality

Inventory (p. 483)

objective (p. 483)

caution (p. 483)

Application of Psychology: Situational Influences on Personality in Everyday Life
Considerable research supports the importance of _____
in determining human behavior.

situations (p. 487)

CONCEPT CHECK

Fill in the missing components of the following concept box. The answers are shown below the box.

Major Theories of Personality

I. Theorist	II. Approach	III. Basic Components of Theory
a. Freud	a. Psychoanalytic	a. Emphasis on id, ego, superego; importance of displacement and identification; and five stages of personality development: oral, anal, phallic, latency, and genital.
b. Jung	b. Psychoanalytic	b.
c.	c. Psychoanalytic	c. Effort to overcome feelings of inferiority is primary emphasis.
d. Horney	d.	d. Anxious insecurity is the source of all conflicts.
e. Bandura	e. Social learning	e.
f.	f. Humanistic	f. Importance is placed on self, self-concept, and ideal self.
g. Maslow	g.	g. Self-actualization and peak experiences are primary components.
h. Allport	h. Trait theory	h.
i.	i. Trait theory	i. Emphasis is on traits, ability traits, and dynamic traits.

Answers:

IIIb. Emphasis on extroversion/introversion traits, personal unconscious, and collective unconscious.
Ic. Adler
IId. Psychoanalytic
IIIe. Personality is learned but reciprocally determined. This theory emphasizes the role of cognition in personality development.
If. Carl Rogers
IIg. Humanistic
IIIh. Concerns cardinal, central, and secondary traits.
Ii. Cattell

Multiple-Choice Questions

1. Which of the following helps define the term *personality?*
   a. characteristics that are typical for a person
   b. characteristics that make a person unique
   c. acting, thinking, and feeling
   d. all of the above
   (p. 460) LO 1

2. According to Freud, primitive instinctual motives and repressed memories are stored in the
   a. conscious mind
   b. preconscious mind
   c. unconscious mind
   d. superego
   (p. 461) LO 2

3. The executive of the personality, which operates according to the reality principle, is the
   a. id
   b. ego
   c. superego
   d. none of the above
   (p. 463) LO 3

4. According to Freud, which part of the mind is dominated by the pleasure principle?
   a. the id
   b. the ego
   c. superego
   d. the superid
   (p. 463) LO 3

5. According to Freud, which part of the mind corresponds roughly to conscience?
   a. the id
   b. the ego
   c. the superego
   d. the superid
   (p. 463) LO 3

6. All of the following are examples of sublimation *except*
   a. competing in contact sports
   b. robbing a bank
   c. painting nude portraits
   d. competing in business
   (p. 464) LO 4

7. According to Freud, the Oedipus complex and the Electra complex develop during the
   a. oral stage
   b. anal stage
   c. phallic stage
   d. genital stage
   (p. 466) LO 5

8. According to Freud, lasting relationships revolving around sexual and romantic interests are possible during what stage?
   a. the oral stage
   b. the anal stage
   c. the phallic stage
   d. the genital stage
   (p. 466) LO 5

9. According to Jung, the unconscious mind with which all humans are born is called the
   a. preconscious
   b. personal conscious
   c. collective unconscious
   d. none of the above
   (p. 468) LO 6

10. According to Adler, to develop a healthy personality it is necessary to learn to express
    a. the social interest
    b. the selfish interest
    c. the superego
    d. sexual and aggressive motives
    (p. 468) LO 7

11. According to Karen Horney
    a. Anxious insecurity is the source of all conflicts.
    b. Self-actualization is a basic human motive.
    c. Conflict is the inevitable result of the inborn motives of the id.
    d. We each possess both a personal unconscious and a collective unconscious.
       (p. 469) LO 8

12. To the social learning theorist, each of the following processes is important in the development of personality *except*
    a. classical conditioning
    b. operant conditioning
    c. modeling
    d. feelings of inferiority
       (p. 470) LO 9

13. According to Bandura, self-efficacy and self-regulation emphasize the importance of what determinant of behavior?
    a. learning
    b. traits
    c. situations
    d. cognitions
       (p. 471) LO 9

14. The mutual interaction between a person's behavior and his or her social learning environment is called
    a. reciprocal determination
    b. self-efficacy
    c. self-regulation
    d. efficient regulation
       (p. 472) LO 9

15. The humanistic view states that
    a. humans possess an inner-directedness
    b. humans possess an objective view of reality
    c. people should not frustrate themselves by continually trying to change and improve
    d. personality is dominated by an active unconscious
       (p. 473) LO 10

16. Rogers believes that differences between the self and the ideal self
    a. are uncomfortable
    b. lead to incongruence
    c. lead to unsymbolized feelings
    d. all of the above
       (p. 474) LO 11

17. According to Maslow, all of the following are characteristics of a self-actualizing person *except*
    a. a high level of moral development
    b. a romanticized view of people and life
    c. a commitment to some cause or task
    d. openness and honesty
       (p. 475) LO 12

18. Each of the following is associated with Maslow *except*
    a. self-actualization
    b. peak experiences
    c. social learning
    d. humanistic psychology
       (p. 475) LO 12

19. Which approach to psychology is referred to as the "third force"?
    a. psychoanalysis
    b. social learning theory
    c. humanistic theory
    d. trait theory
       (p. 473) LO 13

20. Humanistic psychologists believe that people are born _____, while social learning theorists believe that people are born

    _____.
    a. good, selfish
    b. selfish, good
    c. neutral, good
    d. good, neutral
       (p. 476) LO 13

21. Allport calls the traits that influence and organize much of our behavior
    a. cardinal traits
    b. central traits
    c. secondary traits
    d. source traits
       (p. 478) LO 14

22. According to Cattell, our effectiveness in satisfying motives such as intelligence and social skills is related to
    a. dynamic traits
    b. ability traits
    c. surface traits
    d. temperament traits
       (p. 479) LO 14

23. Each of the following is considered to be one of the "big five" personality traits *except*
    a. neuroticism
    b. extraversion
    c. conscientiousness
    d. friendliness
       (p. 479) LO 15

24. The view that behavior is influenced by characteristics of both the person and the situation is called
    a. situationism
    b. interactionism
    c. the trait approach
    d. a and b above
       (p. 479) LO 16

25. Which of the following is a problem with the use of interviews as a method of personality assessment?
    a. They are subjective.
    b. They are artificial situations.
    c. They may bring out atypical behavior.
    d. all of the above
       (p. 482) LO 17

26. Which method of personality assessment attempts to delve into unconscious areas?
    a. projective tests
    b. interviews
    c. objective tests
    d. none of the above
       (p. 482) LO 18

27. Which of the following is an example of a projective personality test?
    a. *Thematic Apperception Test (TAT)*
    b. *Minnesota Multiphasic Personalty Inventory (MMPI-2)*
    c. *Rorschach inkblot test*
    d. a and c above
       (p. 483) LO 18

28. Which of the following characterizes the MMPI-2?
    a. It consists of multiple-choice and fill-in questions.
    b. It is designed to reveal unconscious conflicts.
    c. It allows for objective interpretation of the results.
    d. The items are divided into 25 different "scales."
       (p. 483) LO 19

29. Which of the following statements is correct?
    a. Projective tests are generally good predictors of behavior.
    b. Psychologists generally agree about the usefulness of personality tests.
    c. Objective personality tests are generally more effective than projective tests in distinguishing among groups with different traits.
    d. Projective tests are generally more effective than objective tests in distinguishing among groups with different traits.
       (p. 483) LO 20

30. According to the text, most personality researchers agree that personality is influenced strongly by
    a. traits
    b. situations
    c. situations and personal characteristics
    d. human altruism
       (p. 485) LO 21

Multiple-Choice Answers

1. The answer is *D*. Although it might appear contradictory on the surface, the definition focuses on characteristics that are typical for the person, yet make the individual different from others.
2. The answer is *C*. According to Freud, the conscious mind contains our present awareness, but is actually just the "tip of the iceberg" of our mind. The preconscious mind, just below the surface, contains memories of which we are not currently conscious, but can easily be brought into our consciousness. The unconscious mind contains information that is not easily brought into consciousness.
3. The answer is *B*. According to Freud, the id is composed primarily of life instincts and death instincts. Life instincts consist largely of sexual and aggressive urges. The ego attempts to find realistic ways of satisfying the id's urges. The superego, the moral part of the mind, strives to attain a goal of perfection.
4. The answer is *A*. According to Freud, the id is the selfish beast of the mind, seeking immediate gratification and the avoidance of pain at any cost.
5. The answer is *C*. The superego develops as restrictions are placed on the actions of the id and ego, and parental punishment helps to establish the conscience.
6. The answer is *B*. Sublimation is a form of displacement in which a socially desirable goal is substituted for a socially harmful goal.
7. The answer is *C*. According to Freud, during the phallic stage, the genitals become the child's chief source of pleasure. It is during this stage that the child also experiences an intense love for the opposite-sex parent. These attractions bring about the Oedipus and Electra complexes.
8. The answer is *D*. The genital stage is the adult stage of development, characterized by concern about the welfare of loved ones in addition to oneself.
9. The answer is *C*. According to Jung, the personal unconscious contains threatening motives, conflicts, and information that have been repressed, while the collective unconscious is the unconscious mind with which all humans are born.
10. The answer is *A*. According to Adler, the social interest is an inborn motive to establish loving, helpful relationships with other people.
11. The answer is *A*. According to Horney, if parents are indifferent, harsh, or overprotective, the child will lose confidence in parental love and become anxiously insecure.
12. The answer is *D*. Social learning theorists hold that our personalities are formed primarily through interactions with other members of society. Thus, the basic learning concepts presented in chapter 5, such as classical and operant conditioning and modeling, are the important forces in shaping personality.
13. The answer is *D*. According to Bandura, important determinants of personality are the cognitions both about ourselves and our relationships with others.
14. The answer is *A*. According to Bandura, reciprocal determination implies that we play an active role in our own lives.
15. The answer is *A*. Humanistic psychology, sometimes called the third force in psychology (the first two are psychoanalysis and behaviorism), suggests that humans have freedom to make choices. Inner-directedness is an internal force that pushes people to grow and to improve.
16. The answer is *D*. According to Rogers, the self is the person you believe yourself to be, while the ideal self is the person you wish to be. Although Rogers' theory suggests that slight differences between the self and ideal self are okay, major discrepancies can lead to difficulties.
17. The answer is *B*. According to Maslow, self-actualizing people have an accurate, rather than a romanticized view of life.
18. The answer is *C*. Maslow was a humanistic psychologist who wrote about self-actualization and peak experiences. He was *not* considered a social learning theorist.
19. The answer is *C*. Humanistic theory burst on the psychological scene relatively late in psychology's history: in the 1950s, after psychoanalysis and behaviorism were already established forces.
20. The answer is *D*. Humanistic psychologists believe that the inner-directedness with which we are born is basically a positive force. Social learning theorists, however, judge our slate to be clean (neutral) at birth; we can learn to be good or bad.

21. The answer is *B*. According to Allport, cardinal traits are those that dominate a person's life. Relatively few people possess cardinal traits. Secondary traits are those that are more specific but less important in an overall view of a person's personality.

22. The answer is *B*. According to Cattell, dynamic traits are motivational traits relating to our values, while temperament traits are the largely inherited aspects of our behavior, such as energy level and speed of action. Surface traits are relatively unimportant clusters of behaviors that go together.

23. The answer is *D*. A considerable degree of consensus exists among trait theorists that there are five basic personality traits.

24. The answer is *B*. As a counterpoint to the trait approach offered by Allport and Cattell, situationism suggests that behavior is consistent only as long as situations (especially those regarding other people) remain consistent. Interactionism represents a compromise view between the trait and situationism approaches.

25. The answer is *D*. The interview is the most universally used, yet one of the most limited, methods for obtaining information about personality.

26. The answer is *A*. Projective tests ask the individual to interpret ambiguous stimuli. They assume that the individual will project his or her unconscious needs into the interpretation of the stimulus.

27. The answer is *D*. Projective personality tests use ambiguous stimuli in an effort to get the client to project his or her unconscious mind. The TAT asks the client to make up a story about ambiguous pictures. The Rorschach presents the client with a series of symmetrical inkblots.

28. The answer is *C*. The MMPI-2 is an objective test—no effort is made by the test to consider what the respondent meant by each answer. Items on the test are presented as true–false questions and are divided into 10 scales, each measuring a different aspect of personality.

29. The answer is *C*. Research suggests that projective test are generally not successful in distinguishing between individuals with and without psychological problems; objective tests fare somewhat better. The results suggest that caution be used in the interpretation of personality tests.

30. The answer is *C*. The research cited in the "Application" section strongly supports the influence of person × situational factors in determining personality.

Chapter **12** Stress and Health

Learning Objectives

1. Describe the goals of the field of health psychology.
2. Define stress and list the sources of stress.
3. Distinguish among the following types of conflict: approach-approach, avoidance-avoidance, approach-avoidance, and double approach-avoidance.
4. Discuss the relationship between life events and stress.
5. Describe the stages of Hans Selye's general adaptation syndrome: alarm reaction, resistance stage, and exhaustion stage.
6. Explain the relationship between stress and the immune system.
7. List and describe four major factors that influence reactions to stress.
8. Describe cognitive factors in stress reactions and distinguish between sensitizers and repressors.
9. Identify the characteristics of the Type A personality and explain the relationship between Type A personality and heart disease.
10. List and describe three effective methods of coping with stress.
11. List and describe three ineffective strategies of coping with stress.
12. Distinguish among the major defense mechanisms.
13. Describe progressive relaxation training.
14. Describe the challenges faced by psychologists in helping people to improve the quality of their diets.
15. Describe the relationship between health and regular aerobic exercise.
16. Explain the relationship between health practices and mortality.
17. (From the "Application" section) Summarize the role health psychology can play in the prevention and treatment of AIDS.

Chapter Overview

Health psychology is a relatively new field in psychology; health psychologists attempt to prevent health problems by helping individuals cope with stress and by helping to promote healthy lifestyles. Stress is any event that strains or exceeds an individual's capacity to cope. Among the major sources of stress in our lives are frustration, the inability to satisfy a motive, and conflict, the result of two or more incompatible motives. Four types of conflict are (1) approach-approach conflict, (2) avoidance-avoidance conflict, (3) approach-avoidance conflict, and (4) double approach-avoidance conflict. Pressure, an additional source of stress, arises from the threat of negative events. Another source of stress comes from the positive and the negative changes that occur in our lives. There is also growing evidence that environmental stresses, such as heat, cold, and air pollution, can be stressful. Reactions to stress are very similar whether the stress is physical or psychological. Selye has identified a consistent pattern of bodily responses to stress called the general adaptation syndrome. This syndrome consists of three stages: the alarm stage, the resistance stage, and the exhaustion stage. Stress affects our emotions, our immune system, our motivations, and our cognition.

Events are generally less stressful when we have had some prior experience with them, when they are predictable, when we have some control over them, and when we receive social support. The characteristics of individuals also affect their reactions to stress. Cognitive factors are important in our reaction to stress. Sensitizers and repressors react differently to stress.

Much research has been conducted on the Type A personality and its link to heart disease. Hostility seems to be the dangerous component of type A behavior.

Our efforts to cope with stress can be either effective or ineffective. Effective methods of coping with stress include removing the source of stress, cognitive coping, and managing our reactions to stress. Ineffective coping strategies include withdrawal, aggression, and the use of defense mechanisms.

A major goal of health psychology is to prevent health problems. Relaxation training is one technique used to achieve this goal. Health psychologists also seek to reduce health risks by helping individuals exercise properly, eat a healthy diet, and properly follow their medical treatments.

Some health psychologists seek to treat health problems. Psychologists have recently become involved with the AIDS epidemic through efforts to understand and control behavioral aspects of the transmission of AIDS and through efforts to slow the progress of the disease in those who are infected.

Key Terms Exercise

For each of the following exercises, match the key terms on the left with the correct definitions on the right. Page references to the text follow the terms so that you may refer to the text for any items you answer incorrectly or do not understand completely. You may check your responses immediately by referring to the answers that follow each exercise.

Stress: Challenges to Coping (I)

_____ 1. immune system (p. 497)
_____ 2. health psychology (p. 498)
_____ 3. stress (p. 498)
_____ 4. frustration (p. 498)
_____ 5. conflict (p. 498)

a. any event that strains or exceeds an individual's ability to cope
b. occurs when two or more motives cannot be satisfied because they interfere with each other
c. the complex bodily system of defense against illness
d. the field within psychology that seeks to promote healthy life-styles
e. occurs when we are unable to satisfy a motive

ANSWERS
1. c   4. e
2. d   5. b
3. a

Stress: Challenges to Coping (II)

_____ 1. approach-approach conflict (p. 498)
_____ 2. avoidance-avoidance conflict (p. 499)
_____ 3. approach-avoidance conflict (p. 499)
_____ 4. double approach-avoidance conflict (p. 500)
_____ 5. pressure (p. 501)
_____ 6. life events (p. 501)
_____ 7. general adaptation syndrome (G. A. S.) (p. 504)

a. the individual must choose between two negative outcomes
b. the changes in our lives that require readjustment and coping
c. the individual must choose between two alternatives that each contain both positive and negative consequences
d. conflict in which achieving a positive goal will produce a negative outcome as well
e. the individual must choose between two positive goals
f. a pattern of responses used by the body to ward off stress
g. the stress that arises from the threat of negative events

ANSWERS

1. e	5. g
2. a	6. b
3. d	7. f
4. c	

Factors that Influence Reactions to Stress

_____ 1. social support (p. 509)
_____ 2. person variables (p. 511)
_____ 3. repressors (p. 511)
_____ 4. sensitizers (p. 511)
_____ 5. Type A personality (p. 512)

a. differences between people that help to explain our different reactions to stress
b. persons who seek out information and think about stressful events
c. having somebody to whom one can talk, as well as receive advice and reassurance
d. persons who tend to avoid information and don't think about stressful events
e. a personality characterized by intense competitiveness, hostility, and a sense of time urgency

ANSWERS

1. c	4. b
2. a	5. e
3. d	

_____ 1. coping (p. 514)
_____ 2. defense mechanisms (p. 576)
_____ 3. progressive relaxation (p. 518)
_____ 4. alcohol abuse (p. 524)
_____ 5. acquired immune deficiency syndrome
      (AIDS) (p. 526)

a. a method of learning to deeply relax the muscles of the body
b. consumption of alcohol in any manner that is harmful to the individual
c. a disease caused by the human immune deficiency virus (HIV)
d. according to Freud, the ego's effort to discharge tension
e. efforts to deal with the source of stress or to control reactions to stress

ANSWERS

1. e   4. b
2. d   5. c
3. a

Guided Review

Stress: Challenges to Coping

The field that has emerged within psychology that seeks to promote healthy life-styles is called _____ _____.

     health psychology (p. 498)

     Any event that strains or exceeds an individual's capacity to cope is called _____. One major source of stress occurs when we are not able to satisfy a motive; this is called

     stress (p. 498)

_____. Another source of stress occurs when two motives cannot be satisfied because they interfere with one

     frustration (p. 498)

another; this is referred to as _____. There are four major types of conflict: (1) when the individual must choose between two positive goals of approximately equal value, this is

     conflict (p. 498)

a(n) _____-_____ conflict; (2) when we must choose between two or more negative outcomes, this is referred to

     approach-approach (p. 498)

as a(n) _____-_____ conflict; (3) when obtaining a positive goal necessitates a negative outcome, this is

     avoidance-avoidance (p. 499)

called a(n) _____-_____ conflict; (4) when an individual must choose between alternatives that contain both positive and negative consequences, this is termed a(n)

     approach-avoidance (p. 499)

_____ _____-_____ conflict.

     double approach-avoidance (p. 500)

A third source of stress arises from the threat of negative events; this is called _____. Another type of stress comes from changes in our lives, both positive and negative; these are referred to as _____ _____.

Negative life events, small daily hassles, and even _____ life events are all important sources of stress. Holmes and Rahe developed a scale that measures the amount of stress from life events in terms of _____ _____ _____. They found that Navy personnel who had experienced high levels of stress during the previous year were more likely to develop _____ problems. The scale, however, was developed using _____ subjects and may not apply equally well to _____. There is growing evidence that air temperature, air pollution, and other aspects of the _____ can be sources of stress.

Our reactions to stress are influenced by the following recent findings: (1) stress produces both _____ and _____ reactions; and (2) our reactions to stress are very similar whether the stress is _____ or _____.

Hans Selye has identified a pattern of bodily responses to stress called the _____ _____ _____. This syndrome consists of three stages: (1) the body begins to mobilize its resources in the _____ _____ stage; (2) the body's resources are fully mobilized in the _____ stage; and (3) the individual's resources are depleted and resistance to stress is lowered in the _____ stage. Although the GAS is helpful in dealing with emergencies and disease, prolonged stress can lead to dangerous changes in the _____ system. Although stress can harm the functioning of the immune system, in some cases _____ _____ can restore immune system functioning.

The psychological reactions to stress include changes in emotions, _____, and cognitions.

pressure (p. 501)

life events (p. 501)

positive (p. 502)

life
change units (p. 502)

medical (p. 502)

male (p. 502)

women (p. 502)

environment (p. 503)

psychological (p. 503)

physiological (p. 503)

physical (p. 503)/psychological (p. 503)

general adaptation
syndrome (p. 504)

alarm
reaction (p. 504)

resistance (p. 504)

exhaustion (p. 504)

cardiac (p. 506)

stress management (p. 506)

motivations (p. 506)

Factors that Influence Reactions to Stress

Stress reactions are generally less severe when the individual has had some _____ _____ with the stress. The impact of stress is also affected by the _____ and _____ levels of those experiencing stress. Also, events are generally less stressful when they are _____, when we perceive that we have some degree of _____ over the stress, and when we have _____ _____ from friends and family members. One of the important benefits of social support appears to be having someone in whom to _____; social support can also help us to make _____ decisions.

    Individuals also differ in the ways they _____ about stressful events. Those who seek information and think about stressful events are _____ while those who avoid information about stressors are _____. Repressors tend to cope well with stress in the short run, but are less effective in the _____ run.

    The person with a Type A personality shows many of the following characteristics: highly _____, works _____, workaholic, speaks _____, perfectionistic and _____, and hostile or _____. An important Type A characteristic appears to be a particular kind of _____; individuals who react to frustration with _____ or _____ aggression seem to be at risk for coronary heart disease. Type A behavior appears to be indirectly linked to heart disease through two major factors: high _____ _____ and _____.

prior experience (p. 508)

ages (p. 508)

developmental (p. 508)

predictable (p. 508)

control (p. 508)

social support (p. 509)

confide (p. 510)

stressful (p. 510)

think (p. 511)

sensitizers (p. 511)

repressors (p. 511)

long (p. 511)

competitive (p. 512)

hurriedly (p. 512)/loudly (p. 512)

demanding (p. 512)

aggressive (p. 512)

hostility (p. 513)

verbal (p. 513)/physical (p. 513)

blood pressure (p. 513)

cholesterol (p. 513)

Coping with Stress

Effective methods of coping with stress include removing the _____ of stress, _____ coping, and managing our _____ to stress. Psychological counseling involving all three methods has been successful in modifying

source (p. 514)/cognitive (p. 515)

reactions (p. 516)

_____ behavior. Ineffective coping strategies include _____, aggression, and the use of _____. According to Freud, the major defense mechanisms include (1) directing aggressive or sexual feelings toward someone safe, called _____, (2) converting impulses into sexually approved activities, called _____; (3) viewing one's own unacceptable desires as the desires of others, termed _____; (4) unconsciously transforming desires into the opposite desires, called _____ _____; (5) returning to an infantile pattern of behavior, termed _____; (6) "explaining away" stressful events, called _____; (7) keeping stressful, unacceptable desires out of consciousness, called _____; (8) blocking information that is threatening from conscious awareness, called _____; and (9) reducing the emotional nature of threatening events to cold logic, called _____.

A major goal of health psychology is to _____ health problems by helping individuals modify behaviors that create health risks. One example involves teaching individuals to relax. Individuals are taught to deeply relax their large body muscles in a technique called _____ _____ training. This technique has been found to be effective in treating _____, both tension and _____ headaches, and high blood pressure. Relaxation training has also been shown to reduce the recurrence of genital _____ infections.

It is increasingly clear that diet plays an important role in our health, but most Americans do not eat a healthy diet. Although part of the reason is _____, psychologists have sometimes found difficulty in getting people to change their diets. Likewise, although the health benefits of regular exercise are well established, the majority of Americans do not get regular _____ exercise. Research suggests that the following factors can help individuals adhere to a regular exercise program; social _____, setting _____ _____, and avoiding excessively _____ exercise. Other health

Type A (p. 516)

withdrawal (p. 516)/defense mechanisms (p. 516)

displacement (p. 517)

sublimation (p. 517)

projection (p. 517)

reaction formation (p. 517)

regression (p. 517)

rationalization (p. 517)

repression (p. 517)

denial (p. 517)

intellectualization (p. 517)

prevent (p. 518)

progressive relaxation (p. 518)

insomnia (p. 519)/migraine (p. 519)

herpes (p. 519)

ignorance (p. 519)

aerobic (p. 521)

support (p. 521)/personal goals (p. 521)

strenuous (p. 521)

psychologists help implement programs to help patients comply with their _____ _____ .

     doctor's orders (p. 521)

In the future, health psychology may play an important role in fighting _____ disease, cancer, and _____ .

     heart (p. 523)/AIDS (p. 523)

An important issue for the field of health psychology is this: How much impact can _____ factors have on our health?

     psychological (p. 523)

Research done on adults in Alameda county suggests that changes in life-style can produce dramatic improvements in _____ and _____ . Psychologists can help

     health (p. 524)/longevity (p. 524)

moderate health care costs by helping to _____ serious

     prevent (p. 524)

health problems and by providing effective psychological services.

Application of Psychology: The Prevention and Treatment of AIDS

AIDS is caused by the human _____ _____

     immune deficiency (p. 526)

virus (HIV). The period from infection to full-blown AIDS averages _____ years. According to the World Health

     8 to 10 (p. 526)

Organization, as of July, 1990, _____ million people had

     8 to 10 (p. 526)

been infected with HIV. HIV infection leads to the destruction of immune cells called _____ , thus rendering useless the

     lymphocytes (p. 526)

important _____ of the immune system. The HIV virus

     B-cells (p. 526)

is spread through _____ _____ . The most

     bodily fluids (p. 526)

common means of transmission is through _____

     sexual

_____ . Other modes of transmission include

     intercourse (p. 526)

_____ drug use and transmission from an infected

     intravenous (p. 527)

mother to her infant during birth. There is virtually no chance of acquiring AIDS if a person is not sexually active or is involved in a completely _____ sexual relationship with a partner who

     monogamous (p. 527)

is not infected with HIV and does not use intravenous drugs. A study conducted by Kelly demonstrates the effectiveness of _____ for individuals engaging in high-risk sexual

     counseling (p. 527)

behaviors. In the future, _____-_____

     stress-management (p. 528)

training may prove useful in slowing the progress of the HIV infection.

CONCEPT CHECK

Fill in the missing components of the following concept box. The answers are shown below the box.

Sources of Stress

I. Name	II. Description
a.	a. Inability to satisfy a motive.
b. Conflict	b.
c.	c. The threat of negative events.
d. Life events	d.

Answers

Ia.   Frustration
IIb.   Occurs when two motives cannot be satisfied because they interfere with each other. Four major types include approach-approach, avoidance-avoidance, approach-avoidance, and double approach-avoidance.
Ic.   Pressure
IId.   Negative life events, small daily hassles, and even positive life events are all important sources of stress.

Multiple-Choice Questions

1. A health psychologist would agree with all of the following *except*
   a. The functioning of the body is linked to psychological factors.
   b. Health psychologists seek to promote healthy life-styles.
   c. Stress is less of a factor in health psychology than it was a few years ago.
   d. Our patterns of behavior have direct impact on our health.
   (p. 498) LO 1

2. Stress has been linked to
   a. heart disease
   b. strokes
   c. decreased immunity to infections
   d. all of the above
   (p. 498) LO 2

3. A source of stress characterized by the inability to satisfy a motive is called
   a. conflict
   b. life events
   c. frustration
   d. pressure
   (p. 498) LO 2

4. Conflicts that require choosing "the lesser of two evils" are
   a. approach-approach conflicts
   b. avoidance-avoidance conflicts
   c. approach-avoidance conflicts
   d. double-approach-avoidance conflicts
   (p. 499) LO 3

5. As Jennifer approaches the end of her senior year in college, she is excited about the prospects of graduating but scared about being "on her own." Jennifer is experiencing
   a. an approach-avoidance conflict
   b. an approach-approach conflict
   c. an avoidance-avoidance conflict
   d. the exhaustion stage of the general adaptation syndrome
   (p. 499) LO 3

6. The Holmes and Rahe Social Readjustment Rating Scale explores the relationship between stressful life events and
   a. mental illness
   b. physical illness
   c. daily hassles
   d. success in daily living
   (p. 502) LO 4

7. In which stage of the general adaptation syndrome is resistance to stress lowered?
   a. the resistance stage
   b. the exhaustion stage
   c. the alarm stage
   d. the defensive stage
   (p. 505) LO 5

8. In which stage of the GAS are the body's resources fully mobilized and resistant to stress?
   a. alarm reaction
   b. resistance stage
   c. exhaustion stage
   d. any of the above
   (p. 504) LO 5

9. Research suggests that immune system functioning can be affected by
   a. stress
   b. stress management
   c. depression
   d. all of the above
   (p. 506) LO 6

10. Which of the following factors is known to depress immune system functioning?
    a. heavy alcohol consumption
    b. stress
    c. depression
    d. all of the above
    (p. 506) LO 6

11. In general, stress events are less stressful when they are
    a. predictable
    b. unpredictable
    c. controllable
    d. a and c
    (p. 508) LO 7

12. Research on sharing negative feelings with others ("getting it off your chest") found that participants
    a. had elevated blood pressure immediately after venting their feelings
    b. reported feeling better immediately after venting their feelings
    c. were less ill and visited the health center less often during the following six months
    d. a and c above
    (p. 510) LO 7

13. Each of the following is true of social support *except*
    a. Individuals with social support react to stress with less depression and anxiety
    b. The ability to confide in others is an important benefit of social support.
    c. There is little proven health benefit in sharing negative feelings with others.
    d. Social support can help us when we have to make stressful decisions.
    (p. 510) LO 7

14. According to Taylor's research on women coping with breast cancer, the most successful strategies involved
   a. finding a positive lesson in the experience
   b. developing a sense of positive control
   c. finding favorable comparisons
   d. all of the above
      (p. 515) LO 8

15. Research on handling stress by repressors and sensitizers indicates that
   a. repressors do better in the long run
   b. sensitizers do better in the long run
   c. sensitizers do better in the short run
   d. there are no significant differences between repressors and sensitizers
      (p. 511) LO 8

16. "If I ignore it, maybe it'll go away." This reaction to a stressful event is most likely to be spoken by
   a. sensitizers
   b. repressors
   c. cognitive appraisers
   d. interactionists
      (p. 511) LO 8

17. Which of the following components of type A behavior has a strong negative effect on cardiac functioning?
   a. hostile/verbally aggressive
   b. hostile/suspicious
   c. highly competitive
   d. perfectionistic
      (p. 512) LO 9

18. Research on Type A behavior suggests that the link to heart disease may stem from
   a. high blood pressure
   b. high cholesterol
   c. poor dietary habits
   d. a and b above
      (p. 513) LO 9

19. After being promoted to department head, Bill found the job to be uncomfortable and highly stressful. Ultimately, Bill resigned from the position and returned to his former job, where he reported being much happier. Which method of coping with stress did Bill use?
   a. managing stress reactions, an effective coping method
   b. withdrawal, an ineffective coping method
   c. removing stress, an effective coping method
   d. excessive use of defense mechanisms, an ineffective coping method
      (p. 515) LO 10

20. Each of the following is an effective method of coping with stress *except*
   a. removing stress
   b. cognitive coping
   c. defense mechanisms
   d. managing stress reactions
      (p. 515) LO 10

21. Each of the following is considered to be an ineffective method of coping with stress *except*
   a. withdrawal
   b. aggression
   c. use of defense mechanisms
   d. cognitive coping
      (p. 516) LO 11

22. The process of blocking out of consciousness any upsetting thoughts is the defense mechanism called
   a. projection
   b. reaction formation
   c. denial
   d. intellectualization
      (p. 517) LO 12

23. When Ken called Barbie to ask her for a date, Barbie said, "I'm sorry, but I think I'm busy for the rest of my life!" Ken has decided that he is really relieved because Barbie has lots of faults anyway. Which defense mechanism is he using?
    a. displacement
    b. repression
    c. rationalization
    d. suppression
    (p. 517) (LO 12)

24. Which of the following has been successfully treated with progressive relaxation?
    a. insomnia
    b. tension and migraine headaches
    c. high blood pressure
    d. all of the above
    (p. 519) LO 13

25. Research suggests that when people are presented with accurate information concerning proper eating habits
    a. most people permanently change their eating habits
    b. many people change their eating habits only briefly
    c. few people change their eating habits
    d. none of the above
    (p. 519) LO14

26. According to psychologists, which of the following would be good advice for keeping a commitment to an exercise program?
    a. social support
    b. setting clear personal goals
    c. avoiding excessively strenuous exercise
    d. all of the above
    (p. 521) LO 15

27. In which of the following ways can psychologists help reduce health care costs?
    a. by helping to prevent serious problems
    b. by reducing recurrences of certain medical problems
    c. by increased use of clinical psychologists
    d. all of the above
    (p. 524) LO 16

28. AIDS impairs the body's immune system by destroying or disabling the immune cells called
    a. T-4 helper cells
    b. B-cells
    c. DNA
    d. a and b above
    (p. 526) LO 17

29. Health psychologists can lessen the negative impact of the AIDS epidemic by
    a. helping individuals change their high-risk behaviors
    b. helping to cure those with the HIV infection by counseling
    c. teaching stress management techniques to help slow the progression of AIDS
    d. a and c above
    (p. 527) LO 17

30. The study of health practices in Alameda County suggested
    a. health psychologists can be effective at getting people to increase the number of positive health practices
    b. a strong relationship between health practices and mortality
    c. that stress and life-style practices can minimize the impact of infectious diseases
    d. that sleeping and exercise were not strongly related to improving health
    (p. 523) LO 16

1. The answer is *C*. According to the text, stress is "perhaps the key factor that must be understood if psychology is to improve our health and happiness."
2. The answer is *D*. Research has implicated stress in a wide variety of diseases and maladies in addition to those listed in the question.
3. The answer is *C*. While frustration refers to the inability to satisfy a motive, conflict refers to a situation in which motives cannot be satisfied because they interfere with one another.
4. The answer is *B*. Situations in which we are faced with having to choose between two or more negative outcomes are called avoidance-avoidance conflicts.
5. The answer is *A*. Approach-approach conflict refers to situations in which the individual must choose between two positive goals; in avoidance-avoidance conflict, the individual must choose between two negative outcomes (the expression "stuck between a rock and a hard place" applies).
6. The answer is *B*. The scale was originally presented to Navy personnel. Holmes and Rahe found that those who reported higher levels of life stress were more likely to develop medical problems than subjects reporting lower levels of life stress.
7. The answer is *B*. According to Selye, the body's resources begin to be mobilized in the stage called the alarm reaction. During the second stage, called the resistance stage, the body's resources are fully mobilized. In the final stage, the exhaustion stage, the individual's resources have become exhausted; thus resistance to stress is lowered.
8. The answer is *B*. The resistance stage, the second in the GAS, fully mobilizes the body's resources but leaves it vulnerable to further stress.
9. The answer is *D*. The negative impact of stress on the immune system is most striking in those who become severely depressed under stress.
10. The answer is *D*. Although these factors can have an adverse impact on immune system functioning, stress management can actually restore immune system functioning in some cases.
11. The answer is *D*. Stressful events are less stressful both when they are predictable *and* when the individual can exert some control over the stress.
12. The answer is *D*. Although student participants felt sad and experienced a rise in blood pressure immediately after venting their feelings, the same students reported being ill less in the following six months. The research supports the value of "getting it off your chest."
13. The answer is *C*. The study by Pennebaker and Beall described in the text on page 510 suggests that there are positive health benefits in sharing negative feelings with others.
14. The answer is *D*. Each of these coping strategies is a cognitive strategy. Thus, Taylor has found that the interpretation of the stress of breast cancer can help reduce the stress.
15. The answer is *B*. Repressors tend to cope effectively with stress in the short run, but they pay a price for their denial in the long run.
16. The answer is *B*. Whereas sensitizers actively seek out information and think about stressful events, repressors tend to avoid information and do not think about stressors. Generally, repressors tend to cope with stress better in the short run, but actually cope less effectively in the long run.
17. The answer is *A*. While characteristics of the Type A personality include each of those listed in the question, research suggests that those who express their hostility with verbal or physical aggression are at risk for coronary heart disease.
18. The answer is *D*. One theory advanced to explain this suggests that Type A personalities react physiologically more to stress than do others.
19. The answer is *C*. Three effective methods for coping with stress are removing stress, cognitive coping, and managing stress reactions. When Bill resigned his position, he removed the source of stress.
20. The answer is *C*. The use of defense mechanisms is often an ineffective method for coping with stress.
21. The answer is *D*. Cognitive coping, or changing how we think about stress, is considered to be an effective method for coping with stress.

22. The answer is *C*. Denial is commonly seen with individuals who have problems with health, drugs and relationships.
23. The answer is *C*. Ken has successfully "explained" or justified to himself and others why he is relieved about Barbie. As the text suggests, the use of defense mechanisms, when used in moderation, can be relatively harmless. Problems begin when people rely too heavily on defense mechanisms.
24. The answer is *D*. Progressive relaxation training teaches people to deeply relax their large body muscles.
25. The answer is *B*. Thus far, most research suggests that psychologists have been able to get people to change their unhealthy eating habits for only a limited period of time.
26. The answer is *D*. As is true with changing unhealthy eating habits, many people know about the importance of regular exercise, but adhering to behavioral changes seems to be difficult.
27. The answer is *D*. Research has shown that providing psychological services can help reduce the cost of medical care.
28. The answer is *D*. HIV invades the T-4 Helper cells, thereby disabling the B-cells from identifying and destroying hostile bacteria and viruses.
29. The answer is *D*. While psychologists have had limited success thus far in helping people to change their high-risk behavior and in teaching skills to slow the progression of the disease, there is as yet no cure for AIDS.
30. The answer is *B*. The Alameda study, which isolated seven positive health practices, found that those who engaged in few of these practices tended to have higher death rates than those who engaged in most of the practices.

Chapter **13** **Abnormal Behavior**

Learning Objectives

1. Define abnormal behavior and distinguish between the continuity hypothesis and the discontinuity hypothesis.
2. Discuss the historical views of abnormal behavior, including supernatural theories, biological theories, and psychological theories.
3. Describe the issues involved in the use of the term *insanity*.
4. Distinguish among simple phobias, social phobias, and agoraphobia.
5. Distinguish between generalized anxiety disorder and panic anxiety disorder.
6. Describe the causes and effects of posttraumatic stress disorder.
7. Distinguish between obsessions and compulsions.
8. Identify the following somatoform disorders: somatization disorders, hypochondriasis, conversion disorders, and somatoform pain disorders.
9. Distinguish between psychogenic amnesia and psychogenic fugue.
10. Describe the symptoms of depersonalization.
11. Discuss the symptoms of multiple personality.
12. Describe the characteristics of major depression and discuss the importance of cognitive factors in depression.
13. Discuss the results of research into postpartum depression.
14. Identify the characteristics of bipolar affective disorder.
15. Identify and describe the three major areas of abnormality in schizophrenia.
16. Distinguish among the following types of schizophrenia: paranoid schizophrenia, disorganized schizophrenia, and catatonic schizophrenia.
17. Discuss delusional disorder and describe how it differs from schizophrenia.
18. Describe the characteristics of the personality disorders, including schizoid personality disorder and antisocial personality disorder.
19. (From the "Application" section) Discuss the psychological implications of homelessness and physician-assisted suicide.

Chapter Overview

Abnormal behavior includes actions, thoughts, and feelings that are harmful to the person and/or to others. Historically, the causes of abnormal behavior have been explained by supernatural theories, biological theories, and psychological theories. Contemporary psychologists view abnormal behavior as a natural phenomenon with both biological and psychological causes. The term *insanity* is a legal term with several different meanings.

Anxiety disorders, characterized by excessive anxiety, include the following: (1) phobias, which are intense and unrealistic fears; (2) general anxiety disorders, which are characterized by free-floating anxiety; (3) panic anxiety disorders, which involve attacks of intense anxiety; (4) posttraumatic stress disorders, a reaction to the stress of war or rape, and (5) obsessive-compulsive disorders, characterized by persistent, anxiety-provoking thoughts and by urges to repeatedly engage in a behavior.

Somatoform disorders are conditions in which the individual experiences symptoms of health problems that are psychological rather than physical in origin. One type of somatoform disorder is referred to as somatization disorder. This disorder involves multiple minor symptoms of illness that indirectly create a high risk of medical complications; hypochondriasis is characterized by excessive concern with health. Another type of somatoform disorder is the conversion disorder. This involves serious specific somatic symptoms without any physical cause; somatoform pain disorders involve pain without any physical cause.

In the various types of dissociative disorders, there is a change in memory, perception, or identity. For example, psychogenic amnesia and fugue states are characterized by memory loss that has psychological rather than physical causes. Individuals experiencing depersonalization feel that they or their surroundings have become distorted or unreal. Individuals who exhibit multiple personalities appear to possess more than one personality in the same body.

Affective disorders are disturbances of mood. The individual experiencing major depression is deeply unhappy and lethargic. In the condition known as bipolar affective disorder, periods of mania alternate irregularly with periods of severe depression.

Schizophrenia involves three major areas of abnormality: cognitive disorders, emotional disturbances, and social withdrawal. The major types of schizophrenia include (1) paranoid schizophrenia, in which the individual holds false beliefs or delusions—usually of grandeur and persecution—that seriously distort reality; (2) disorganized schizophrenia, which is characterized by extreme withdrawal from normal human contact, fragmented delusions and hallucinations, and a shallow "silliness" of emotion; and (3) catatonic schizophrenia, which is marked by stupors during which the individual may remain in the same posture for long periods of time. Psychologists believe that schizophrenia may have biological causes such as deterioration of the cortex and abnormal prenatal development. Psychologists also view stress as a trigger for the disorder in those who are genetically predisposed to schizophrenia.

Personality disorders are thought to result from personalities that developed improperly during childhood rather than from breakdowns under stress. Schizoid personality disorders are characterized by a loss of interest in proper dress and social contact, a lack of emotion, and an inability to hold regular jobs. The antisocial personality frequently violates social rules and laws, is often violent, takes advantage of others, and feels little guilt about it.

Two important societal issues that have important implications for psychology are homelessness and physician-assisted suicide.

Key Terms Exercise

For each of the following exercises, match the key terms on the left with the correct definitions on the right. Page references to the text follow the terms so that you may refer to the text for any items you answer incorrectly or do not understand completely. You may check your responses immediately by referring to the answers that follow each exercise.

Anxiety Disorders

_____ 1. anxiety disorders (p. 542)
_____ 2. phobia (p. 542)
_____ 3. agoraphobia (p. 542)
_____ 4. generalized anxiety disorder (p. 543)
_____ 5. panic anxiety disorder (p. 543)
_____ 6. obsessive-compulsive disorders (p. 546)

a. a phobic fear of leaving home or other familiar places
b. disorders involving anxiety-provoking thoughts and irresistible urges
c. an uneasy sense of general tension and apprehension that is almost always present
d. psychological disorders that involve excessive levels of nervousness, tension, worry, and anxiety
e. an intense, irrational fear
f. an anxiety pattern in which long periods of calm are broken by an attack of anxiety

ANSWERS

1. d	4. c
2. e	5. f
3. a	6. b

Somatoform Disorders/Dissociative Disorders

_____ 1. somatoform disorders (p. 546)
_____ 2. somatization disorders (p. 546)
_____ 3. hypochondriasis (p. 547)
_____ 4. conversion disorders (p. 547)
_____ 5. somatoform pain disorders (p. 548)
_____ 6. dissociative disorders (p. 548)

a. chronic symptoms of somatic illness that have no physical cause
b. disorders in which the individual experiences symptoms of physical health problems that have psychological causes
c. somatoform disorders characterized by serious somatic symptoms, such as blindness and deafness
d. characterized by excessive concerns about one's health
e. somatoform disorders characterized by a specific and chronic pain
f. conditions involving sudden cognitive changes, such as changes in memory, perception, or identity

ANSWERS

1. b	4. c
2. a	5. e
3. d	6. f

Mood Disorders/Schizophrenia/Personality Disorders

_____ 1. mood disorders (p. 551)
_____ 2. major depression (p. 551)
_____ 3. bipolar affective disorder (p. 554)
_____ 4. schizophrenia (p. 555)
_____ 5. paranoid schizophrenia (p. 556)
_____ 6. delusional disorder (p. 556)
_____ 7. disorganized schizophrenia (p. 556)
_____ 8. catatonic schizophrenia (p. 557)
_____ 9. personality disorders (p. 558)
_____ 10. schizoid-personality disorder (p. 558)
_____ 11. antisocial personality disorder (p. 558)

a. a psychological disorder involving cognitive and emotional disturbance and social withdrawal
b. an affective disorder characterized by episodes of deep unhappiness, loss of interest in life, and other symptoms
c. psychological disorders involving disturbances of mood
d. a condition characterized by periods of mania alternating with periods of severe depression
e. a type of schizophrenia characterized by shallow "silliness," extreme social withdrawal, fragmented delusions and hallucinations
f. a type of schizophrenia in which the individual spends long periods of time in an inactive, statuelike state
g. a type of schizophrenia characterized by false beliefs or delusions that seriously distort reality
h. a disorder characterized by delusions of grandeur and persecution that are more logical than those of paranoid schizophrenics and involve no hallucinations
i. a personality disorder characterized by smooth social skills and a lack of guilt about violating social rules and laws
j. psychological disorders believed to result from personalities that develop improperly in childhood
k. a personality disorder characterized by blunted emotions, little interest in social relationships, and social withdrawal

ANSWERS

1. c.	7. e
2. b	8. f
3. d	9. j
4. a	10. i
5. g	11. k
6. h	

Guided Review

Abnormal Behavior

Actions, thoughts, and feelings that are harmful to the person or to

others are called _____ behaviors. This definition is   abnormal (p. 536)

_____ because (1) it is difficult to decide whether an   subjective (p. 536)

individual's problems are _____ enough to be harmful,   severe (p. 536)

and (2) it is difficult to define what is _____ .   harmful (p. 536)

    The belief that abnormal behavior is just a more severe form

of normal psychological problems is called the _____   continuity (p. 536)

hypothesis; the belief that abnormal behavior is entirely different

from normal psychological problems is called the _____   discontinuity (p. 536)

hypothesis.

    The oldest writings about behavior indicate that abnormal

behavior was believed to be caused by _____   evil

_____ . In medieval Europe, abnormal behavior was   spirits (p. 536)

treated by _____ . Hippocrates believed that abnormal   exorcism (p. 537)

behavior resulted from an imbalance of the body's

_____ . Although inaccurate, Hippocrates' theory   humors (p. 537)

influenced other scientists to search for _____ causes of   natural (p. 537)

abnormal behavior.

    In the 1800s, Krafft-Ebing's discovery of the relationship

between paresis and syphilis contributed to the formation of the

medical specialty of _____ . Krafft-Ebing's discovery led   psychiatry (p. 538)

to expectations that other forms of abnormal behavior also had

_____ causes.   biological (p. 438)

    Pythagoras, an ancient Greek, believed that abnormal behavior

was caused by _____ factors. Although others   psychological (p. 538)

throughout history have also advocated psychological factors, this

approach did not become widely accepted until _____   Freud's (p. 538)

theory was published. The contemporary view is that both

_____ and _____ factors are involved in   biological (p. 538)/psychological (p. 538)

many psychological disorders.

    The term _____ is a _____ term. The   insanity (p. 540)/legal (p. 540)

term *insane* has three different legal meanings: (1) as a

_____ defense in some states, not guilty by reason of insanity; (2) in hearings regarding _____ to stand trial; and (3) in hearings to determine involuntary _____ to mental institutions.

Ten to fifteen million Americans experience the disruptive levels of anxiety called _____ _____. An anxiety disorder characterized by intense, irrational fear is called a _____. A specific phobic fear is called a _____ phobia, while a phobic fear of social interactions is called a _____ phobia. the most damaging of all the phobias involves a phobic fear of leaving familiar places; this is termed _____.

While phobias are linked to specific situations, free-floating anxiety is experienced by individuals with _____ _____ _____. People who experience this anxiety feel uncomfortable because of its almost _____ _____.

An anxiety in which periods of calm are broken by an anxiety attack is called _____ _____ _____. Many individuals experience an occasional _____ attack. While uncomfortable, they should not be a serious concern unless they are _____ or severe.

Reactions that many soldiers experience to the stress of war are called _____ _____ _____. Another highly stressful event that often leads to PTSD is _____.

Obsessive-compulsive disorders are two separate problems that often occur together. Anxiety-provoking thoughts that will not go away are called _____, while irresistible urges to engage in irrational behaviors are termed _____.

Disorders in which the individual experiences the symptoms of physical health problems that have psychological causes are called _____ disorders. There are four types of somatoform disorders, which are presented on the following page.

1. Intensely and chronically uncomfortable conditions that involve many symptoms of bodily illness are called _____ disorders.

   somatization (p. 546)

2. A mild form of somatization disorder marked by excessive concern for health is called _____.

   hypochondriasis (p. 547)

3. Dramatic somatoform disorders which involve serious symptoms, such as functional blindness and paralysis are _____ disorders. Some individuals with conversion disorders are not upset by their condition; this characteristic is known as ____ _____ _____.

   conversion (p. 547)

   la belle indifference (p. 548)

   Conversion disorders usually begin during periods of acute stress and generally provide some kind of _____ to the individual.

   benefit (p. 548)

4. Finally, disorders which cause pain that has no physical cause are called _____ _____ disorders.

   somatoform pain (p. 548)

   Conditions in which there are sudden cognitive changes, such as changes in memory or perception, are called _____ disorders. A dissociative disorder in which there is a memory loss that is psychologically caused is called _____ _____. A state of amnesia that is so complete the individual cannot remember his or her previous life is a _____ _____. The fugue episode may also involve a period of "wandering." Another type of dissociative disorder in which the individual feels that his or her body has become distorted or unreal, or that the surroundings have become unreal, is called _____. Experiences of depersonalization are common in _____ adults. Individuals who shift abruptly from one "personality" to another are exhibiting a rare dissociative disorder called _____ _____.

   dissociative (p. 548)

   psychogenic

   amnesia (p. 548)

   psychogenic fugue (p. 548)

   depersonalization (p. 549)

   young (p. 549)

   multiple personality (p. 549)

Mood Disorders

The two primary types of mood disorders are _____ and _____.

   depression (p. 551)

   mania (p. 551)

   Extreme unhappiness and loss of interest in life are symptoms of _____ _____. This disorder affects about

   major depression (p. 551)

10 million Americans. Most cases of depression are mild; severe cases may require _____. hospitalization (p. 552)

Aaron Beck and others emphasize the importance of _____ in emotional problems. Beliefs that trouble many depressed people are _____ demands. Research has found that, under some circumstances, people who are depressed engage in _____ cognitive distortions than those who are not depressed.

cognition (p. 552)

perfectionistic (p. 553)

fewer (p. 553)

Episodes of major depression in women that are associated with the birth of a child are called _____ _____. Recent research has questioned whether the postpartum period is truly a time of _____ depression for women.

postpartum
depression (p. 554)
increased (p. 554)

Individuals who have periods of mania that alternate irregularly with periods of severe depression are experiencing _____ _____ disorder. The portion of this experience characterized by euphoria and unrealistic optimism is called _____.

bipolar affective (p. 554)

mania (p. 554)

Schizophrenia

Schizophrenia involves the following three characteristics:
(1) _____ disorders, (2) _____ disturbance, and (3) _____ withdrawal. According to the DSM-IV, there are three subtypes of schizophrenia: (1) _____ schizophrenia, characterized by false beliefs, delusions of grandeur, delusions of persecution, and hallucinations; (2) _____ schizophrenia, characterized by extreme withdrawal from normal human contact and a shallow "silliness" of emotion; and (3) _____ schizophrenia, an inactive, statuelike state, frequently broken by periods of agitation.

cognitive (p. 555)/emotional (p. 555)

social (p. 555)
paranoid (p. 556)

disorganized (p. 556)

catatonic (p. 557)

Paranoid delusions of grandeur and persecution characterize a rare disorder called _____ disorder. In this disorder, the delusions are less illogical and there are no hallucinations.

delusional (p. 557)

Personality Disorders

Although schizophrenia and other disorders are breakdowns in relatively normal personalities, the results of improperly developed personalities are called _____ _____. All personality disorders share these characteristics: (1) they begin _____ in life; (2) they are _____ to the person or to others; and (3) they are very _____ to treat. One example, _____ _____ _____, is characterized by extreme social withdrawal and a loss of interest in social conventions. Another personality disorder, in which the individual has smooth social skills but violates social rules and takes advantage of others without feeling guilty, is called _____ _____ _____. The primary harmfulness of this disorder is in the damage done to _____.

    Other personality disorders, as listed in the DSM-IV, are (1) characterized by few friendships and strange ideas, called the _____ personality disorder; (2) suspiciousness, irritability, and coldness, called _____ personality disorder; (3) self-centered and manipulating by exaggerating feelings, called the _____ personality disorder; (4) unrealistic sense of self-importance, requiring constant attention and praise, called the _____ personality disorder; (5) impulsive and unpredictable with unstable relationships, called the _____ personality disorder; (6) extremely shy and withdrawn and low self-esteem, called the _____ personality disorder; (7) passive dependence on others for support and low self-esteem, called the _____ personality disorder; (8) perfectionistic, dominating, and excessively devoted to work, called the _____-_____ personality disorder; and (9) while not overtly aggressive, nonetheless resists the demands of others by forgetting and procrastinating, called the _____-_____ personality disorder.

personality disorders (p. 558)

early (p. 558)/disturbing (p. 558)

difficult (p. 558)

schizoid personality

disorder (p. 558)

antisocial personality

disorder (p. 559)

others (p. 559)

schizotypal (p. 559)

paranoid (p. 559)

histrionic (p. 560)

narcissistic (p. 560)

borderline (p. 650)

avoidant (p. 560)

dependent (p. 560)

obsessive-compulsive (p. 560)

passive-aggressive (p. 560)

Application of Psychology: Abnormal Psychology and Civil Liberties

Research has found a high rate of serious psychological disorders

among _____ people. Psychologists are divided on the   homeless (p. 562)

issue of whether psychological treatment for homeless people with

psychological disorders should be _____ or   mandatory (p. 563)

_____ . Another issue with strong implications for civil   voluntary (p. 563)

liberties is _____-_____ _____ .   physician-assisted suicide (p. 563)

CONCEPT CHECK

Fill in the missing components of the following box. The answers are shown on the following page.

Major Disorders

I. Category	II. Description	III. Examples
a. Anxiety	a. The person suffering from anxiety is nervous, tense, and worried.	a. Phobias, generalized and panic anxiety disorders, PTSD, and obsessive-compulsive.
b. Somatoform	b. The individual experiences physical health problems that have psychological rather than physical causes.	b.
c. Dissociative disorders	c.	c. Amnesia, fugue, depersonalization, and multiple personality.
d. Mood disorders	d. Individual has disturbances of positive or negative moods.	d.
e. Schizophrenia	e.	e. Paranoid, disorganized, and catatonic.
f. Personality disorders	f. Beginning early in life, these individuals are disturbing to themselves or others and are difficult to treat.	f.

Answers

IIIb.   Somatization, hypochondriasis, conversion disorder, and somatization pain disorder.
IIc.   Those suffering from a somatoform disorder may have sudden alterations in cognition, characterized by a change in memory, perception, or identity.
IIId.   Major depression, bipolar disorder.
IIe.   Persons with schizophrenia experience cognitive disorders, emotional disturbance, and social withdrawal.
IIIf.   Schizoid, antisocial, schizotypal, paranoid, histrionic, narcissistic.

Multiple-Choice Questions

1. In what ways are subjective judgments used to define abnormal behavior?
   a. deciding whether problems are severe enough to be harmful
   b. deciding what is harmful
   c. a and b above
   d. none of the above
      (p. 536) LO 1

2. Throughout history the prevailing view of the cause of abnormal behavior was
   a. evil spirits
   b. biological theories
   c. psychological theories
   d. none of the above
      (p. 536) LO 2

3. Each of the following is an application of the term insanity *except*
   a. not guilty by reason of insanity
   b. insanity due to genetic inheritance
   c. incompetent to stand trial
   d. involuntary commitment
      (p. 540) LO 3

4. Mary feels extremely uncomfortable walking outside her home, even to check the mail or to pick up the morning newspaper. A psychologist might suggest she is experiencing
   a. agoraphobia
   b. social phobia
   c. obsessive-compulsive disorder
   d. simple phobia
      (p. 543) LO 4

5. A usually mild, but relentless type of rare-floating anxiety is experienced by those with
   a. panic anxiety disorder
   b. phobic disorder
   c. generalized anxiety disorder
   d. a and c above
      (p. 543) LO 5

6. A disorder in which long periods of calm are broken by sharp, intense periods of anxiety is called
   a. phobic disorder
   b. simple anxiety
   c. panic anxiety disorder
   d. generalized anxiety disorder
      (p. 543) LO 5

7. Posttraumatic stress disorder has been linked to
   a. war veterans
   b. rape victims
   c. concentration camp survivors
   d. all of the above
      (p. 545) LO 6

8. Obsessions refer to
   a. thoughts
   b. behaviors
   c. psychotic behavior
   d. insane behavior
      (p. 546) LO 7

9. Each of the following is a compulsion *except*
   a. repeatedly washing one's hands
   b. checking and rechecking the locks on doors
   c. touching a spot on one's shoulder over and over
   d. uncontrollable thoughts about somebody
   (p. 546) LO 7

10. Individuals whose symptoms include chronic aches and pains, fever, fatigue, and anxiety are experiencing
   a. dissociative disorder
   b. somatization disorder
   c. conversion disorder
   d. fugue disorder
   (p. 546) LO 8

11. Each of the following is a type of somatoform disorder *except*
   a. somatization disorder
   b. hypochondriasis
   c. conversion disorder
   d. obsessive-compulsive disorder
   (p. 546) LO 8

12. Jim has begun to talk exclusively about the state of his health. Furthermore, he tries to see two or three doctors daily, although none can find anything wrong with him. He has also started wearing white gloves as a precaution against contact with germs. A psychologist might consider that Jim is experiencing
   a. hypochondriasis
   b. somatization disorder
   c. la belle indifference
   d. none of the above
   (p. 547) LO 8

13. "La belle indifference" is experienced by those suffering from
   a. hypochondriasis
   b. somatization disorder
   c. conversion disorder
   d. somatoform pain disorder
   (p. 548) LO 8

14. Individuals who suffer pain that has no physical cause are experiencing
   a. conversion disorder
   b. somatoform pain disorder
   c. obsessive pain disorder
   d. a and b above
   (p. 548) LO 8

15. Which of the following dissociative disorders involves an inability to remember one's previous life and involves "wandering"?
   a. psychogenic amnesia
   b. psychogenic fugue
   c. depersonalization
   d. multiple personality
   (p. 548) LO 9

16. The sensation of leaving one's body may occur to the individual who is experiencing
   a. depersonalization
   b. psychogenic amnesia
   c. psychogenic fugue
   d. all of the above
   (p. 549) LO 10

17. Multiple personality is considered to be a type of
   a. depersonalization
   b. neurotic disorder
   c. somatization disorder
   d. dissociative disorder
   (p. 549) LO 11

18. Reasonably strong evidence exists that multiple personality is an extreme reaction to
   a. psychedelic drugs
   b. childhood sexual abuse
   c. adolescent trauma
   d. the pressures of our society
   (p. 550) LO 11

19. Mary, age 47, has begun experiencing deep unhappiness, frequent lethargy, and sleep problems. A psychologist might consider that she is experiencing
   a. bipolar affective disorder
   b. a mood disorder
   c. major depression
   d. b and c above
   (p. 551) LO 12

20. Which of the following has been identified as a cognitive factor in depression?
    a. perfectionistic demands
    b. repressive coping
    c. obsessive behavior
    d. a and b above
       (p. 553) LO 12

21. A study of postpartum depression found that this type of depression
    a. occurs in most women immediately after they give birth
    b. can be prevented with a variety of medications
    c. may be a myth
    d. none of the above
       (p. 554) LO 13

22. The results of recent research conducted on postpartum depression indicate
    a. The problem may be more widespread than anticipated
    b. virtually all mothers experience some postpartum depression
    c. most of the women who experience some depression are only mildly affected
    d. the average onset of depression occurs about four days after giving birth
       (p. 554) LO 13

23. Which affective disorder involves periods of mania that alternate with periods of depression?
    a. bipolar affective disorder
    b. major depression
    c. schizophrenia
    d. a and b above
       (p. 554) LO 14

24. All of the following are characteristics of schizophrenia *except*
    a. cognitive disorders
    b. emotional disturbance
    c. social withdrawal
    d. alternating between two or more personalities
       (p. 555) LO 15

25. Delusions of grandeur, delusions of persecution, and hallucinations characterize
    a. paranoid schizophrenia
    b. disorganized schizophrenia
    c. catatonic schizophrenia
    d. undifferentiated schizophrenia
       (p. 536) LO 16

26. A type of schizophrenia characterized by long periods in an inactive, statuelike state is called
    a. paranoid schizophrenia
    b. disorganized schizophrenia
    c. catatonic schizophrenia
    d. undifferentiated schizophrenia
       (p. 537) LO 16

27. Which of the following distinguishes delusional disorder from paranoid schizophrenia?
    a. Delusional disorder is not accompanied by hallucinations.
    b. The delusions in delusional disorder are not as illogical as in paranoid schizophrenia.
    c. Delusional disorders occur far more often than paranoid schizophrenia.
    d. a and b above
       (p. 557) LO 17

28. Which personality disorder is characterized by an unrealistic sense of self-importance and preoccupation with fantasies about future success?
    a. schizotypal
    b. histrionic
    c. narcissistic
    d. borderline
       (p. 560) LO 18

29. Which of the following characterizes the antisocial personality disorder?
    a. smooth social skills
    b. little interest in social contact
    c. lack of guilt about violating social customs
    d. a and c above
       (p. 559) LO 18

30. Recent studies of homeless people in large cities support the idea that the homeless
    a. for the most part are just individuals who are down on their luck
    b. have high rates of chronic mental disorders
    c. have high rates of substance abuse disorders
    d. b and c above
       (p. 562) LO 19

Multiple-Choice Answers

1. The answer is *C*. The inherent subjectivity of judgments is a continual problem for psychologists who study abnormal behavior.
2. The answer is *A*. Consider an important implication of this question—the treatment and "cures" for those exhibiting abnormal behavior has been strongly influenced by the perceived causes of the abnormal behavior.
3. The answer is *B*. Remember that the term *insanity* is a legal rather than a psychological term.
4. The answer is *A*. Agoraphobia is an intense fear of leaving one's home or other familiar places.
5. The answer is *C*. While a person experiencing generalized anxiety disorder has a continual, gnawing sense of uneasiness, the person with panic anxiety disorder usually has periods of calm that are broken by an explosive attack of anxiety.
6. The answer is *C*. While generalized anxiety disorder is characterized by free-floating anxiety that almost always seems to be present, panic anxiety disorder is characterized by a sharp and intense anxiety, although it is not continually present.
7. The answer is *D*. The upsetting recollections, combined with feelings of guilt, disgust, and terrible dreams are all, unfortunately, components of PTSD.
8. The answer is *A*. Whereas obsessions refer to thoughts, compulsions refer to behaviors.
9. The answer is *D*. Compulsions are irresistible urges to engage in behaviors, while obsessions refer to seemingly unstoppable thoughts. They usually go together to form obsessive-compulsive behavior.
10. The answer is *B*. The category of somatoform disorders contains (a) somatization disorder, (b) hypochondriasis, (c) conversion disorder, and (d) psychogenic pain disorder.
11. The answer is *D*. In the question, the missing type of somatoform disorder is somatoform pain disorder.
12. The answer is *A*. The individual experiencing hypochondriasis is dominated by concerns about his or her health.
13. The answer is *C*. "The beautiful indifference" refers to the fact that, although individuals with conversion disorder appear to be suffering serious symptoms, such as paralysis or blindness, they often are not upset with their condition.
14. The answer is *B*. Somatoform pain often occurs to the person who is experiencing high levels of stress, and the condition may be beneficial to the individual in some way.
15. The answer is *B*. While psychogenic amnesia involves a loss of memory, a psychogenic fugue involves such a complete loss of memory that the individual cannot remember his or her identity or previous life. Often, during the fugue episode, the individual will take on a new personality.
16. The answer is *A*. During a depersonalization episode, the individual feels that he or she has become distorted or unreal in some way. The experience of leaving one's body is also a common experience in depersonalization.

17. The answer is *D*. Recall that the category of dissociative disorders consists of amnesia, fugue, depersonalization, and multiple personality. The common feature is that all involve a change in memory, perception, or identity.
18. The answer is *B*. Multiple personality remains a rare, though often highly publicized disorder.
19. The answer is *D*. To answer this question correctly, you need to know that major depression is a type of mood disorder.
20. The answer is *D*. In addition to the cognitive factors described in the question, research suggests that having a positive opinion of oneself makes depression less likely following stressful life events.
21. The answer is *C*. Although 10 percent of the women in the study developed serious depression, this percentage was not higher than in the non-childbearing group.
22. The answer is *C*. The research on postpartum depression cited in the text found that many women experience little or no postpartum depression; most of the women who experience depression are only mildly affected; and the depression lasted for a relatively brief period of time.
23. The answer is *A*. Bipolar affective disorder, formerly known as manic-depressive behavior, is a type of mood disorder. Although the manic period can be enjoyable to the person in the short run, it can have disastrous consequences. When mania is recurrent, it alternates with severe depression.
24. The answer is *D*. One of the biggest misconceptions in the field of abnormal psychology continues to be the notion that schizophrenics have a "split" personality.
25. The answer is *A*. Disorganized schizophrenia is also marked by hallucinations and delusions, but the cognitive processes of the individual are extremely disorganized. Disorganized schizophrenia is also characterized by a shallow, silly affect. The catatonic schizophrenic spends long periods of time in a statuelike state often described as "waxy flexibility."
26. The answer is *C*. Catatonic schizophrenics exhibit a "waxy flexibility" while in this stuporous condition.
27. The answer is *D*. The delusions that accompany delusional disorder are more subtle and believable than those that accompany paranoid schizophrenia. Delusional disorders are also rare.
28. The answer is *C*. The schizotypal is characterized by few friendships and strange ideas; the histrionic is self-centered and uses exaggerated expression of emotions; the borderline is impulsive, unpredictable and has an almost constant need to be with others.
29. The answer is *D*. In fact, many individuals with antisocial personality disorder have disarmingly smooth social skills.
30. The answer is *D*. Research conducted on the homeless living in New York and in Los Angeles has revealed that a majority of these people have mental and/or substance abuse disorders.

Learning Objectives

1. Define psychotherapy.
2. Identify and describe ethical standards for psychotherapy.
3. Discuss the following psychoanalytic techniques: free association, dream interpretation, interpretation of resistance, interpretation of transference, and catharsis.
4. Describe Carl Rogers' client-centered approach to psychotherapy.
5. Discuss the goals and techniques of Gestalt therapy.
6. Distinguish between the following behavior therapy methods for reducing fear: systematic desensitization and flooding.
7. Explain the goals and techniques of social skills training and assertiveness training.
8. Describe aversive conditioning techniques and discuss why these techniques are not widely used.
9. Identify and describe the maladaptive cognitions that, according to Beck, contribute to depression.
10. Identify and describe the fundamental concepts of feminist psychotherapy.
11. Discuss the advantages of group therapy.
12. Describe the goals and assumptions of family therapy.
13. Explain the following types of medical therapies: drug therapy, electroconvulsive therapy, and psychosurgery.
14. Describe the goals and techniques of the community mental health movement.
15. (From the "Application" section) Discuss guidelines for selecting a psychotherapist, research regarding the most effective form of psychotherapy, and ethnic and gender issues in seeking psychotherapy.

Chapter Overview

Psychotherapy is a form of therapy in which a trained professional uses methods based on psychological theories to help a person with psychological problems. One form of psychotherapy, founded by Sigmund Freud, is called psychoanalysis. Psychoanalysis tries to help the patient bring unconscious conflict into consciousness. The following techniques are used in psychoanalysis: (1) free association, which is used to relax the censorship of the ego; (2) dream interpretation, in which the symbols of the manifest content of dreams are interpreted to reveal their latent content; (3) resistance, which refers to any form of patient opposition to psychoanalysis; (4) transference, which refers to the development of a relatively intense relationship between patient and therapist during therapy; and (5) catharsis, the release of emotional energy related to unconscious conflicts.

Humanistic psychotherapists attempt to help the client seek more complete self-awareness to allow the client's inner-directed potential for growth to be realized. One type of humanistic psychotherapy is client-centered therapy. The goal of the client-centered therapist is to create an atmosphere that encourages clients to explore their unsymbolized feelings. Another humanistic approach, Gestalt psychotherapy, helps the individual achieve greater self-awareness by using directive techniques, such as questioning and challenging the client.

Another approach to psychotherapy is called behavior therapy. Behavior therapists help their clients to unlearn abnormal behavior and learn adaptive ways of thinking, feeling, and acting. Among the techniques used by behavior therapists are (1) systematic desensitization and flooding, two commonly used methods of fear reduction; (2) social skills training and developmental skills training, two approaches that teach new, adaptive skills using operant conditioning; (3) assertiveness training, techniques to increase assertive rather than aggressive ways of expressing feelings; and (4) aversive conditioning, a controversial technique that uses unpleasant, negative stimuli to eliminate abnormal habits.

Cognitive therapy, a relatively new approach to therapy, assumes that faulty cognitions are the cause of abnormal behavior.

Other models of therapy include feminist psychotherapy, which has evolved from the philosophical foundation of feminism.

Group therapy, generally conducted with one or two therapists and four to eight clients, makes efficient use of therapists' time and provides an opportunity for clients to benefit from interactions with each other. Family therapy is a variation of group therapy that attempts to reestablish proper functioning within a family.

Medical therapies are designed to correct a physical condition that is believed to be the cause of a psychological disorder. Medical therapies include drug therapy, electroconvulsive therapy, and psychosurgery.

The community mental health movement was initiated by congressional legislation in 1963. It established facilities to provide services for individuals with psychological problems in their own communities. Additionally, community mental health centers emphasize prevention of psychological disturbances.

Key Terms Exercise

For each of the following exercises, match the key terms on the left with the correct definitions on the right. Page references to the text follow the terms so that you may refer to the text for any items you answer incorrectly or do not understand completely. You may check your responses immediately by referring to the answers that follow each exercise.

Psychoanalysis

_____ 1. psychotherapy (p. 570)
_____ 2. psychoanalysis (p. 572)
_____ 3. free association (p. 572)
_____ 4. dream interpretation (p. 573)
_____ 5. resistance (p. 574)
_____ 6. transference (p. 574)
_____ 7. catharsis (p. 574)

a. occurs when a patient in psychoanalysis reacts to a therapist in ways that resemble the patient's reaction to other significant adults
b. the method of psychotherapy developed by Sigmund Freud
c. the use of a variety of psychological methods to help a patient with psychological problems
d. the release of emotional energy related to unconscious conflicts
e. A Freudian method that attempts to reveal the latent content of dreams
f. A Freudian method that encourages the patient to talk about whatever comes to mind
g. patient opposition to psychoanalysis

ANSWERS

1. c	5. g
2. b	6. a
3. f	7. d
4. e	

Humanistic Psychotherapy and Behavior Therapy

_____ 1. client-centered psychotherapy (p. 577)
_____ 2. reflection (p. 577)
_____ 3. Gestalt therapy (p. 578)
_____ 4. behavior therapy (p. 580)

a. psychotherapy based on social learning theory
b. a humanistic therapy that tries to create a safe environment for clients so they can discover feelings of which they are unaware
c. a humanistic theory in which the therapist takes an active role in helping the client become more aware of feelings
d. a technique in which the therapist reflects clients emotions in order to help clients clarify their feelings

ANSWERS

1. b   3. c
2. d   4. a

Behavior Therapy Techniques

_____ 1. systematic desensitization (p. 580)
_____ 2. flooding (p. 581)
_____ 3. social skills training (p. 582)
_____ 4. assertiveness training (p. 582)
_____ 5. aversive conditioning (p. 582)
_____ 6. cognitive therapy (p. 585)

a. a behavior therapy method that teaches the client to overcome phobias by relaxing in response to increasingly threatening stimuli
b. a behavior therapy method that teaches individuals assertive ways of dealing with situations
c. an approach that teaches individuals new cognitions to eliminate abnormal behavior
d. a behavior therapy method that uses unpleasant stimuli to eliminate abnormal habits
e. a behavior therapy method that teaches the client to overcome phobias by presenting the client with high levels of the phobic stimulus
f. using operant conditioning techniques to teach social skills

ANSWERS

1. a   4. b
2. e   5. d
3. f   6. c

Other Models of Therapy

_____ 1. group therapy (p. 591)
_____ 2. family therapy (p. 592)
_____ 3. drug therapy (p. 593)
_____ 4. electroconvulsive therapy (p. 593)
_____ 5. psychosurgery (p. 594)

a. a medical therapy that induces controlled convulsive seizures to alleviate some mental disorders
b. a medical therapy that uses drugs to treat abnormal behavior
c. a medical therapy that involves operating on the brain to alleviate some mental disorders
d. an approach to psychotherapy that emphasizes an understanding of the roles of each family member
e. psychotherapy conducted in groups

ANSWERS

1. e   4. a
2. d   5. c
3. b

Who Am I?

Match the psychologists on the left with their contributions to the field of psychology on the right. Page references to the text follow the names of the psychologists so that you may refer to the text for further review of these psychologists and their contributions. You may check responses immediately by referring to the answers that follow each exercise.

_____ 1. Sigmund Freud (p. 572)
_____ 2. Carl Rogers (p. 577)
_____ 3. Frederick Perls (p. 578)
_____ 4. Aaron Beck (p. 586)

a. Gestalt therapy
b. psychoanalysis
c. client-centered therapy
d. cognitive therapy

ANSWERS

1. b   3. a
2. c   4. d

Guided Review

Psychoanalysis

A trained professional uses psychological methods to help a person with psychological problems in the process called _____.   psychotherapy (p. 570)

The following ethical guidelines must be followed by psychotherapists: (1) the _____ of treatment must be   goals (p. 570)

considered with the client; (2) the choices for alternative treatments should be carefully considered; (3) the therapist must treat only the problems that he or she is _____ to treat;   qualified (p. 571)

(4) the _____ of the treatment must be evaluated in   effectiveness (p. 571)

some way; (5) the rules and laws regarding _____ must be fully explained to the client; (6) the therapist must not _____ the client in sexual or other ways; (7) the therapist must treat clients with dignity and respect differences among people.

confidentiality (p. 571)

exploit (p. 571)

Psychoanalysts feel that abnormal behavior is the result of _____ conflicts among the id, ego, and superego. According to Freud, problems can be solved only when unconscious conflicts are brought into _____ . This can occur only when the ego's guard is temporarily _____. The job of the psychoanalyst is to (1) relax the censorship of the _____ and (2) _____ the revelations of the unconscious mind.

unconscious (p. 572)

consciousness (p. 572)

relaxed (p. 572)

ego (p. 572)/interpret (p. 572)

Freud's primary tool of therapy was to encourage the individual to talk about whatever comes to mind, a technique called _____ _____. The "glimpse of the unconscious" revealed during free association must be _____ to the patient by the psychoanalyst. Freud believed that another "window" to the unconscious was provided by _____ _____. Psychoanalysts believe that the manifest content of dreams symbolically masks the true or _____ _____ of dreams.

free association (p. 572)

interpreted (p. 573)

dream interpretation (p. 573)

latent content (p. 573)

Freud also placed significance on any patient opposition to psychoanalysis, a process he called _____. Intense relationships often develop between therapist and patient. The patient often reacts to the therapist in ways that resemble how he or she would react to other authority figures. Freud called this process _____. Releasing emotional energy related to unconscious conflicts is called _____.

resistance (p. 574)

transference (p. 574)

catharsis (p. 574)

Humanistic Psychotherapy
Humanists view full self-awareness as necessary for the complete realization of our inner-directed potential; according to humanists, therapy is "growth in _____."

awareness (p. 576)

The therapy approach associated with Carl Rogers is
called_____-_____ psychotherapy. According   client-centered (p. 577)
to Rogers, growth in awareness comes when the client feels safe
enough to explore _____ _____. Rogers   hidden emotions (p. 577)
believes that the therapist must be _____, able to accept   warm (p. 577)
their clients _____, and able to share their client's   unconditionally (p. 577)
emotions, a process called _____. The closest thing to a   empathy (p. 577)
technique in client-centered therapy is the process of
_____. Client-centered therapists strictly avoid giving   reflection (p. 577)
_____ to clients.   advice (p. 577)

　　Frederick Perls developed a type of humanistic therapy called
_____ therapy. In this type of therapy, the therapist   Gestalt (p. 578)
takes a more active role to help the client become more aware of
his or her _____. Gestalt therapists often deal with their   feelings (p. 578)
clients in a challenging manner, a technique Perls called a
_____ _____.   safe emergency (p. 578)

Behavior Therapy

The approach to psychotherapy based on social learning theory is
called _____ therapy. This approach views abnormal   behavior (p. 580)
behavior as _____ behavior. The therapist, who plays   learned (p. 580)
the role of a teacher, helps the client to unlearn abnormal behavior
and to learn more _____ ways to behave.   adaptive (p. 580)

　　Several behavior therapy methods are used to treat phobias.
One technique, developed by Joseph Wolpe, is called
_____ _____. In this technique, fear-   systematic desensitization (p. 580)
provoking stimuli are arranged in a _____. Then the   hierarchy (p. 580)
client is taught to relax using _____ _____   progressive relaxation
_____. Finally, while deeply relaxed, the client is asked   training (p. 580)
to imagine the phobic scenes in the hierarchy. By repeatedly
pairing phobic stimuli with relaxation, the client is conditioned to
_____ in the response to the stimuli.   relax (p. 580)

　　An alternative to systematic desensitization is called
_____. This technique confronts the client with high   flooding (p. 581)
levels of the phobic stimulus until fear is _____.   extinguished (p. 581)

A major emphasis of behavior therapy is on the teaching of new skills using methods derived from _____ _____. For example, people who have difficulties interacting with other people might benefit from _____ _____ training. One technique, in which the therapist and client act as if they are people in problematic situations, is called _____ _____. Using this technique, the therapist might take the role of the client and _____ appropriate behavior. The therapist also provides _____ _____ for the client by praising the good aspects of the client's behavior.

    A technique that is used to develop assertive rather than aggressive ways of dealing with others is called _____ training.

    A controversial behavior therapy technique, which uses unpleasant negative stimuli to eliminate abnormal behavior, is called _____ _____. This approach has been used to eliminate _____ and deviant _____ behavior. Aversive conditioning is used less widely today than in the past.

    A new approach to therapy teaches individuals new cognition—beliefs, expectations, and ways of thinking—to eliminate abnormal behavior. This approach is called _____ therapy. Cognitive therapists believe that behavior therapists can be more effective if they teach both more adaptive _____ and _____.

    According to the cognitive therapy program developed by Aaron Beck, depression is caused by the following erroneous patterns of thinking: (1) basing one's thoughts on a detail taken out of context, called _____ _____; (2) reaching a general conclusion based on a few bits of evidence, called _____; (3) reaching a conclusion based on little or no logical evidence, called _____ _____; (4) blowing statements out of proportion or minimizing their importance, called _____/_____;

operant
conditioning (p. 582)
social
skills (p. 582)

role playing (p. 582)
model (p. 582)
positive
reinforcement (p. 582)

assertiveness (p. 582)

aversive conditioning (p. 582)
alcoholism (p. 582)/sexual (p. 582)

cognitive (p. 585)

behavior (p. 586)
cognition (p. 586)

selective abstraction (p. 586)

overgeneralization (p. 586)
arbitrary inference (p. 586)

magnification/minimization (p. 586)

(5) reasoning that external events are directly related to one's behavior, called _____; and (6) thinking in all-or-nothing terms, called _____ thinking.

personalization (p. 587)

absolutistic (p. 487)

Other Models of Therapy

An approach to understanding and treating the psychological problems of women that evolved from feminism is called _____ psychotherapy. Its basic concepts include: (1) an equal relationship between client and therapist; (2) encouragement for women clients to see the ways in which society has limited their development; (3) encouragement to become aware of _____ as a result of living in a sexist society; (4) help in defining women in ways that are _____ of their roles as wife, mother, and daughter; (5) skills to increase women's sense of self-worth and _____-_____; (6) encouragement to develop _____ not traditionally encouraged in women.

feminist (p. 589)

anger (p. 590)

independent (p. 590)

self-esteem (p. 590)

skills (p. 590)

Therapy conducted with groups, usually four to eight clients at a time, is called _____ _____. Some of the advantages of group therapy are (1) _____ from other group members; (2) learning that a person is not alone in his or her problems; (3) learning from the _____ of others; and (4) learning new ways to _____ with others.

group therapy (p. 591)

encouragement (p. 591)

advice (p. 591)

interact (p. 591)

Another form of group therapy is conducted with parents, children, and other family members living in the home; this approach is called _____ therapy. One approach to family therapy assumes that the psychological problems of the individual can be understood only by knowing the role of that individual in the _____ _____. This systems approach suggests that an individual's problems are often caused by problems within the _____ and that they may serve a _____ in the family system. The family therapist attempts to improve the functioning of the family system by (1) giving family members _____ into the workings of the family system; (2) increasing the amount of warmth and

family (p. 592)

family system (p. 592)

family (p. 592)

function (p. 592)

insight (p. 592)

_____ among family members; (3) improving

_____ among family members; and (4) helping family

members establish a set of _____ for the family.

    When a physical condition is believed to cause a psychological

disorder, _____ _____ are used. The most

widely used medical therapy is _____ therapy, which

uses chemicals to treat abnormal behavior. A drug that has been

successfully used in the treatment of schizophrenia is

_____. Some drugs have serious side effects; others are

highly addictive.

    The use of electrical current to induce controlled convulsive

seizures that help alleviate some mental disorders is called

_____ _____ (ECT). Although side effects

such as _____ loss and _____ are relatively

common, studies have shown that ECT is somewhat effective in

treating _____.

    The most controversial approach to medical therapy, operating

on the brain to alleviate some mental disorders, is called

_____. The most common type of psychosurgery, the

_____ _____, cuts the neural fibers that

connect the frontal region of the cerebral cortex with the

hypothalamus. The procedure is performed infrequently today, and

its use is still hotly debated.

    In 1963, Congress passed the _____

_____ _____ _____ Act that

established mental health centers in every part of the country.

These centers allow people to receive psychological treatment

while remaining ____ _____, thereby allowing patients

to remain in regular contact with family and friends. These patients

can avoid living in the sometimes dreary and regimented

institutions and can avoid the stigma of _____.

    Other community-based programs focus on former residents of

mental hospitals; these programs have provided _____

programs to help with the transition to independent living.

intimacy (p. 592)

communication (p. 592)

rules (p. 593)

medical therapies (p. 593)

drug (p. 593)

Thorazine (p. 593)

electroconvulsive therapy (p. 593)

memory (p. 594)/confusion (p. 594)

depression (p. 593)

psychosurgery (p. 594)

prefrontal lobotomy (p. 594)

Community
Mental Health Center (p. 595)

at home (p. 595)

institutionalization (p. 595)

aftercare (p. 596)

One successful example is the _____ _____   Community Lodge

_____. The community psychology movement consists of   Program (p. 596)

psychologists who work with large groups of people. These

psychologists seek to _____ psychological problems by   prevent (p. 596)

identifying and eliminating the aspects of a community that

contribute to psychological disorders.

Application of Psychology: What to Do if You Think You Need Help

The following are important considerations in deciding whether to

use professional mental health services. An important issue

concerns the _____ surrounding seeking professional   stigma (p. 598)

help. A second consideration is where to get help. Many colleges

and universities have a student counseling or mental health center.

Services are also provided by professionals in _____   private (p. 598)

practice. Referrals and board _____ are other guides in   certification (p. 599)

helping select a professional. Research by Smith and Glass has

confirmed that various types of psychotherapy all produced positive

treatment effects, although there was variation in the size of the

effects. There are important _____ and   ethnic (p. 600)

_____ inequities in terms of receiving psychological   gender (p. 600)

services in the United States.

CONCEPT CHECK

Fill in the missing components of the following box. The answers are shown below the box.

Approaches to Therapy

I. Psychologists	II. Type of Therapy	III. Techniques
a. Freud	a. Psychoanalysis	a. Free association, catharsis, and interpretation of dreams, resistance, and transference.
b. Rogers	b. Humanistic (client-centered)	b.
c.	c. Humanistic (Gestalt)	c. Focus is on active involvement in client's conversations during sessions, feelings, and creating a "safe emergency."
d. Wolpe	d.	d. This is a fear reduction method that involves relaxation, construction of a fear hierarchy, and conditioning a new response to the phobic stimulus.
e. Ellis and Beck	e. Cognitive therapy	e.

Answers

IIIb.   Focus is on the ability of clients to help themselves; the therapist tries to create an emotionally safe atmosphere; the therapist must show warmth, unconditional acceptance, and empathy.

Ic.   Perls

IId.   Systematic desensitization

IIIe.   In this therapy, faulty cognitions are seen as the cause of abnormal behavior. Some examples of erroneous patterns of thinking include selective abstraction, overgeneralization, arbitrary inference, magnification/minimization, personalization, and absolutistic thinking.

Multiple Choice Questions

1. Each of the following is part of the definition of psychotherapy *except*
   a. trained professional
   b. psychological methods
   c. medical treatment methods
   d. based on psychological theory
   (p. 570) LO 1

2. According to the Association for Advancement of Behavior Therapy, each of the following is an ethical consideration in the use of psychotherapy *except*
   a. the goals of treatment
   b. the fees (splitting the fees when necessary)
   c. the choice of treatment methods
   d. client confidentiality
   (p. 570–571) LO 2

3. Ann's therapist asks her to lie on a couch and talk about whatever comes to mind. The technique being used by her therapist is
   a. catharsis
   b. resistance
   c. free association
   d. transference
   (p. 573) LO 3

4. According to Freud, when the patient reacts to the therapist in ways that resemble how he or she would react to other authority figures, the process is called
   a. resistance
   b. catharsis
   c. free association
   d. transference
   (p. 574) LO 3

5. In psychoanalysis, the release of emotional energy related to unconscious conflicts is called
   a. resistance
   b. catharsis
   c. free association
   d. transference
   (p. 574) LO 3

6. According to Rogers, the ability of the therapist to share the client's emotions is an important process called
   a. reflection
   b. empathy
   c. catharsis
   d. b and c above
   (p. 577) LO 4

7. The role of the client-centered therapist is to
   a. interpret the client's unconscious conflicts
   b. create a safe atmosphere for clients to express feelings
   c. confront and challenge the client and point out inconsistencies
   d. help the client unlearn abnormal ways of behaving
   (p. 577) LO 4

8. Which of the following techniques is a client-centered therapist most likely to use?
   a. analysis
   b. giving advice
   c. reflection
   d. aversive conditioning
   (p. 577) LO 4

9. In Gestalt therapy, when a therapist confronts the client, it is called (a)
   a. cathartic experience
   b. empathy
   c. safe emergency
   d. reflection
   (p. 578) LO 5

10. The techniques used by Gestalt therapists include
    a. interpreting the client's unconscious conflicts
    b. creating a safe atmosphere for clients to express feelings
    c. confronting and challenging the client and pointing out inconsistencies
    d. helping the client unlearn abnormal ways of behaving
    (p. 578) LO 5

11. Systematic desensitization and flooding are two techniques used to treat
    a. schizophrenia
    b. phobias
    c. bipolar disorder
    d. depression
       (p. 580) LO 5

12. Constructing a hierarchy of phobic stimuli and training in progressive relaxation are important steps in
    a. flooding
    b. systematic desensitization
    c. reflection
    d. a and b above
       (p. 580) LO 6

13. Flooding is often used in the treatment of
    a. PTSD
    b. depression
    c. schizophrenia
    d. generalized anxiety
       (p. 591) LO 6

14. Richard frequently feels that he is being "used" by others; he has been told by his friends that he is too passive. He might benefit from
    a. developmental skills training
    b. assertiveness training
    c. aversive conditioning
    d. none of the above
       (p. 582) LO 7

15. Behavior therapy teaches skills based on methods derived from
    a. classical conditioning
    b. operant conditioning
    c. information-processing theory
    d. a and b above
       (p. 582) LO 7

16. Aversive conditioning has been used to treat
    a. phobias
    b. alcoholism
    c. deviant sexual practices
    d. b and c above
       (p. 583) LO 8

17. After Mike got to college, the first two people he called to ask for a date forcefully told him "No!" Mike has concluded he will never have a date. Beck would say Mike is engaging in
    a. selective abstraction
    b. personalization
    c. overgeneralization
    d. none of the above
       (p. 586) LO 9

18. With which disorders has cognitive therapy been shown to be effective?
    a. anxiety disorders
    b. bulimia
    c. major depression
    d. all of the above
       (p. 588) LO 9

19. Persuading clients to abandon their erroneous ways of thinking is a goal of
    a. aversive conditioning
    b. cognitive therapy
    c. systematic desensitization
    d. social skills training
       (p. 587) LO 9

20. Which of the following is a fundamental concept of feminist psychotherapy?
    a. an equal relationship between therapist and client
    b. an awareness of anger over living in a sexist society
    c. encouragement to consider the clients' needs as valid and worthy
    d. all of the above
       (p. 590) LO 10

21. Group therapists tend to follow which orientation?
    a. humanistic
    b. psychoanalytic
    c. behavioral
    d. any of the above
       (p. 591) LO 11

22. Each of the following is an advantage of group therapy *except*
    a. It allows people with complex problems to have the therapist's full attention.
    b. It can provide encouragement from other group members.
    c. It permits learning from the advice of others.
    d. Members can learn new ways to interact with others.
    (p. 591) LO 11

23. Which of the following describes the position of the family systems view?
    a. Individual problems are often caused by problems within the family.
    b. An individual's problems may serve a function within the family system.
    c. Family problems are usually caused by too many rule and regulations within the family.
    d. a and b above
    (p. 592) LO 12

24. The drug Thorazine has been helpful to many individuals suffering from
    a. depression
    b. schizophrenia
    c. obsessive-compulsive disorder
    d. agoraphobia
    (p. 593) LO 13

25. Electroconvulsive therapy is believed by most psychiatrists to be useful for patients who are
    a. severely schizophrenic
    b. epileptic
    c. bipolar
    d. suicidally depressed
    (p. 593) LO 13

26. A side effect of electroconvulsive therapy is
    a. memory loss
    b. increased depression
    c. increased tendency to have seizures
    d. a and c above
    (p. 594) LO 13

27. The emphasis of the community psychology movement is on
    a. solving psychological problems in a community
    b. providing psychological treatment at no charge to the client
    c. preventing psychological problems
    d. all of the above
    (p. 595) LO 14

28. Which of the following would be good advice for someone considering a therapist?
    a. Eclectic therapists are best because they can provide the widest variety of services.
    b. Student counseling centers are usually staffed by students and recent graduates who don't have much experience.
    c. Anybody can call themselves a "psychologist."
    d. Referrals can be a good guide in choosing a psychologist.
    (p. 599) LO 15

29. According to research conducted by Smith and Glass, which type of therapy produced the smallest magnitude of treatment effect?
    a. Adlerian psychoanalytic
    b. operant skills training
    c. Gestalt therapy
    d. eclectic psychotherapy
    (p. 599) LO 15

30. Research suggests inequities in receiving psychotherapy based on one's
    a. gender
    b. ethnicity
    c. race
    d. all of the above
    (p. 600) LO 15

Multiple-Choice Answers

1. The answer is *C*. The definition of psychotherapy technically does not include medical treatment methods such as medication or surgery.
2. The answer is *B*. The issue of fees for providing psychological services is not addressed in the text. It is, however, of special interest to consumers of psychological services.
3. The answer is *C*. At upwards of $100 per hour, why do they call it *free* association?) Catharsis refers to the release of pent-up emotional energy. Resistance occurs when patients express opposition to the process of psychoanalysis. In transference, the patient in psychoanalysis comes to regard the therapist in ways that resemble the patient's feelings toward other significant adults.
4. The answer is *D*. Transference should be interpreted by the psychoanalyst to give the patient additional insight into his or her situation.
5. The answer is *B*. Catharsis is not really a technique of psychoanalysis; instead, this brief relief from psychic discomfort is considered a benefit.
6. The answer is *B*. Empathy, genuine warmth, and unconditional positive regard are important in client-centered therapy in creating a safe atmosphere.
7. The answer is *B*. According to client-centered therapists, the emphasis is on the ability of clients to help themselves. The goal of the therapist is to create an atmosphere conducive to this process. This is considerably different from the goal of psychoanalysis (option *A* of the question), or Gestalt therapy (option *C*), or behavior therapy (option *D*).
8. The answer is *C*. Client-centered therapists steadfastly avoid giving advice to clients. They believe that clients can solve their own problems once the problems have entered awareness.
9. The answer is *C*. The confrontational approach used in Gestalt therapy strongly differs from the warm atmosphere created in client-centered therapy.
10. The answer is *C*. The goal of Gestalt therapy is to help the client achieve greater self-awareness. Unlike the client-centered approach, Gestalt therapy is done by challenging and confronting the client.
11. The answer is *B*. Although they differ widely in their approaches, both systematic desensitization and flooding try to extinguish phobic responses and substitute relaxation responses.
12. The answer is *B*. Systematic desensitization is a process in which the client learns not to fear a formerly phobic stimuli. The procedure involves learning to relax in the presence of progressively more threatening stimuli. Flooding attempts to achieve the same goal, but does so by "flooding" the client with high levels of the phobic stimulus.
13. The answer is *A*. Flooding is a rather unpleasant procedure, and it requires clients who are highly motivated to solve their problems.
14. The answer is *B*. Assertiveness training seeks to teach individuals how to more effectively express feelings to others and/or to deal with interpersonal problems. Role playing is often used in this situation.
15. The answer is *D*. The assumption of behavior therapy is that abnormal behavior has been learned. Therapy, then, is largely a product of learning new behaviors.
16. The answer is *D*. Aversive conditioning uses the principles of classical conditioning to stop people from engaging in destructive behaviors.
17. The answers is *C*. Overgeneralization is the process of reaching a general conclusion based on a few specific bits of evidence. Don't give up, Mike!
18. The answer is *D*. In most studies, cognitive therapy was found to be superior to either the traditional psychoanalytic or humanistic approaches.
19. The answer is *B*. The assumption of cognitive therapy is that it is a person's maladaptive beliefs and expectations about situations, rather than the situations themselves, that cause abnormal behavior.
20. The answer is *D*. In addition, feminist psychotherapy encourages women to view themselves as powerful and to define themselves independently of their roles as wives, mothers, and daughters.
21. The answer is *D*. Group therapists can follow any of these approaches to psychotherapy.
22. The answer is *A*. Individual therapy is probably more appropriate for those with complex problems.

23. The answer is *D*. The family therapist attempts to solve the problems of each family member by focusing on the functioning of the family as a whole.
24. The answer is *B*. Thorazine belongs to a class of drugs called the phenothiazines. The introduction of these drugs in the 1950s helped to revolutionize the treatment of schizophrenia.
25. The answer is *D*. Although ECT seems to be effective with suicidally depressed patients, nobody seems to know exactly why.
26. The answer is *A*. Temporary or permanent memory loss and confusion continue to be side effects of ECT.
27. The answer is *D*. The passage of the Community Mental Health Center Act in 1963 changed the emphasis to *prevention* of psychological disturbances and attempted to bring psychological services to communities.
28. The answer is *D*. Eclectic therapists are skilled in a variety of therapeutic techniques. This doesn't necessarily make them "the best." Student counseling centers generally provide high-quality services to students at moderate cost. It is true that in many states virtually anybody can call themselves a counselor or therapist, but only licensed individuals can call themselves "psychologists" or "psychiatrists."
29. The answer is *C*. According to the Smith and Glass study, systematic desensitization had the largest average effect. As a group, behavior therapy techniques also seemed to provide the largest average effect.
30. The answer is *D*. Research suggests that the quality of treatment and whether or not one is receiving necessary treatment depend to a large extent on one's ethnicity, gender, and race.

Chapter **15**   Social Psychology

Learning Objectives

1. Define social psychology.
2. Distinguish between situational attributions and dispositional attributions.
3. Describe the fundamental attribution error.
4. Describe the process of deindividuation.
5. Discuss the steps that are involved in a decision tree; describe the social factors that influence a decision tree.
6. Describe the following group processes: social loafing, social facilitation, and social impairment.
7. Identify the following group phenomena: polarization and groupthink.
8. Define conformity and discuss the results of research on conformity.
9. Discuss Zimbardo's prison study and describe the importance of social roles.
10. Discuss Milgram's "shocking" research on obedience.
11. Identify the components of attitudes.
12. Describe how characteristics of the speaker, the message, and the listener affect persuasion.
13. Explain Leon Festinger's cognitive dissonance theory.
14. Discuss the relationship between stereotypes and prejudice; explain how stereotypes affect our attributions about other people's behavior.
15. Describe the primacy effect and discuss the factors that can reduce its impact.
16. Describe the roles played by expectations and equity in maintaining relationships.
17. (From the "Application" section) Discuss the implications of the sex discrimination lawsuit filed against Price Waterhouse.

Chapter Overview

Social psychology is the branch of psychology that studies individuals as they interact with others. One topic of interest to social psychologists is the influence that others have on individual behavior. Social behavior is strongly influenced by the attribution process. The fundamental attribution error involves our tendency to underestimate the impact of situations on others while more easily seeing its impact on ourselves. Among the group processes discussed are deindividuation, social loafing, social facilitation, social impairment, group polarization, and groupthink.

Social psychologists have also studied group phenomena such as our tendency to conform to group pressure, the importance of social roles in our lives, and our tendency to obey authority figures.

Attitudes are beliefs that predispose us to behave in certain ways. Attitudes are learned from direct experience and from others. The persuasiveness of messages is determined by the characteristics of the speaker (credibility, attractiveness, and intent), the message (fear appeals and two-sided arguments), and the listeners (intelligence, need for social approval, esteem, and audience size).

Leon Festinger's cognitive dissonance theory has been proposed to explain the process of attitude change.

Prejudice is a negative attitude based on inaccurate generalizations about a group of people. The inaccurate generalization on which the prejudice is based is called a stereotype. Stereotypes are harmful . because they take away our ability to treat each member of a group as an individual and because they lead to faulty attributions.

Friendship and love are powerful social phenomena based on the process of person perception. The process of person perception is complicated by the ways in which we gather and use information about others. Different people will perceive the same individual differently because of differences in interpreting the individual's characteristics. Negative information is generally weighted more than positive information in person perception. First impressions, also known as the primacy effect, generally influence person perception more than information learned about the person at a later date. Prolonged exposure to the person, the passage of time, and knowledge about primacy effects all can reduce the effects of the primacy effect. Person perception is also influenced by the emotional state of the perceiver.

Although many factors ensure that each individual's perception of an individual will be unique, there are some general factors that partly determine to whom we will be attracted: similar and complementary characteristics, competence, physical attractiveness, and mutual liking. The attribution process is also involved in the perception of others. One aspect of the attribution process is deciding if a person's behavior is caused by the situation (a situational attribution) or by a trait of the person (a dispositional attribution).

Two major factors that determine whether a relationship will last are the differences between what you expect to find in a relationship and what you actually find, and the degree to which the relationship is equitable.

According to Susan Fiske, there are three sources of gender-based job discrimination (1) evaluations of job performance are influenced by gender stereotypes; (2) narrow expectations for behavior created by stereotypes lead to discrimination; and (3) faulty attributions based on gender stereotypes operate in the workplace.

Key Terms Exercise

For each of the following exercises, match the key terms on the left with the correct definitions on the right. Page references to the text follow the terms so that you may refer to the text for any items you answer incorrectly or do not understand completely. You may check your responses immediately by referring to the answers that follow each exercise.

_____ 1. social psychology (p. 608)
_____ 2. deindividuation (p. 609)
_____ 3. diffusion of responsibility (p. 611)
_____ 4. conformity (p. 613)
_____ 5. obedience (p. 613)

a. a process in which group membership leaves one feeling anonymous and unidentifiable
b. the effect of being in a group that reduces an individual's sense of personal responsibility
c. doing what one is told to do by people in authority
d. yielding to group pressure even when no direct request to comply has been made
e. the branch of psychology that studies individuals as they interact with each other

ANSWERS
1. f   4. d
2. a   5. c
3. b

Social Influence

_____ 1. social loafing (p. 611)
_____ 2. group polarization (p. 612)
_____ 3. groupthink (p. 612)
_____ 4. social facilitation (p. 612)
_____ 5. social impairment (p. 612)
_____ 6. attitudes (p. 618)
_____ 7. persuasion (p. 618)
_____ 8. sleeper effects (p. 169)
_____ 9. cognitive dissonance (p. 622)

a. changing another person's attitudes through arguments and other related means
b. the tendency for individuals to work less hard as a member of a group
c. beliefs that predispose an individual to act a certain way
d. the discomfort that results from inconsistencies between one's attitude and behavior
e. the potential for low credibility speakers to gain credibility after a period of time
f. improved performance on individual projects that sometimes occurs as a member of a group
g. lowered individual performance that occurs while working in the presence of a group
h. the tendency for group discussion to make beliefs and attitudes more extreme
i. faulty group decision making that often occurs in tightly knit, cohesive groups

ANSWERS

1. b	6. c
2. h	7. a
3. i	8. e
4. f	9. d
5. g	

Attitudes and Social Behavior/Interpersonal Attraction

_____ 1. prejudice (p. 624)
_____ 2. stereotype (p. 624)
_____ 3. attribution theory (p. 624)
_____ 4. person perception (p. 626)
_____ 5. primacy effect (p. 627)
_____ 6. situational attribution (p. 609)
_____ 7. dispositional attribution (p. 609)
_____ 8. fundamental attribution error (p. 608)
_____ 9. equity theory (p. 635)

a. the process of forming impressions of others
b. a negative attitude based on inaccurate generalizations about a group of people
c. an explanation for behavior that is based on an external cause
d. the theory that partners will be comfortable in a relationship only when the ratio between their perceived contributions and benefits is equal
e. an inaccurate generalization on which a prejudice is based
f. the tendency to weigh first impressions heavily in forming opinions about other people
g. an explanation for behavior that is based on a characteristic of the individual
h. the theory that people tend to look for explanations for their own behavior and that of others
i. the tendency to underestimate the impact of social situations on some while more easily seeing the impact on others

ANSWERS

1. b	6. c
2. e	7. g
3. h	8. i
4. a	9. d
5. f	

Guided Review

The branch of psychology that studies individuals as they interact
with others is called _____ psychology.   social (p. 608)

Social Influence and the Attribution Process

The tendency to underestimate the impact of situations on others,
while more easily seeing it in ourselves is called the

_____ _____ error. When an explanation for   fundamental attribution (p. 608)
behavior is based on an external cause, it is called a

_____ attribution; when the explanation is based on an   situational (p. 609)
internal motive, it is called a _____ attribution. We tend dispositional (p. 609)
to attribute the behavior of others to _____ causes.   dispositional (p. 609)

The group process in which a person feels anonymous and
unidentifiable is called _____. According to Latané and   deindividuation (p. 609)
Darley, bystanders who are considering helping out in an
emergency use a _____ _____ with several   decision tree (p. 610)
steps. The first step is noticing; the second step is interpreting the
situation as an emergency, and finally the bystander must assume
_____ for helping. Social factors affect the second and   responsibility (p. 611)
third stages of the decision process. Groups can create a
_____ of _____.   diffusion (p. 611)/responsibility (p. 611)

When group performance is measured, individuals tend to
exert less effort than when individual effort is measured; this
phenomenon is called _____ _____. Working   social loafing (p. 611)
individually in the presence of others sometimes improves
performance; this is called _____ _____.   social facilitation (p. 162)
Under some circumstances, working in the presence of others
impairs performance; this is termed _____   social
_____. Research suggests that the presence of others   impairment (p. 612)
improves performance on _____ tasks and impairs   easy (p. 612)
performance on _____ tasks. We generally offer less   difficult (p. 612)
risky advice when we are alone with the person seeking advice;
when groups discuss the same issues, however, they are more likely
to offer _____ advice. Group discussion of issues often   riskier (p. 612)

pushes our opinions toward the extremes, a process called

_____. According to Janis, faulty group decision making,   polarization (p. 612)

especially in cohesive groups, is called _____.   groupthink (p. 612)

Under many circumstances, individuals yield to group pressure,

even when no direct request to comply has been made; this is

called _____. A study of conformity conducted by Asch   conformity (p. 613)

found that subjects conformed to the group at least part of the

time in _____ percent of the cases.   74 (p. 613)

Sherif's study involving autokinetic effects, which presented

subjects with an ambiguous situation, found that subjects not only

went along with others' judgments, but actually _____   changed (p. 613)

their own judgments. Zimbardo's prisoner-guard study underscored

the importance of _____ _____ in our lives.   social roles (p. 613)

Stanley Milgram has conducted research on _____.   obedience (p. 615)

Subjects believed they were participating in a learning experiment

and were asked to administer electric shocks to a "learner" when

the learner made a mistake. Milgram found that _____   65 (p. 616)

percent of the subjects participated until they had given the highest

possible shock. Further studies found that the percentage of

obedient subjects declined (1) when the victim was in the same

room, (2) when the _____ of the experimenter was   prestige (p. 616)

reduced, (3) when the experimenter gave instructions by

_____, and (4) when the subject was in the presence of   telephone (p. 616)

other _____ subjects. Although groups can produce   disobedient (p. 616)

negative effects, they can also be _____.   advantageous (p. 616)

Attitudes, Persuasion, and Social Influence

Beliefs that predispose people to act and feel in certain ways are

called _____. This definition has three important   attitudes (p. 618)

components: (1) _____, (2) _____, and   beliefs (p. 618)/feelings (p. 618)

(3)_____ to behave. Attitudes are learned from our   dispositions (p. 618)

experiences and from others.

Logic may be one of the least important qualities in

determining the _____ of a communication. The   persuasiveness (p. 618)

qualities of persuasive communication fall into three categories:

characteristics of the _____, of the _____, speaker (p. 618)/listener (p. 618)

and of the _____. Among the characteristics of the message (p. 618)

speaker, Aronson and Golden found that the speaker's

_____ is important to the persuasiveness of the credibility (p. 619)

communication. The key is whether the speaker is a credible

source of _____ about the specific argument. Although information (p. 619)

speakers who are low in credibility are ineffective at first, they

often influence opinions after a period of time through

_____ _____. sleeper effects (p. 619)

When advertisers use glamorous celebrities to help sell their

products, they are using another persuasive characteristic of the

speaker-_____. The persuasiveness of attractive attractiveness (p. 619)

speakers is limited to relatively _____ issues. unimportant (p. 619)

When the speaker is obviously trying to change an opinion, he

or she will be less persuasive. This characteristic is referred to as

_____ and helps to explain the use of the intent (p. 619)

"_____ _____" testimonials in television hidden camera (p. 619)

commercials.

The characteristics of the message that are determinants of

persuasiveness include _____ appeals and fear (p. 620)

_____-_____ arguments. Listeners will two-sided (p. 620)

respond favorably to a fear-inducing persuasive communication

only if (1) the emotional appeal is _____, (2) the strong (p. 620)

listeners believe the fearful outcome is likely to happen to them,

and (3) the message offers a way to _____ the fearful avoid (p. 620)

outcome.

When speaking to an audience that agrees with your position,

the message will be more persuasive if you do not present

_____ _____ of the argument; however, it's both sides (p. 620)

generally better to give both sides of the argument if the audience

is initially _____ to your position. unfavorable (p. 620)

The way in which problems are _____ has a strong framed (p. 620)

influence on how we solve these problems.

The following characteristics of listeners help to determine the

persuasiveness of an argument. (1) Generally, less

_____ people are easier to persuade; however, if the message is complex, more intelligent listeners are easier to persuade. (2) People with a high need for _____ _____ are generally easier to persuade. (3) People with low _____-_____ are sometimes easier to persuade. (4) People are easier to persuade when listening to the message in a _____; larger groups are easier to persuade than smaller groups; (5) recent studies have found no gender differences in _____.

intelligent (p. 622)

social
approval (p. 622)

self-esteem (p. 622)

group (p. 622)

persuasibility (p. 622)

Sometimes, important differences exist between our attitudes and our _____. When behavior and attitudes are inconsistent, _____ often change to become more consistent with behavior. Cognitive dissonance theory, proposed by Festinger, states that inconsistencies between attitudes and behavior are _____; people will change their attitudes to reduce this discomfort. To demonstrate cognitive dissonance, Festinger asked subjects to perform a boring _____-_____ task for an hour, and then to tell the next subject that the task was interesting. Half of the subjects were paid $20 and half were paid $1. When subjects were asked how interesting the task really was, the most positive attitudes were expressed by the group that experienced cognitive dissonance—those that were paid _____.

behavior (p. 622)

attitudes (p. 622)

uncomfortable (p. 622)

spool-
stacking (p. 623)

$1 (p. 623)

A harmful attitude that is based on generalizations about a group of people is called _____. The inaccurate generalization on which the prejudice is based is called a _____. Stereotypes are harmful for three reasons: (1) they take away our ability to treat each member of a group as an individual; (2) they lead to narrow _____ for behavior; and (3) they lead to faulty _____. Attribution theory states that people tend to attribute all behavior to some _____.

prejudice (p. 624)

stereotype (p. 624)

expectations (p. 624)

attributions (p. 624)

cause (p. 624)

Interpersonal Attraction: Friendship and Love

The process of forming impressions of others is called

_____ _____. People seem to go through a — person perception (p. 626)

process of "_____ _____" to help calculate — cognitive algebra (p. 626)

perceptions of others. Other things being equal, a person's

_____ qualities are weighted more heavily than the — negative (p. 627)

_____ qualities. — positive (p. 627)

The tendency to weigh first impressions heavily in forming

opinions of other people is called the _____ — primacy

_____. The impact of the primacy effect is reduced by — effect (p. 627)

(1) prolonged _____ to a person, (2) passage of — exposure (p. 628)

_____, and (3) _____ of the primacy effect. — time (p. 628) /knowledge (p. 628)

The emotional state we are in also affects person perception.

_____ emotional states lead to greater attraction to — Positive (p. 628)

others than negative emotions do.

The attribution process is subjected to the fundamental

attribution error, that is, underestimating the impact of

_____ _____ on others but not on ourselves. — social situations (p. 630)

Males and females tend to use different _____ for their — attributions (p. 630)

successes and failures.

There are several general determinants of interpersonal

attraction. We are attracted to those people who have

_____ values, interests, and attitudes. We are attracted — similar (p. 630)

to opposites, however, when those opposite characteristics

_____ our own characteristics. It's also more flattering — complement (p. 630)

and attractive to be liked by someone who holds _____ — opposite (p. 630)

views than by someone holding similar views.

With regard to competence, we are more attached to

_____ than to incompetent people; however, we are less — competent (p. 630)

attracted to those who are too competent.

Concerning physical attractiveness, people tend to be attracted

to physically _____ people. In the early stages of — beautiful (p. 631)

attraction between dates, physical attractiveness seems to be the

_____ important factor. In a study in which men — most (p. 631)

thought they were talking to beautiful women, the men talked in a more _____ way. Furthermore, the men apparently induced the women to act in a more _____ way.

sociable (p. 632)

likable (p. 632)

People tend to choose mates who closely match themselves in _____ _____. Physical beauty is a highly _____ quality. As we get to like people better, we begin to think they are more beautiful. Liking somebody often leads to liking in return; this is the basis for _____ _____.

physical attractiveness (p. 632)

subjective (p. 632)

mutual

liking (p. 632)

Recent surveys suggest that both men and women tend to feel that being in love is necessary for marriage. However, women tend to place more emphasis on their romantic partner's _____, character, and education; men place a greater emphasis on _____ _____. People tend to evaluate the same characteristics in others in the different ways.

intelligence (p. 633)

physical attractiveness (p. 633)

Two factors are important in maintaining relationships. The first concerns the difference between expectations and _____ in relationships. One common source of unfilled expectations is the shift from passionate love to _____ love. The second factor is whether the partners in a relationship feel that the ratio of their perceived contributions and benefits is _____. This is called _____ _____. Although the benefits the two people receive from one another do not have to be equal, the _____ between the benefits and contributions must be equal. Also, the benefits and contributions each person receives are based on their _____. If either member of the relationship perceives the relationship to be inequitable, he or she will either try to restore _____ or leave the relationship.

reality (p. 634)

companionate (p. 634)

equal (p. 635)/equity theory (p. 635)

ratio (p. 635)

perceptions (p. 635)

equity (p. 635)

Application of Psychology: Gender Stereotypes—Gender Discrimination in the Workplace

According to Susan Fiske, there are three sources of gender-based job discrimination: (1) evaluations of job performance are influenced by the _____ we hold regarding the two genders; (2) the narrow expectations for appropriate behavior encouraged by stereotypes can contribute to workplace

stereotypes (p. 638)

_____; and (3) faulty attributions based on _____ _____ operate in the workplace. The courts have upheld lawsuits brought against employers who discriminate against employees based on _____.

discrimination (p. 638)

gender stereotypes (p. 638)

gender (p. 638)

CONCEPT CHECK

Fill in the missing components of the following concept box. The answers are shown below the box.

Classic Social Psychology Research

I. Psychologist	II. Social Psychology Area	III. Research Findings
a. Asch	a. Conformity	a. Conformity to group pressure was widespread.
b. Zimbardo	b. Social roles	b.
c. Milgram	c. Obedience	c.
d. Festinger	d.	d. Subjects participated in a boring spool-stacking experiment; those who were paid the least expressed the most positive attitudes.

Answers

IIIb.   Zimbardo's mock prison experiment had to be stopped after six days because subjects lost the ability to differentiate between role playing and self.

IIIc.   Milgram found that a majority of subjects were willing to obediently shock another participant to the maximum 450-volt level.

IId.   Cognitive dissonance

Multiple-Choice Questions

1. Which of the following topics would be studied by a social psychologist?
   a. attractions to other people
   b. the influence of groups on individual behavior
   c. the formation of stereotypes and prejudices
   d. all of the above
   (p. 608) LO 1

2. Ron is a salesman who just made a big sale. He tells another salesman, "The reason I'm such a successful salesman is that I'm cheery, friendly, kind, and loyal." Which type of attribution is Ron using?
   a. equitable attribution
   b. dispositional attribution
   c. situational attribution
   d. none of the above
   (p. 609) LO 2

3. Which of the following is a component of the fundamental attribution error?
   a. the tendency to underestimate the impact of situations on others' behavior
   b. the tendency to overestimate the impact of situations on others' behavior
   c. the tendency to attribute our own behavior to situations
   d. a and c above
   (p. 608) LO 3

4. The process in which group membership makes a person feel anonymous and unidentifiable is called
   a. deindividuation
   b. social facilitation
   c. social impairment
   d. polarization
   (p. 609) LO 4

5. Each of the following is part of Latané and Darley's decision tree *except*
   a. noticing that something is out of the ordinary
   b. interpreting an event as an emergency
   c. assuming responsibility
   d. consulting with other bystanders
   (p. 610) LO 5

6. According to Latané and Darley, the diffusion of responsibility created by groups affects what part of the decision tree?
   a. noticing that something is out of the ordinary
   b. assuming responsibility for helping
   c. interpreting the event as an emergency
   d. deciding whether or not the bystander knows how to help
   (p. 611) LO 5

7. When individual effort decreases in a group project (such as a group tug-of-war) this is referred to as
   a. deindividuation
   b. social loafing
   c. social impairment
   d. social facilitation
   (p. 611) LO 6

8. Social impairment is generally more likely to occur on what types of tasks?
   a. easy tasks
   b. well-learned tasks
   c. tasks that involve motor skills
   d. difficult tasks
   (p. 612) LO 6

9. According to Latané and others, how does the effort exerted by individual members of a group compare with the effort exerted by individuals acting alone?
   a. Individuals exert more effort when in a group than when alone.
   b. There are no significant differences.
   c. Individuals exert less effort when in a group than when alone.
   d. Approximately half work harder when in a group and half work harder when alone.
   (p. 611) LO 6

10. Which of the following is more likely to occur with easily accomplished tasks?
    a. social impairment
    b. social facilitation
    c. group polarization
    d. deindividuation
    (p. 612) LO 6

11. In a heated group discussion of politics, Carla is somewhat surprised to hear herself arguing for a more extreme position than she usually does. According to social psychologists, this is due to
    a. polarization
    b. groupthink
    c. social loafing
    d. a and c above
       (p. 612) LO 7

12. Which of the following is a common result of group discussion?
    a. polarization
    b. taking more extreme positions
    c. suggestions involving riskier options
    d. all of the above
       (p. 612) LO 7

13. The study of conformity by Asch found that
    a. most subjects refused to conform
    b. most subjects conformed at least part of the time
    c. subjects conformed both privately and outwardly
    d. b and c above
       (p. 613) LO 8

14. Zimbardo's prison experiment has underscored
    a. the inherent aggressive potential of humans
    b. the kindness of some individuals in spite of a hostile environment
    c. the extent to which our behavior is influenced by social situations
    d. all of the above
       (p. 614) LO 9

15. In Milgram's research on obedience, which of the following factors decreased subjects' willingness to deliver shocks?
    a. when the prestige of the experimenter was reduced
    b. when the experimenter gave instructions by telephone
    c. when the subject was in the presence of other subjects who refused to deliver shocks
    d. all of the above
       (p. 615) LO 10

16. Each of the following is a component of the term *attitude except*
    a. beliefs
    b. facts
    c. feelings
    d. dispositions to behave
       (p. 618) LO 11

17. Sleeper effects refer to the persuasiveness of
    a. speakers who are low in credibility
    b. speakers who are high in credibility
    c. intelligent listeners
    d. emotional appeals
       (p. 619) LO 12

18. Which of the following approaches can make a fear-inducing communication more powerful?
    a. if the emotional appeal is strong
    b. if the listeners believe the feared outcome is likely to happen to them
    c. if the message offers a way to avoid the fearful outcome
    d. all of the above
       (p. 620) LO 12

19. Each of the following is true regarding characteristics of an audience and persuasiveness of a message *except*
    a. more intelligent audiences are generally easier to persuade
    b. audiences with a high need for approval are generally easier to persuade
    c. bigger audiences generally are easier to persuade
    d. audiences with moderate levels of self-esteem are easier to persuade than people with high self-esteem
       (p. 622) LO 12

20. According to Festinger, cognitive dissonance is a phenomenon that
    a. we seek because it makes us comfortable
    b. we seek to avoid because it makes us uncomfortable
    c. occurs when attitudes and behavior are consistent with each other
    d. none of the above
       (p. 622) LO 13

21. According to Festinger and others, cognitive dissonance results in
    a. attitudes shifting to become more consistent with behavior
    b. attitudes shifting to become less consistent with behavior
    c. behavior shifting to become more consistent with attitudes
    d. behavior shifting to become less consistent with attitudes
       (p. 622) LO 13

22. Stereotypes influence our explanations of behavior, according to
    a. cognitive dissonance theory
    b. attribution theory
    c. attitudinal modification theory
    d. dispositional modification theory
       (p. 624) LO 14

23. Which of the following is a harmful effect of stereotypes?
    a. Stereotypes permit us to treat each member of a group as an individual.
    b. Stereotypes take away our ability to treat each member of a group as an individual.
    c. Stereotypes lead to faulty attributions.
    d. b and c above
       (p. 624) LO 14

24. Which of the following expressions best summarizes interpersonal attraction?
    a. "Birds of a feather flock together"
    b. "Opposites attract"
    c. both a and b above
    d. none of the above
       (p. 630) LO 14

25. The expression "First impressions are lasting impressions" refers to which person perception variable?
    a. the primacy effect
    b. negative information
    c. individual differences in the evaluation of others
    d. emotional states
       (p. 627) LO 15

26. Which of the following can reduce the impact of the primacy effect?
    a. prolonged exposure
    b. passage of time
    c. knowledge of primacy effects
    d. all of the above
       (p. 628) LO 15

27. With regard to romantic attraction, women place more emphasis than men on each of the following factors *except*
    a. intelligence
    b. character
    c. physical attractiveness
    d. education
       (p. 632) LO 16

28. According to the text, many relationships move predictably from
    a. companionate to passionate
    b. passionate to companionate
    c. romantic to passionate
    d. sublime to ridiculous
       (p. 634) LO 16

29. Equity theory states that partners will be comfortable in their relationship when the ratio between their perceived contributions and benefits is
    a. balanced
    b. uneven
    c. similar
    d. equal
       (p. 635) LO 16

30. The evidence presented by psychologist Susan Fiske in the Ann Hopkins lawsuit against Price Waterhouse suggested which of the following as a source of gender-based job discrimination?
    a. Job performance is influenced by stereotyped beliefs about the genders.
    b. Narrow expectations for behavior encouraged by gender stereotypes can contribute to workplace discrimination.
    c. Faulty attributions based on gender stereotypes operate in the workplace.
    d. all of the above
       (p. 638) LO 17

1. The answer is *D*. Social psychology studies individuals as they interact with others; therefore, all the topics mentioned in the question, and many others, are studied by social psychologists.
2. The answer is *B*. Situational attributions explain behavior as based on some external (environmental) cause, while dispositional attributions explain behavior as based on personal characteristics of the person. If Ron would have attributed his selling success to a superior product, he would be using a situational attribution.
3. The answer is *D*. The fundamental attribution error involves attributing others people's behavior to dispositional causes (that's just how they are) while readily attributing our own behavior to situations.
4. The answer is *A*. Deindividuation has helped explain behavior as dramatic as lynching.
5. The answer is *D*. A fourth part of the bystander's decision tree, in addition to choices *A, B,* and *C* in the question, is deciding whether or not the bystander knows how to help.
6. The answer is *C*. Diffusion of responsibility tends to "divide up" responsibility among all bystanders, making it less likely that any *one* bystander will assume all the responsibility for acting.
7. The answer is *B*. Can you think of other examples of social loafing?
8. The answer is *D*. The reason for social impairment on difficult tasks apparently has to do with levels of arousal that become too high for the task.
9. The answer is *C*. This phenomenon has been given the descriptive term *social loafing*.
10. The answer is *B*. This finding is consistent with the optimal levels of arousal, which indicate that easier tasks are easier to do when people are aroused.
11. The answer is *A*. Polarization refers to the fact that group discussions often lead its participants to take more extreme positions. Groupthink, a related process, refers to the fact that group decision making is subject to distorted, polarized thinking.
12. The answer is *D*. Group discussions can change opinions in subtle, but powerful ways.
13. The answer is *B*. Although Asch's study found that the majority of subjects conformed to the group, most of the conformity was outward. When subjects were allowed to make their judgments in private, there was little group conformity.
14. The answer is *C*. Zimbardo and his colleagues were surprised at the extent to which the subjects assumed their roles. In a short time, many of the "guards" exhibited very aggressive behavior and many of the "prisoners" became despondent.
15. The answer is *D*. An additional factor that lowered subjects' obedience was when the "victim" was in the same room as the subject.
16. The answer is *B*. According to the text, attitudes are beliefs that predispose one to act and feel in certain ways.
17. The answer is *A*. Research has suggested that even speakers who are low in credibility can come to influence opinion after a period of time. This has been referred to as the sleeper effect.
18. The answer is *D*. Emotional appeals can be highly persuasive if all of the elements mentioned in the question are present.
19. The answer is *A*. Research suggests that less intelligent people are generally easier to persuade, except when the message is complex and difficult to understand.
20. The answer is *B*. When our attitudes and behavior are inconsistent, we are motivated to reduce the resulting discomfort. One way to accomplish this involves changing our attitudes.
21. The answer is *A*. According to cognitive dissonance theory, when attitudes and behavior are inconsistent, it creates discomfort; this discomfort is reduced when attitudes are modified to become consistent with behavior.
22. The answer is *B*. Attribution theory also explains why attitudes shift to become consistent with behavior, but the focus here is on our need to explain everything that happens or to attribute events to some cause.
23. The answer is *D*. Stereotypes are inaccurate generalizations that serve as the basis for prejudice.

24. The answer is *C.* This seemingly contradictory answer can be explained as follows: Although we are attracted to people who hold similar values and attitudes, we also are attracted to opposites when those opposite characteristics complement our own.
25. The answer is *A.* The impact of the primacy effect can be reduced with prolonged exposure, the passage of time, or knowing about primacy effects.
26. The answer is *D.* Most of us are relieved to note that certain factors can reduce the impact of the primacy effect.
27. The answer is *C.* The emphasis on different factors in romantic relationships holds up across different generations in the United States and across other cultures as well.
28. The answer is *B.* Companionate love, while less intense than passionate love, is a blend of friendship, intimacy, commitment, and security.
29. The answer is *D.* According to equity theory, the actual perceived benefits people receive from each other don't have to be equal, but the *ratio* of these perceived benefits and contributions must be equal.
30. The answer is *D.* The suit, brought successfully against Price Waterhouse, was the first suit in which psychological testimony on gender stereotyping was introduced as evidence.

Learning Objectives

1. Describe the work of industrial-organizational psychologists.
2. List and discuss the types of measures that are commonly used for employee selection and evaluation.
3. Compare the validity of various job selection measures.
4. Describe the challenges involved in the fair selection of minority employees.
5. Describe the relationship between job satisfaction and productivity; describe the strategies that are designed to improve both.
6. Identify the goals of human factors engineering.
7. Describe the role of health psychology in the workplace.
8. Describe the work of environmental psychologists.
9. Discuss the characteristics of defendants and jury members that affect conviction rates.
10. Discuss the importance of psychological factors in courtroom evidence.
11. Describe the work of educational psychologists.
12. Describe and evaluate both mastery learning and intelligent tutoring systems.
13. Identify Project Follow Through.
14. Describe criterion-referenced testing.
15. Discuss the goals of mainstreaming.
16. (From the "Application" section) Discuss the role of environmental psychology in preventing the destruction of our environment.

Chapter Overview

Psychologists who work for businesses are known as industrial-organizational psychologists. They are frequently found in personnel departments and are involved in employee selection and training. Interviews play an important role in the evaluation of job applicants and in the assessment of current employees for possible promotion. Industrial-organizational psychologists have helped to educate managers about the nature and limitations of interviews. Biographical data, or biodata, are sometimes used by large companies to match the characteristics of applicants with those who are successfully performing the same type of job. Paper-and-pencil tests, which measure personality and intellectual ability, are used in the assessment and selection process. Tests that measure specific skills and abilities are also frequently used. Performance tests, which measure actual manual performance, are used to predict behavior on the job.

Techniques that are used to assess the performance of current employees include such job performance ratings as multiple-step rating scales and checklists. Assessment centers are frequently used to evaluate applicants for management positions. Research has indicated that intellectual ability tests are the most valid method of evaluating applicants for complex jobs, but performance tests are more valid when the job is less complex. Psychologists have suggested techniques to ensure the fair selection of minority applicants and employees.

Psychologists have helped improve employee satisfaction and productivity by improving supervisory style, managerial organization, and physical conditions. Health psychologists have also worked with businesses to improve the health-related aspects of the work environment. Other psychologists have worked to improve the efficiency of training techniques, including the use of computer simulation.

In recent years, environmental psychologists have become involved in the effort to create environments where people can live and work more happily, healthily, and productively. For example, environmental psychologists have helped design workspaces, and have helped evaluate alternative designs of college dormitories.

In recent years, psychologists have also begun to apply their methods to the practice of law in the courtroom. They have found that the characteristics of defendants affect the likelihood of conviction and the harshness of the sentence. They have also found that certain types of jury members are more likely to vote for conviction and to recommend harsher sentences than other types. Psychological factors are involved in the effectiveness of courtroom evidence. Eyewitness testimony is the most convincing evidence, but eyewitnesses can and do make mistakes. Research has also determined that the order in which testimony is presented can make a difference in the outcome of a trial.

Psychologists serve the field of education in three ways: as professors who help train teachers, as consultants on testing programs, and as school psychologists employed by school systems. One recent development is mastery learning, based on Benjamin Bloom's belief that children should progress from one learning task to the next only when they have fully mastered the previous one. Another development is Project Follow Through, a federally funded experiment to test new ways of educating economically disadvantaged children. An approach to testing called criterion-referenced testing is designed to determine if a child can meet the minimum criteria for a specific educational objective. Public Law 94–142, the mainstreaming law, established that every child has a right to public education, regardless of his or her handicap.

Environmental psychologists are working to change human behavior in order to solve environmental problems. Three areas of particular concern involve overpopulation, resource depletion, and pollution.

Key Terms Exercise

For each of the following exercises, match the key terms on the left with the correct definitions on the right. Page references to the text follow the terms so that you may refer to the text for any items you answer incorrectly or do not understand completely. You may check your responses immediately by referring to the answers that follow each exercise.

Psychology and Work (I)

_____ 1. industrial-organizational psychology (p. 646)
_____ 2. interview (p. 647)
_____ 3. biodata (p. 648)
_____ 4. performance test (p. 650)
_____ 5. job performance ratings (p. 650)
_____ 6. assessment center (p. 651)

a. a conversational method of assessment
b. a test that measures actual manual performance
c. the branch of psychology that studies organizations and seeks to improve the human benefits of business
d. an evaluation system usually conducted by upper managers and consultants that makes use of simulated management tasks
e. biographical information used by potential employers to evaluate a job candidate
f. designed by industrial-organizational psychologists to transform a supervisor's rating of actual job performance into a numerical evaluation

ANSWERS
1. c   4. b
2. a   5. f
3. e   6. d

Psychology and Work (II)

_____ 1. simulated management task (p. 651)
_____ 2. in-basket exercise (p. 651)
_____ 3. structuring (p. 656)
_____ 4. participative management (p. 656)
_____ 5. management by objectives (p. 656)
_____ 6. human factors engineering (p. 656)

a. a management method in which employees are given specific tasks to accomplish
b. activities of managers that organize and direct the work of employees
c. the branch of industrial-organizational psychology interested in the design of machines to be operated by humans
d. a simulation in which the candidate is given a problem that might show up in a manager's "in-basket"
e. a management method that involves all employees in decision making
f. an evaluation method in which the candidate plays the role of a manager

ANSWERS

1. f   4. e
2. d   5. a
3. b   6. c

Environmental Psychology and Psychology Applied to Education

_____ 1. environmental psychology (p. 661)
_____ 2. educational psychology (p. 668)
_____ 3. school psychologist (p. 668)
_____ 4. mastery learning (p. 669)
_____ 5. intelligent tutoring systems (p. 669)
_____ 6. Project Follow Through (p. 670)
_____ 7. criterion-referenced testing (p. 671)
_____ 8. mainstreaming (p. 671)

a. the branch of psychology that deals with learning and educational testing
b. a program designed to help educate economically disadvantaged children
c. the practice of integrating handicapped children into regular classrooms
d. specialists who are employed by school systems
e. testing that determines if a child meets the minimum standards of a specific educational objective
f. the concept that children should never progress to the next learning task until they have mastered the more basic one
g. the field that evaluates human reactions to the physical environment
h. a computerized, individualized tutoring system based on the mastery approach

ANSWERS

1. g   5. h
2. a   6. b
3. d   7. e
4. f   8. c

Guided Review

Psychology and Work: Employees and Managers Are People

A psychologist who studies organizations and seeks to improve the

human benefits of work is an _____-_____   industrial-organizational (p. 646)

psychologist. Industrial-organizational psychologists are often found

in _____ departments.   personnel (p. 646)

    The traditional heart of the process of evaluating job

applicants and assessing current employees for possible promotion

is the _____. Interviews are more or less   interview (p. 647)

_____ conversations. Interviews have some inherent   structured (p. 647)

flaws. Industrial-organizational psychologists have found that the

_____ in which applicants are interviewed may influence   order (p. 647)

the interviewer's opinions of the applicants. Also, one study found

that interviewers tended to rate _____-looking   attractive (p. 648)

applicants and _____ applicants higher.   male (p. 648)

    The biographical information used by potential employers to

evaluate a job candidate is called _____. Biodata are   biodata (p. 648)

often used to find characteristics in new applicants that match the

characteristics of successful employees. Biodata are generally used

by _____ companies.   large (p. 648)

    Tests of cognitive ability, personality tests, and sales aptitude

tests are examples of _____-____-_____   paper-and-pencil (p. 649)

tests frequently used to evaluate job candidates. Tests that measure

the actual manual performance necessary for the job to be

performed are called _____ tests.   performance (p. 650)

    The most widely used method of assessing current employees

is the _____ _____ rating. For example,   job performance (p. 650)

employees are rated on different dimensions of job performance in

_____-_____ _____   multiple-step rating

_____. In another approach, the supervisor checks those   scales (p. 650)

items that are characteristic of the employee; this approach uses a

_____.   checklist (p. 651)

Candidates for management positions are often evaluated by a team of upper managers and outside psychological consultants in an evaluation technique that takes place at _____ _____. This approach evaluates candidates while they are carrying out _____ _____ tasks. A frequently used simulation presents the candidate with problems that might show up in the "in basket" of the new management position. This simulation is called the ____-_____ _____.

A summary of research on the validity of job selection measures indicates that paper-and pencil tests of _____ _____ are the best predictors of job success. The least valid selection method is the _____. No validity at all was found for _____ tests and handwriting analyses. According to a model proposed by Schmidt and Hunter, intellectual ability has its greatest impact by influencing how well and how quickly the employee _____ the job. While tests for intellectual ability are best for selecting employees for more complex jobs, the best selection techniques for less complex jobs are _____ tests. Schmidt and Hunter have also found that employees who score high in _____ learn job knowledge more quickly and perform their jobs better.

Since the use of intellectual ability tests might be unfair to some minority applicants, Hunter and Hunter recommend setting _____ for each minority group and then hiring the most qualified applicants in each group. This approach, like others that deal with the issue of minority applicants, is controversial both from _____ and _____ standpoints.

Psychologists working in business have two goals: to improve the job _____ of employees and to improve their _____. Researchers have determined that job satisfaction is not usually related to how well employees perform. In spite of this, high job satisfaction can improve business profits in the following ways: (1) reducing the rate at which employees quit, called _____; (2) reducing the rate at which employees

assessment
centers (p. 651)
simulated management (p. 651)

in-basket
exercise (p. 651)

intellectual
ability (p. 652)
interview (p. 652)
projective (p. 652)

learns (p. 652)

performance (p. 652)
conscientiousness (p. 652)

quotas (p. 654)

ethical (p. 654)/legal (p. 654)

satisfaction (p. 654)
productivity (p. 654)

turnover (p. 655)

fail to show up for work, called _____; (3) improving   absenteeism (p. 655)

relations between labor and _____; (4) improving the   management (p. 655)

ability of businesses to _____ good employees; and   recruit (p. 655)

(5) improving the _____ of the business.   reputation (p. 655)

    Managers have developed several strategies to improve job
satisfaction and productivity. The supervisory style of effective
managers includes being considerate and communicative; in
addition, they spend time organizing and directing the work of
their employees, called _____.   structuring (p. 656)

    Another strategy to improve job satisfaction and productivity
focuses on managerial organization. For example, employees at
every level are actively involved in decision making in the
_____ _____ method. In another approach,   participative management (p. 656)
employees are given specific goals, but are provided considerable
freedom in how they meet those goals; this approach is called

_____ ____ _____.   management by objectives (p. 656)

    Another approach to improving job satisfaction and
productivity focuses on understanding the influence of lighting,
noise, and other _____ _____. A branch of   physical conditions (p. 656)
industrial-organizational psychology whose goal is the design of
machines that can be more easily and efficiently operated by
human beings is called _____ _____   human factors (p. 656)
engineering. Many American businesses have found that programs
to improve employee health are not only good for employees, but
lead to greater _____ and fewer _____   productivity (p. 654)/absences (p. 655)
among employees.

    Psychological principles have been used in developing various
training methods for employees. Many training procedures
currently make use of _____ _____.   computer simulation (p. 659)
Psychologists have also contributed to the fields of
_____ and _____.   advertising (p. 659)/marketing (p. 659)

Environmental Psychology

Psychologists who are involved in the field that strives to create
environments where people can live and work more happily,

healthily, and productively are called _____

psychologists. For example, environmental psychologists have

helped to evaluate the effectiveness of a popular type of office

design called the _____ _____ format.

Psychologists have also helped to evaluate the design of college

dormitories. One study found that the architecture of college

dormitories can influence _____ over long periods of

time.

Psychology and Law: The Behavior of Juries and Witnesses

Psychologists and the legal profession have worked together for

many years, in testimony at trials and in hearings to commit

patients to mental hospitals. Recently, psychologists have turned

their attention to the practice of law in the _____. Thus

far, the most extensive psychological study has focused on the

_____ _____.

Research findings on the characteristics of defendants suggest

that justice is not _____. Juries tend to be influenced by

characteristics of defendants such as _____,

_____, and _____.

Certain types of jury members are more likely to vote for

conviction and to recommend harsher sentences than others.

Generally, juries are "_____ to their own kind." There

is also evidence that jurors who believe in the _____

_____ are more likely to convict than those who do not.

The outcome of a trial can be affected by the _____ in

which evidence is presented. Police also use psychological

techniques in _____ criminal suspects.

Psychology Applied to Education: Better Teaching and Testing

Although educational psychology is an old field, its current

excitement stems from recent innovations that may enhance the

education of the _____-_____ children.

Benjamin Bloom has proposed an educational concept which

suggests that children should never progress to a new learning task

environmental (p. 661)

office landscape (p. 661)

friendships (p. 662)

courtroom (p. 664)

criminal trial (p. 664)

equal (p. 665)

income (p. 665)

attractiveness (p. 665)/race (p. 665)

kinder (p. 665)

death (p. 665)

penalty (p. 665)

order (p. 667)

interrogating (p. 667)

slowest-learning (p. 668)

until they have fully mastered the more basic one. This approach, called _____ _____, is effective for slow-learning children and does not penalize _____ children. The use of computers to serve as individual tutors for students is called the _____ tutoring system.

    Each year in school, children from disadvantaged families learn about _____-_____ of what the average child learns. A program designed to help educate economically disadvantaged children was _____ _____ _____. The most successful Follow Through project used a teaching method that included _____ _____.

    The concepts relating to person × situation interaction also apply to the _____.

    A new approach to testing, designed to determine if a child can meet the minimum standards of a specific educational objective is called _____-_____. These tests play an important rule in _____ and _____ teaching methods.

    During the 1970s, Public Law 94–142 established that every child has a _____ to public education, regardless of his or her special needs. Whenever possible, children with special needs must be integrated into regular classrooms; this practice is called _____.

    Environmental psychologists are working to change human behavior in order to solve environmental problems. Three areas of particular concern involve _____, resource depletion, and _____.

mastery learning (p. 669)

brighter (p. 669)

intelligent (p. 669)

two-thirds (p. 670)

Project Follow
Through (p. 670)
positive
reinforcement (p. 670)

classroom (p. 670)

criterion-referenced
testing (p. 671)
evaluating/improving (p. 671)

right (p. 674)

mainstreaming (p. 673)

overpopulation (p. 673)

pollution (p. 674)

CONCEPT CHECK

Fill in the missing components of the following concept box. The answers are shown below the box.

Techniques to Select and Evaluate Employees

I. Technique	II. Description
a. Interviews	a.
b.	b. Biographical data; these data are used to match an applicant's characteristics with the characteristics of those who are successful employees.
c. Paper-and pencil tests	c.
d. Performance tests	d.
e. Job performance ratings	e.
f.	f. Evaluate candidates while they carry out simulated management tasks, such as the in-basket exercise.

Answers

IIa.   Interviews are structured conversations in which the employee or applicant is asked about prior training and education, future goals, and so on. Interviews are subject to a number of biases, such as the primacy effect, physical attractiveness, gender, and ethnicity.

Ib.   Biodata

IIc.   These consist of general intellectual ability and personality tests, and tests to measure specific skills and abilities.

IId.   Performance tests are based on the assumption that the most valid way to evaluate applicants is while they are actually working.

IIe.   This approach evaluates employees on a number of different dimensions of job performance.

If.   Assessment centers

Multiple-Choice Questions

1. Which of the following statements regarding industrial-organizational psychologists is true?
   a. They seek ways to help businesses produce more goods and services.
   b. They seek to increase job satisfaction.
   c. They try to fit the right person for the right job.
   d. all of the above
      (p. 646) LO 1

2. Assessment centers often evaluate candidates for promotion while they are
   a. eating lunch
   b. carrying out orders from their supervisors
   c. performing simulated management tasks
   d. none of the above
      (p. 651) LO 2

3. Which of the following is a biasing factor in interviews?
   a. primacy effects
   b. physical attractiveness
   c. gender
   d. all of the above
      (p. 647) LO 2

4. Which of the following is an example of a simulated management task?
   a. the in-basket exercise
   b. biodata
   c. job performance ratings
   d. a and b above
      (p. 651) LO 2

5. A "big five" personality trait that is associated with good job performance is
   a. extroversion
   b. conscientiousness
   c. neuroticism
   d. intelligence
      (p. 652) LO 3

6. Researchers have concluded that the most valid predictors of later job performance and success in job-training programs are
   a. paper-and-pencil tests of intellectual ability
   b. information contained in biodata
   c. performance tests
   d. projective personality tests
      (p. 649) LO 3

7. According to Schmidt and Hunter, the most useful measure for selecting employees for most jobs is
   a. biodata
   b. assessment centers
   c. tests of intellectual ability
   d. interviews
      (p. 652) LO 3

8. According to Hunter and Hunter, the most reasonable way to use tests of intellectual ability and promote fair hiring of members of minority groups is to
   a. lower the required scores on the tests
   b. assign different minimal scores for different groups
   c. set quotas for each group and hire the most qualified in each group
   d. none of the above
      (p. 654) LO 4

9. The process of actively involving employees at every level in decision making is called
   a. management by objectives
   b. participative management
   c. structuring
   d. a and c above
      (p. 656) LO 5

10. According to the text, all of the following strategies are used to improve both job satisfaction and productivity *except*
    a. raising employees' salaries
    b. improving supervisory style
    c. improving managerial organization
    d. improving physical conditions
       (p. 656) LO 5

11. Which of the following is characteristic of management of objectives?
    a. Employees are given specific goals to achieve.
    b. Employees are given freedom in how they achieve their goals.
    c. Meeting and exceeding objectives often leads to bonuses.
    d. all of the above
    (p. 656) LO 5

12. Each of the following is an advantage of having employees with high job satisfaction *except*
    a. reduced employee turnover
    b. reduced absenteeism
    c. improved productivity
    d. improved labor-management relations
    (p. 655) LO 5

13. The goal of human factors engineering is
    a. to find people in an organization who can work compatibly on projects
    b. to design machines that can be more easily and efficiently operated by people
    c. to design consumer products and packaging so that people will be more likely to purchase them
    d. all of the above
    (p. 656) LO 6

14. Computer simulation has been effectively used in training
    a. sailors to operate submarines
    b. pilots to fly aircraft
    c. physicians to practice medical diagnoses
    d. all of the above
    (p. 659) LO 7

15. Psychologists who work in marketing and advertising deal with
    a. package design
    b. advertising effectiveness
    c. surveys of consumer preference
    d. all of the above
    (p. 659) LO 7

16. Companies who make the health of their employees a priority find
    a. they can attract healthy employees who will incur fewer health-related costs
    b. they can save money by keeping employees healthy
    c. that facilities for aerobic workouts and healthy foods offered in the cafeterias are used only by a small group of workers
    d. a and b above
    (p. 659) LO 7

17. Environmental psychologists might conduct research on which of the following?
    a. an office landscape format
    b. the design of college dormitories
    c. psychological reactions to different wall colors
    d. all of the above
    (p. 661) LO 8

18. Research on office space organized around the office landscape concept found that workers
    a. were more productive
    b. were more cooperative
    c. interacted with each other more frequently
    d. all of the above
    (p. 662) LO 8

19. According to research on the design of dormitories, which configuration led to increased interaction with other residents and more time spent in the dorms?
    a. traditional single corridors
    b. alternating rooms with males and females
    c. TV rooms and lounges on each floor
    d. suite design
    (p. 662) LO 8

20. Juries are most likely to acquit defendants with which characteristics?
    a. physically attractive, high social status, and nonwhite
    b. physically attractive, low social status, and white
    c. physically attractive, high social status, and white
    d. physically unattractive, high social status, and nonwhite
    (p. 665) LO 9

21. Which type of jury member is more likely to vote for conviction?
    a. younger
    b. better educated
    c. lower social status
    d. more liberal
    (p. 665) LO 9

22. Research has shown that information that is presented in a courtroom is more potent when
    a. it is presented first
    b. it is presented last
    c. it is presented by a male attorney
    d. it is presented by a female attorney
    (p. 667) LO 10

23. Educational psychologists
    a. treat children who are psychotic
    b. help design educational programs
    c. help design educational testing programs
    d. b and c above
    (p. 668) LO 11

24. The mastery learning approach
    a. is equally effective for all children, regardless of their ability
    b. is particularly effective for bright children
    c. is particularly effective for slow-learning children
    d. works best with children of average ability
    (p. 669) LO 12

25. The most successful Project Follow Through project
    a. designed curriculum based on the skills needed for reading
    b. used positive reinforcement
    c. used practice methods to help students remember what they had learned
    d. all of the above
    (p. 670) LO 13

26. The goal of criterion-referenced testing is to
    a. measure whether a child can meet the minimum standards of an objective
    b. help to compare children
    c. help to determine a child's grade level
    d. all of the above
    (p. 671) LO 14

27. According to research, anxious children perform better
    a. in structured classrooms
    b. in unstructured classrooms
    c. with anxious teachers
    d. with experienced teachers
    (p. 670) LO 14

28. Mainstreaming
    a. refers to integrating children with special needs into regular classrooms
    b. was legislated by Public Law 94–142
    c. requires children to be educated in the "least restrictive environment"
    d. all of the above
    (p. 671) LO 15

29. Each of the following is a common characteristic of an environmentally oriented person according to Borden *except*
    a. dreams or daydreams of being a victim of a nuclear catastrophe
    b. early outdoor experiences
    c. religious convictions related to environmentalism
    d. romantic fantasies derived from books, films, or TV
    (p. 675) LO 16

30. According to the text, which of the following
   represents a threat to the environment?
   a. overpopulation
   b. resource depletion
   c. pollution
   d. all of the above
      (p. 673) LO 16

Multiple-Choice Answers

1. The answer is *D*. Inasmuch as many of us will spend a good portion of our waking hours at work, it seems logical that industrial-organizational psychologists can have a dramatic impact on our lives.
2. The answer is *C*. One type of simulation often used in assessment centers is the in-basket exercise.
3. The answer is *D*. An additional biasing factor in interviews is ethnicity.
4. The answer is *A*. In the in-basket exercise, the candidate is given a simulated problem that might well show up in the "in-basket" of a manager.
5. The answer is *B*. Research suggests that conscientious employees learn job knowledge more quickly and perform their jobs better.
6. The answer is *A*. Hunter and Hunter also found that performance tests, assessment centers, and biodata were valid measures, but were less useful than tests of intellectual ability.
7. The answer is *C*. Intellectual ability tests are most useful in selecting employees for more complex jobs, like sales jobs, managerial positions, and so on.
8. The answer is *C*. According to Hunter and Hunter, this method would ensure balance among members of different groups while hiring the fewest unqualified individuals.
9. The answer is *B*. Structuring refers to those managers who spend much of their time organizing and directing the work of their employees; management by objectives involves setting specific goals for employees to achieve.
10. The answer is *A*. Much research suggests that raising employee's salaries leads to only temporary improvements in job satisfaction and productivity.
11. The answer is *D*. Management by objectives is often used with a participative management strategy.
12. The answer is *C*. an important point in this section of the text is that job satisfaction is *not* related to how productive employees are. The text speculates that productivity is influenced by many factors.
13. The answer is *B*. While choices *A* and *C* might also involve industrial-organizational psychologists, *B* is a specific goal of human factors engineering.
14. The answer is *D*. There seems to be no end to the possible applications for training with the use of computer simulation.
15. The answer is *D*. To be effective and competitive in today's marketplace, businesses consult with psychologists and others in designing product names, packaging, advertising, distribution, etc.
16. The answer is *D*. By keeping employees happy and healthy, businesses typically can reduce turnover costs and increase productivity and profitability.
17. The answer is *D*. Architect and interior designers have often made good use of the findings of environmental psychologists.
18. The answer is *C*. Interestingly, workers who functioned for six months in an office landscape environment report they ere less satisfied with their surroundings.
19. The answer is *D*. The suite design involves four rooms clustered around a lounge and bathroom.
20. The answer is *C*. These same factors also affect the harshness of the sentence; perhaps it is not yet possible for all people to receive equal justice in the court system.
21. The answer is *B*. These are additional characteristics of jurors that make them more likely to vote for conviction: they are white, older, of higher social status, are more conservative, and strongly believe that authority and law should be respected.

22. The answer is *B*. Traditionally, the prosecutor in a trial presents to the jury last.
23. The answer is *D*. Although educational psychologists might help to identify children who are severely disturbed, intensive treatment is typically left to clinical psychologists and psychiatrists.
24. The answer is *C*. The mastery learning approach suggests that a child should not progress from one learning task to the next until they have mastered the more basic task.
25. The answer is *D*. Project Follow Through was designed to help educate economically disadvantaged children.
26. The answer is *A*. Criterion-referenced tests are designed to determine if a child can meet the minimum standards of a specific education objective.
27. The answer is *A*. Research results like these remind us of the importance of the person × situation interaction.
28. The answer is *D*. The guiding principle behind Public Law 94–142 is that every child has the right to a public education, regardless of his or her special need.
29. The answer is *C*. The influence of role models, an emotional experience with the birth or death of animals, and the loss of some special outdoor place were other common characteristics found by Borden.
30. The answer is *D*. The challenge to psychology is to change attitudes and behavior regarding the threats to our environment.